Navigating Dimensions

Reminders for Remembering
Awakening & Ascension Guide Book

Lisa "Transcendence" Brown

DEDICATION

To all who awaken and come to embrace their journey from within; To Ascension Guides, WayShowers, Light Anchors, Galactic Emissaries, and Pioneers, I honor you for your relentless dedication and hard work in fulfilling your missions here as well. So much appreciation, respect and love! I look forward to the next phases for us all in Unity & LOVE!

To my physical family: My son David, "my buddy", you are such a gift and I am so very proud of you. To Rachel, his twin flame, you are such a beautiful heart, to my grandson, Braxton, "my buddy Junior", you are a most definitely a rainbow crystal child and super special indeed! What an absolute honor to have chosen you all for my family here.

To Julie Coraccio, Pat Cole and Tameka Kelly, you have become so much more than friends. Thank YOU for embracing your journey, your continual support, the laughs and for becoming MY family here. You have amazing hearts and are so very appreciated and loved! To my Reiki Teacher, Joy Ayscue, for your unconditional, non-judgmental love while I was activating, clearing and going through my rough days to rebirth my-self and "grow up", along with your mission of BEing and teaching/sharing LOVE!

To my SOUL FAMILY incarnated here that I've had the opportUNITY over my physical lifetime to interact with, activate my own distortions while activating yours, bring through MORE LOVE while realizing what was not, fulfilling contracts, clearing these, activating more… one dimension at a time until I could open them all and exist in them all myself, heart wide open, soul embodied to experience the vast exquisiteness and physical abundance that comes from returning to PURITY within myself. What a GIFT WE all are!!!

To my Facebook & online family, as we have shared so much together over the years, and now we all come together to hold NEW Earth Gridwork in place so that all can experience and contribute too!

Thank YOU ALL for sharing your hearts with me. I love and appreciate you BEYOND!

To our beloved crystal family, the magnificent Na Pali Coastline and awesome Kauai Roosters for your part in this book! LeMUrian Energies embodied, thank you Kauai, for calling me home. ~ Aloha Nui Loa ♥

CONTENTS

PREFACE

From the human perspective, at the time this book was written, the 3rd Dimensional Realm still existed, but was in great dis-Integration. Yet from the higher realms, it no longer exists, and from the highest realms, it never did. It was just an illusion. The further we fell, the more real it became. The key, is to go BEyond Ascension, where it no longer exists again.

Some see the collapse of the 3rd Dimensional realm, some see them merge; some completely leave them all behind, and they just dissipate and dissolve. How you see will be up to you. If your focus is inward, it will not matter. For you will come to exist as your Higher Self again and as you do this, you will exist no lower than the 5th Dimensional realm again. You are here waiting for you to arrive. Your journey home is inside.

New Earth is already here and your higher dimensional version exists here too. It is a visible and actual palpable thing to see, touch, smell and so completely experience in the physical now. Here there is nothing to "do". Here you REMEMBER your way back into until you just REALIZE you are here, that you always have been and that you had just forgotten. This is a place, a sacred space of BE'ing, it is magical, paradise, heavenly and you are all things again. Only love exists here. There is no separation, no lack, no memories of another time. *There* are no teachers, there are no students. All are of an open heart sharing all that they have again. You arrive here by REMEMBERING, which is by way of a pure and open heart. Judgment was left at the gate. For you ascend inside and transcend all human existence from within. Here WE exist in a space of unity, and as one again.

What you will see as you transcend, shall be magnificent beyond that which you could ever imagine or dream. That which becomes visible again does not exist on your old earth. At least it did not, but it is does now. Do not discount anything you hear, feel or see. For absolutely everything is a part of this, especially that which you have yet to believe.

Magic and miracles are just the beginning loves. Come together again to walk in this dream. This dream is your new reality, if you can let go of that which you held onto before. Holding on was the old human way. You do not exist there anymore.

Welcome to NEW EARTH, just the beginning, as WE further transcend to go Galactic and BEyond from here.

I
AM
TRANSCENDENCE

THE VERSIONS OF ME WRITING THIS BOOK

This book may read like it was written by different energies. That would technically be true. For WE exist in so many spaces, places and times still, that in any given moment I can be "as close to a human as me gets", a Channel, a Translator, a Higher Self, Source, an Angel, an Alchemist, a Cosmic Portal, Energy Tuner and more… for WE are ALL THINGS and they are us. The one thing that will be apparent through this book, is that it was written from the heart. At no time will anything other than love and light be introduced here. It is not within our capacity to be any other way.

Everything here is my own perception through my own filter of that which I see, hear, feel, know, and REMEMBER again. My view is as expansive as the entire Universe, for this is what I AM, therefore, you will receive many perspectives and views, all based on frequency and energy. All versions are true in some parallel that translates to human. In the higher realms, none of this matters, for all exist from the heart and how we got there, when, how long, all gone. No one cares.

If you are looking for "proof", you are reading the "wrong" book (one of the few times you will ever see me say "wrong", for WE do not see right or wrong here). Words are only descriptives, as speaking alone is a waste of energy. I await the ability for energetic communication fully again. Until then, I too am limited to what's left of the human existence. As Masters, WE are all bringing this forth, along with teleportation, instant materialization and so many more magnificent BEyond-human REMEMBERED things. When I have managed these, I shall no longer be writing books. I will be pointing my finger and materializing them. Until then, I love my computer. Yet very soon, as all is transpiring very fast!

WRITING AS THE HIGHER REALMS

This book is written from multiple realms, all accessible FROM the 5th Dimensional Realm. For once one fully exists of the 5th Dimension inside, then all other realms are also opened for access from within as well. This is a spiraling journey/process. There is no beginning and no end. It is ever changing, shifting and elevating in frequency. And since WE are IT, so are WE.

I speak in WE, for here there is no separation in anything at all. I do this for this book, while "I" exist in this space in your human reality as well. I have finally come to understand this. It took much time, for I had to expand BEyond the limits of space and time within. All had to dissipate and dissolve within me, as it does for all. Time is but a separation we hold within. It is but only one of the limits we placed on ourselves when we "fell," descended and separated into a gazillion pieces here. Then, we ended up separated in a gazillion places "out there". For "out there" is only a materialization of our own Soul frequencies and I hope to assist with simplifying the understanding of this. I write in what I call "simple". I take the illogical and translate it into terms that hopefully make sense. There are times that I will "wander off into a crop circle". This is my version of "left field".

I write, speak, hear and exist in frequency. This sharing (writing) will also transmit in frequency. Where the frequency is high, the human-thinking-mind will not be able to stay awake to REMEMBER anything at all. The last book I wrote was in such a high frequency that most fell asleep each time they tried to read it (it makes a GREAT sleeping aid), and they REMEMBERED none of that which they read in actual words, for books of this nature are not meant to be read, but absorbed. They activate one's REMEMBERING from inside. Some can just hold the books and absorb the frequencies. Others read and go immediately to sleep. What a great way to get others to buy books. "This book will put you to sleep and you won't REMEMBER anything you read". Yep, that was the last book, yet many carry the book everywhere they go. Why? Because it activates them each time they read it. I am putting "quick reference guides" throughout this book and "simplifying", by way of comparison (which is so totally human) of realm to realm. I write for the logical minds that prefer comparison and bulleted lists, and also those who prefer more explanation than bulleted lists. My intent is to make this book a guide for either BEING that utilizes it; the awakening human BEing or the expanding light BEing, all BEing the same as the Awakening & Ascending Soul.

You will see me write/speak in "again" and "here" terms. This is because we come to exist in a space "again" that we have always been. This is a returning to that which we already know, a space that is expanded from within. It is a place REMEMBERED and held deep within the heart. Then it expands to encompass the entire universe, that has always existed inside. "Here" is where we ALL are and shall come to exist again. It is from this space that I write, for here is where I am used to. It is where I am at home inside. And it is here that I share with you, a place that you also reside.

Along the way, many thought I spoke in metaphor when I spoke like this. Yet I do not, for I speak as I AM; expanded and existing in every dimension is where I actually exist again. All dimensions, all existences, all EVERYTHING exist within us. WE have to unlock this inside to come to BE HERE again.

You will find that in parts I will speak simple, other parts sound "channeled". This is because of the multiple existences that we all now have the capability of "here". The goal is to give a comprehensive, yet simple guidebook, one that provides absolutely everything that I receive as I type it out to you. I do not tend to edit much. I write and when I am done, I publish. This book shall probably be the same. And the next book and so on and so on. The day I materialize an editor and a publisher is the day I will let another handle that. Until then, I type it as it comes through out my fingertips from within.

As my Higher Self/selves (for WE are many), I write from your future; from a time that many have yet to come to experience in the (perceived) physical here. What I understand is way more vast than any human mind can comprehend. Even mine sometimes.

All shall also come to be able to "know this place", for access has been granted, the gates are open, the corridors now traveled by all who come here to "lead the way" (i.e. WayShowers, Ascension Guides, and more). We all exist in the same space in "time", yet all have not yet come to *REMEMBER* this. This too shall change; technically it already has.

These writings are for those who may utilize them to expand BEyond the previously veiled-human-mind limits. It is in embracing this, that the forgotten realities shall materialize in the physical. It is through this, that all who embrace light shall come to transmit the "new" hologram from within. The old hologram is extinct. The new exists inside of you. It has already been created. All you have to do is go inside and unlock it. You do this by believing in the intangible, and honoring your Higher Self by way of that which you feel inside. You listen to your heart. This is your key. This is where freedom and peace reside, under all that has been hidden. And this is where home is. It always has been. Welcome home.

REMINDER: Your light is free, share it with love! ♥

TRANSLATING VS. CHANNELING

No longer technically a channel, I hold REMEMBERING inside of me. It is this way for all, as they integrate to the higher frequencies of the higher realms and hold them inside. Until we become this, it lingers in our energy field waiting for us to hit that frequency and hold it long enough inside for our physical reality to also restructure and materialize to match. This is why so many feel like they are getting downloads from "out/up there". They are, yet not from an outside source "out there". The entire universe exists inside. When the light frequencies activate "in there", when one sleeps, purges, releases and lets go of all identities and separation within, they are able to open a portal inside that brings that information into their BEing. As they do this, they hold this REMEMBERING within. As long as one maintains separation from self, they also remain veiled and separated inside. This limits one's ability to hold this inside, for one cannot be separate and ONE at the same time. For me, I activate the frequencies, sleep to integrate them, observe absolutely every moment & everything that I see. I have come to understand that every thought, every visual, every dream, every exchange, every everything is a memory, therefore it does exist. So if I can think it, see it or it can become visible in any existence that I have access to, it is true and it does exist. I instantly expand my mind to comprehend the most outrageous and unbelievable things. Only then, can I come to hold that inside. This has allowed me to go so far BEyond human comprehension. I have spent the last several years "waiting" for the reality "out there" to catch up to what I know, feel and see inside. This was frustrating for a long time, for I was still either partly or very much human'ish at the time, and as a human we hold lack within. So, while I understood so much more than anyone else could see, I still had to work to transcend my own human beliefs that I too held inside. The only thing that got me through it was my utter and complete trust of that which I received. I learned to honor my higher inner guidance voice of my universe within. I was "trained" by the universe, *MY* universe. While at the time I did not understand this, all becomes clearer as we evolve. As I listened, observed and learned to trust, an entire universe opened up that I had no idea existed. Yet not one universe, but a multitude of them; the multi-verse was inside of me. "Wow" is an understatement indeed.

I "moved so fast" that I went from channeling, to automatic writing instantly to teaching and channeling AS that from inside of me. It was not until others noticed my change in frequency when I spoke, that any of us realized I was "channeling" AS that from inside of me. Freaky cool, this is all I know. I then was shown to start writing and sharing publicly, online to the masses, which I did. Others thought I was getting info elsewhere to share. I had no idea until those who knew me told me that it was perceived that I was speaking in metaphor and not actually from this space. Again, not BEing OF this world, I knew no better. It was all that I understood and knew to be. A constant state of "waiting" for others to catch up, I had no idea what all of this really meant, until that day I heard "you are not from their time, but from their future".... Hmmm, now that took a bit of expanding my mind to comprehend.

I have always heard and translated that which I came to understand from inside of me. I knew no other way. It was "years later" before I even understood that I was "channeling" according to human labels. I did this entire journey backwards. I did it, then I understood, which is how the Soul learns. So I guess you can say that my Soul led this journey. For I truly, my entire 3rd and 4th Dimensional realm version, had only been along for the ride. First as the human, who tried to drive (in a very literal sense, which can be addressed later, if it comes back up), yet got thrown under the bus, hit the "brick wall", got beat upside the head with a 12x12 (yes, my 2x4 was "super-sized") until all that was left was to ride, for there was no energy left. WE (as humans) hit rock-bottom and had to lose everything before we decided to let go. That was the "old human way". The reason many of us, as WayShowers do this, is to create awareness so that others do not have to suffer, and to know that they have choice. It has finally come to a "time" in existence where one has conscious choice. Enough of the veils are lifting inside so that WE can actually assist others PRIOR to losing all in order to ascend.

I share my messages that I received from the Sirians, Galactic High Council, Lyran Energies (and more), as they started coming from within me, as memories, rather than "downloads" from the perceived "other place". Hopefully the words will assist another in understanding this *again*.

MY MESSAGE:
SIRIAN AND GALACTIC HIGH COUNCIL ENERGIES

"You have been given access to the outer realms/higher realms/off-world energies, but no longer from "out there", now rather from within.

For this too was locked behind a "portal" that you had to "open" and now have access anytime you choose.

It is this way for all things, for all you have to do is ask. Then go inside to release anything that surfaces once you do.

The human is given experiences to observe, so that their human mind can truly understand. It is through this observation that one gains access to their forgotten land.

It is up to you to choose to discover, that which lays dormant and hidden inside; for everything transcended or released, further uncovers that which you chose to hide.

There shall be more, if you will, as this journey never ends; it only expands further into the beyond, each time you go within.

You have always HAD access, yet your access is by way of your own vibrational frequency and portals that you unlock from within.

REMINDER: Every thought is a memory. It is either of the human existence or one of a "time" I have yet to REMEMBER within.

REMINDER: All things, all realms, all existences, all earths, all universes, all BEings, all all all, exists inside. Activation of the frequency is mine in light.

REMINDER: The human "receives" messages. This Higher Self BEing REMEMBERS again.

NAVIGATING DIMENSIONS

PORTALS
AND
REALMS
WITHIN

NAVIGATING DIMENSIONS

The concept sounds so BEyond comprehension, yet when one is provided tools, it is so very simple, for it does not conform to the logical mind. True navigation comes from letting go of logic and coming to exist AS your Higher Self again. It is as hard as you perceive it to be, for the human mind is the block to this. Going BEyond THIS is what WE do. So, let go of logic and allow yourself to imagine, feel and believe as you read. Expand your mind as far as you can. It is outside the human mind that this will all make sense. And it is "here" that we all truly exist.

You open dimensions as you open your heart. Consciousness is the action you take through your heart. You navigate by being conscious at all times again. That is the simple explanation. This book is a small portion of the expanded version. A dimension is just a frequency and you exist in frequency. Everything, sound, color, matter ... all just frequency. Some denser than others, the dimensional traveler is all of us, in every moment. The only difference is how dense or how light one is. The dense matter human (unconscious) does not do this at will. The Light Matter human (LightBody) is a walking conscious energy that now walks in Light, in the physical, and exists here in your time on your Earth. This one does this at will and AS love. And before you "think", oh it's not possible, stop and ask "then who wrote this book?"

A REMINDER OF ASKING TO REMEMBER:
I wish to hear, I wish to see
I wish to know, I wish to be
I wish to REMEMBER and be shown
That which was hidden, shall now be known.

SEPARATING DIMENSIONAL REALMS

For the sake of this writing, we shall separate these. Where in fact, there is no separation, the human needs to separate them in order to understand. When one comes to exist in the higher dimensional realms, the lower realms no longer exist. For a time they are still visible, yet have no bearing on existence anymore. Only when one operates at a lower frequency is this even a concern.

The human mind compares and works from a place of separation. For the purpose of understanding, we shall compare in order to assist the human-mind-need to understand. The heart needs no such comparison, therefore while some of this book is written to the human mind, it also is written to assist one in shifting to their heart space at the same time. It is through this "logical understanding" that the human comes to participate in this journey, by allowing the heart to lead. Until then, the human tries to maintain control, offering resistance instead of ease. Letting go is of the Higher Self BEing and is not the human way.

The human will try to "fit" into one dimensional realm or another, yet exist in all realms at all times. There is no "this realm or that realm"; it is all realms simultaneously. The human separates them in order to understand. The more conscious one becomes, the more they come to exist in/as all realms again. They see the illusion of the lower realms, so they just let them go, which is what causes them to dissolve and eventually no longer exist. This is because they existed within us all, and as they no longer do, they will also no longer exist "out there". You are the one who dictates this, by that which you hold onto in the physical from within.

DIMENSIONAL REALM COMPARISON

For the sake of simplifying, we shall speak in lower vs. higher realms or 3rd/4th/5th Dimensional Realm Comparison. If you are reading this book, you are no longer 3rd Dimensional. You are 4th Dimensional, seeking to understand and navigate with greater ease. The first thing to do is to stop associating yourself as a 3rd Dimensional BEing. That is human and is a part of the suppression it creates. The 3rd Dimensional BEing cannot recognize that they are 3rd Dimensional. The 4th Dimensional BEing is awake and asleep all at the same time. When you exist solely from your heart, in present moment, consciously choosing, without judgment, without compromise, without lack and for the purpose of all as one, you are a 5th Dimensional BEing. When you fall "out of this" (descend), you become 4th Dimensional again, seeking to regain consciousness. You may exercise some 3rd Dimensional traits, yet those are just going. Do not shortchange yourself by trying to place yourself in that frequency again. That is human.

3rd and 4th Dimensions have been merged, and if you are reading this book, you have awoken in some way, shape or form and shall find yourself in the middle realm or "the space in-between". The comparisons are to help you identify that which you may not recognize easily on your own. This can assist you in shifting back into your heart-self, a place that is foreign until you learn to do this with much practice of your own.

Some feel bi-polar and all over the place, others just seek to understand why things no longer make sense. Whatever you find, it is perfect for you. It is your chosen journey. Gaining tools of understanding for easier navigation shall assist you. You are curious enough to desire to understand more. Most likely, you have been "working" to exist from your heart, clear blocks and let go of that which has limited or suppressed you thus far. This you should be commended for. This is not an easy journey. It takes heart, much desire for something different and activates a drive inside of you that you may or may not understand.

The 4th Dimensional Aspect is one of continual release, activation, merging and integration. The Higher Self works to expand from within and all things of the dense human aspect reality are pushed up and out so that one can expand as the light that it truly is. This BEing "works" to REMEMBER, whether conscious or not.

Once you become conscious, there is no going back. You may choose not to be conscious for periods of time, yet you will suffer more when you do. This cycle alone will cause you to desire not to be unconscious anymore.

Now, those of us in the 5th Dimensional Realm and higher cannot even see the 3rd Density any longer. We are aware it still exists for others, but we literally cannot see anything at all. It is gone. This occurs for all as they let go of the beliefs that kept them anchored there to start with.

It is important to understand that once you awaken to "there is something more", you become a seeker. Most go on a rampage, gathering a barrage of information, trying to make sense of it all. This is a very important space as well. It is an activation, a gathering of that which you will use later, when you expand as your Higher Self and "split into two" BEings inside your body. This is also where duality, shadow selves and the "denseness" that we all hid from inside emerges as well. Your Soul starts to awaken and this is a whole new ballgame in itself.

No "one" is ever fully just in one realm. One might be unconscious, but all have a heart. It may be blocked, walled up and buried under blackened soot, but it IS there. And it is this tiny spark of light that ignites when the Soul is ready to awaken, expand and emerge. Hold on to your energetic britches, because reality is about to go complete sideways, backwards, inside out and in reverse. It will be so twisted, that you will question your own sanity many times along the way. Crazy is the new reality, for Unicorns and magic DO exist here.

Additional realms may be mentioned when it feels appropriate to do so. We would be remiss in not addressing these most exquisite realms BEyond the 5th Dimension, for they hold the memories that one has forgotten in veiled/separated human form.

UNDERSTANDING DIMENSIONS

A Dimension is a frequency, a realm, a way of BEing. Which dimensional realm one exists in, will depend on the frequency that they are operating, at any given moment in "time".

Time is but a separation, so in order to understand this, one must transcend the limits of time to see from multiple dimensional realms, as a space that is occupied rather than a place to be. From this view, one's existence no longer spans months, years or even lifetimes. One maneuvers dimensions by way of switching frequencies, therefore transcending the limits of human time.

Now, there will come a "time" when separation of dimensions no longer matters; they are no longer separated, because technically they do not exist either. They were separated so that one could come to understand them, to transcend them, to no longer need to see them separately. REMEMBER, separation is a human creation. When you release this human need to separate, you will no longer care either.

No "one" is ever fully in any one dimensional realm, yet instead, all are existent in all realms and all times. This is where "multi-dimensional" comes from. At first, the human realm is the only one visible, for visibility FROM THE HIGHER REALMS is dependent on how expanded and unified one has become inside. As one expands inside, they open portals to an unlimited number of dimensions and realms; each realm a different vibrational frequency. One comes to embody that realm as they release the human aspect that blocked that access to it. Each release further opens these realms until one comes to fully have access again inside at all times.

As one expands, one gets to choose the realms that they prefer to exist in. Human was a lower realm. As one transcends the lower realms, human goes too. Eventually human is no longer visible. The memories quickly fading, the experiences cease to exist. One perceives that "out there" is changing, when in "truth" all have come to exist FROM WITHIN again.

For the sake of understanding that which I speak in this book, I am including a brief section on SIMPLE definitions to help with any confusion. Dependent on where you look, you will find an array of explanations, but I found on my journey that most of what I read made no sense to me. This is because, as humans, much of what we read or find doesn't, yet we keep reading and seeking, for we are called to figure it all out. I REMEMBER looking back and wishing that someone had simplified things for me, tied the puzzle pieces together. There were probably times that they did, yet they were using their own words and this did not make sense to me. So, when I got to a point to see the overall picture, I actually asked for translation to come so that I could translate and assist others with this. Little did I realize that I would BECOME a translator here, in so very many ways. So, I work to simplify, and while these terms in no way encompass the vastness of all that is entailed, the goal here is to give a briefness that is simpler, and then go from there. So these are "one simple" version of many explanations and truths. I hope they assist you in a basic place to start and then expand.

Expand your perceptions and get as expansive as you can. The more you do, the more all of this will make sense!

SIMPLE TERMS

AWAKENING: When the world "out there" no longer makes sense and integrity of all comes into question. When you start realize "there has to be more", but have no idea what that is. This is when your soul wakes up your thoughts get so loud they drive you crazy. It's when the physical world no longer fills the "holes". "Who am I?" and "Why am I here?" questions begin.

REMEMBERING: Ancient memories of other existences and times are buried beneath the walls of your human experience. The more you let go of your human self, the more you come to REMEMBER within, coming to BE who you truly are again and have forgotten your true self again.

ASCENSION: The complete stripping of all human belief systems and rise in frequency to Christ Consciousness within. The journey of an awakening soul and a seeker of truth to come to find that all existed within; The journey back to the 5th Dimensional version of you again. The completion of your human journey on OLD EARTH from within.

HUMAN SELF: The BEing you REMEMBER on earth that has nothing to do with who you truly are inside. This one holds out-of-tune frequencies, discord which can be acted out by the rational and limited thinking mind. Some see this as the ego self. This one holds the emotions, duality and beliefs of the human experience in separation as the individual self of "I" your earthly version of you that exists in all other times but the present one. This one holds judgment and fear within. This one needs tangible, exists in logic, box and need things a certain way. Human is the one who feels alone and has lost humanity, by way of separation, within.

CONSCIOUSNESS: This is what you are when you are present and choosing love over fear and unity over separation. This starts out as thought energy and literally spreads to, and transforms, your entire BEing and physical reality. The more it does, the more every cell of you becomes conscious, present and AS love and unity again. The more you practice, the more you just become this. Every time you step beyond the limited-human-mind-limits to find more perspectives, more choices, options, parallels, you expand. Eventually you are your soul and higher self again. In this state, one is HIGHER CONSCIOUSNESS or EXPANDED CONSCIOUSNESS and it is a way of BEing, rather than a "thing" to achieve. Before you know it, you ARE your true self again. You are "home" inside and out there. You are Source and All-That-Is. This is you in your purest state, living solely from the heart and unified mind as one again. Consciousness is what you practices until you just become it again. Ever expanding, unlimited and free from all previous human belief systems.

HIGHER SELF: Your true essence of who you are; your future you who is always available when you are conscious, present and choosing from the heart. Here to be embodied within and waiting for you to listen. This YOU will emerge from inside as you choose to listen and participate more. This is you when you are present, conscious, aware and making a choice from your higher heart AS love.

SOUL: Another word for your higher self accessible through the depths of your Universal heart. Holds all in frequency, and in light, and is your true divine essence; a sovereign BEing; SOURCE, existing AS All-That-Is; this is emerging from within you in every moment that you breathe. You are a Walking Soul, just waiting to wake up fully to come to BE the higher realms again.

LIGHTBODY: Your energy body that activates as all of your bodies purge the density of the human experience. Eventually enough has restructured and you actually feel lighter, happier and things "turn around" or shift, where you exist from your heart instead of your human thinking mind. Your soul /higher self (which is LIGHT) integrates with your other bodies of consciousness (mental, physical, emotional) to unify and work together as one BEing, instead of 4 separate ones. Each's raise vibrationally to unify and merge. The result is your higher self AS ONE inside of you, "in command" if you will as a Walking Soul here.

MERKABA: Activates as you have achieve unification of all of your bodies, where the frequencies create a spin. This spin is your multi-dimensional vehicle that you can use to travel from realm to realm, dimension to dimension, reality to reality and more. You navigate this when you are conscious, choosing through love and to and come to exist as/in higher realm frequencies inside again.

ORBITRON: Now, after Ascension, I activated what I call an "Orbitron". The Merkaba became obsolete here and the fields all merged. This can be heard, felt and seen when it activates, yet it is much more "advanced" than the Merkaba. It is like being the nucleus of an atom and the electrons speeding up and going so fast that it creates this huge Orbitron that you are in. Magnetism activates and creation is visible from here. I am shown this is the vehicle of the Ascended Masters. More will be shared in upcoming posts and books. Because I do not look outside for answers, I do not worry about details of being proper and correct according to another's views. I share mine, my higher guidance, my understanding, for we all only need honor that which we understand inside. Another may have a different word. Mine is Orbitron! ☺

ADJUSTMENT: What occurs to your reality "out there" when you are out of alignment inside; Used to get your attention and cause you to go within.

TRANSCEND: What you do when you clear, release, leave a denser (old/lower) vibrational frequency inside. Eventually you transcend the entire human existence and go beyond Ascension.

JUDGMENT: Observation with a human opinion attached to it.

THAT: I speak in "that" a lot, as it does not matter what the "thing" is that I speak of, for we all have our own realities. The purpose is to give you a tool, another perspective and have you fill in what "that" is, in your own reality. It is a tool that applies to many things. Limiting "that" to one thing would be human. Here we expand to include all things that apply.

FALL: What we did as souls when we fell; What WE as Lemurians and Atlanteans did. WE fell from grace, fell from consciousness, fell from the stars. They are all true. Just the version you remember first is yours. One you re-experience the fall (descension) again, here in the physical (REMEMBERING), nothing will EVER be the same.

DESCENSION: Relatively the same as "fall", yet we continue to ascend and descend until we have truly ascended again. This is what causes the dramatic ups and downs along the way. Continual ascension & descension is occurring until you no longer forget again.

FORGET: What you do when you allow yourself to separate and become human again. This is when you are not present, not aware, not conscious anymore.

RISE (ASCENSION): This is what we do again, together and individually. Each time we raise in vibration, we ascend a little bit more. Together WE all rise again to BE ascension individually and as WE as one to create the 5th Dimensional Realm, all of our lights together as ONE.

TUNING: This is what we do as Souls in frequency, every time we shift at will to a higher vibrational frequency. Eventually we use this ability to shift realities at will, materialize light particles into form and more.

WALKING SOUL: This is what we are as our Higher Self here in the physical here again. As we merge inside as one we become our Soul in physical body form. The body we wear, our suite, the LightBody, our Merkaba, when fully activated, for walking between realities, realms and worlds. When I refer to Soul, it is the same, yet putting the word "walking" in front of it helps with the visual of what we truly are here in physical form.

DENSITY: Anything of the physical world that is not of light and serving the purpose of unifying all again. Anything out of alignment holds a lower vibration and creates density within and also in particle form "out there".

LIGHT: Us as the sun, Gaia, and the stars that we are, as our soul and higher self. Light is the frequency that we are in purest form. Our return to Higher/Christed (Unity) Consciousness, SOURCE, and Galactic Existences. Anything we bring into our reality that assists in embodying all of this again. WE are LIGHT. Everything we feed ourselves in light feeds us, as our soul, as Light Beings. And yes, literally light. It is that simple. The human mind complicates it though.

WE: All of us unified again as one and becoming WE as the Universal Mind and Heart again. WE holds a frequency of unity and love.

SHIFTING DIMENSIONALLY & CHOOSING REALITIES

You are in every moment shifting. You exist in all spaces, all times, all places at once, simultaneously. The further you fell, the further you separated, the more unconscious you became. It is through consciousness that you get to participate in shifting, by raising your own vibrational frequency and therefore ascending again. This you can do at will, yet in the beginning, it is a challenge and is BEyond your human comprehension. The more one "practices" (or chooses), the more this becomes an "art". Then, eventually it becomes your REMEMBERED (natural state). For you do not "try" to do this; you just REMEMBER through the amount of light that you activate and hold within you.

Dimensions are but a vibrational frequency. You are but many vibrational frequencies; an energy form transmitted by way of light. If a dimension is a frequency and you are a frequency, what does that make you?

Intentional shifting means that you have chosen to be present and to exist in your heart, instead of your human-thinking mind. Separation exists in the limited human mind. To bypass this separation, one must intentionally choose to shift (and exist) in their heart. Until you exist in alchemy, in order to create your reality, you must challenge the reality that you have until you do not believe it anymore. You must dissect the reality in your mind. Look at your human aspect and see it backwards, opposite, in reverse. Find the most expanded perspective that you can in order to see things as they truly are from within. If you wish to exist BEyond human, you must go BEyond human in order to come to exist again; for you are a

34

Human Star BEing here.

For a time, there is too much human emotional energy and memories blocking this. The human sees this as uncomfortable. Yet, the discomfort is the purpose. For when one embraces the discomfort, one creates the ability to transcend that which is not true. The human-mind is created, and fear exists in the human mind/DNA. Therefore this is an untruth that one has come to believe in order to have this human experience. Dissolving the fear requires stepping into it, to see that it is not real. The more that one chooses to do this, the easier this becomes. Fear becomes another energy, easily bypassed when one chooses to shift out of it and into their heart again

When you exist in love and light, you exist in your REMEMBERED state.

To the human, these things are "new", magical and BEyond the physical, for in a way they are, as the lower realm human aspect is not capable of such things. Only in releasing the human aspect, can one come to exist AS this again; for they have forgotten themselves to truly be an Energetic BEing of Light.

The human will see the 5th Dimensional Reality Realm as a new creation. The Light BEing understands that this is what has always been, yet was just forgotten of how to be. The Light BEing understands that they are REMEMBERING and just coming to BE again.

Until the 5th Dimensional Realm exists as one's new reality in totality, then one must choose which dimension to exist in. Where one does not consciously choose, one will "get" the reality that is transmitted by way of one's unconscious frequencies within. This will continue to occur until one REMEMBERS that they actually already exist here. One must also consciously choose to let go of the "old realm version" of their BEing, all that existed there as a result of this BEing and all that was created of a lower realm (3rd or 4th) that exists of a lower frequency no longer compatible with their 5th Dimensional existence.

On one's journey of *REMEMBERING*, one will constantly have to choose. It is the path that one chooses that determines one's experience here. One will choose safe (the human way of fear) or one will choose to listen to their heart (the way of the Higher Self). When one chooses "safe" (fear), then a lesson or experience to learn is necessary. We call this the scenic route. One must "see" more to "prove" that a different route is necessary in order to align within. When one chooses the subtle guidance of the Higher Self, then one chooses the "direct path" vibrationally to transcend the energy through love, light, honor and integrity from within.

Where one chooses not to listen to the subtle guidance along the way, then one starts to get minor "adjustments" to their realities that attempt to "re-route" the unconscious BEing. Where one still ignores these, then a major adjustment is necessary. This is removal of something tangible or that one holds dear to their human existence. Where one places more value on something over their journey, or that of another living thing, these things are considered obstacles and must be removed in order to shift one into alignment with their Higher Self path.

All shall be tested (constantly) to see which version of a reality they believe in. Every tool that one has in their awareness will need to be in place. Presence, awareness and conscious choice will be imperative for all who desire to exist in a REMEMBERED REALITY of creation, magic, bliss, peace and love again.

REMINDER: I will continually be tested to see which reality I truly believe. The reality I came to believe in my head or the one I hold within my heart.

REMINDER: My new reality is one REMEMBERED, BELIEVED and CREATED from within me. I can listen to my head or I can honor my heart. One is true and one is not.

REMINDER: The reality I get, will be the one I believe at any given time.

REMINDER: If I need to REMEMBER, I can just close my eyes and tune into my heart. Here, the human thoughts are silent (or more visible) and allowed to fall away. My Soul (inner voice) holds my truth and emerges from the silence within.

VOID SPACES BETWEEN DIMENSIONAL SHIFTS

Here we feel like a brain-dead zombie. Energy does not move. Thought is just non-existent. Any work or doing at all is not possible. And inspiration, well that is a HUGE joke! You have probably just gone through a HUGE internal fight where your thought energy was rampant & out of control. Your attempt to observe might have produced much for you to see, or it may not have even got off the launch pad. You might have gone "kaput" from the get-go. It doesn't matter, for each void will be different, get shorter and shorter in duration until they are not even visible at all. In the beginning, these lasted for years upon years for some, in human time, while days at a time for others. These are labeled by the human as depression, lack for life, no zest, no luster, hiding from the outside world and down-right never-ending sleep!

VOID spaces are imperative on this journey. You are shifting internally from one dimension to another. The length of time will be indicative of the amount of separation within your soul, from REMEMBERING your true self, AS SOURCE again. Where there is much separation within, these seem to last forever. Where one is doing much inner work or has less human density, these move "faster", as time is perceived to be.

There is a space between dimensions called VOIDS, the "null" zone. Label it what you like, for it does not matter, as the purposes are many and the variations are too. These are a necessity along the journey of the evolving dimensional traveler.

You are "placed into this VOID space" while the old human reality moves out. You are BEing prepared for shifting and moving again. Looking at the spiral of energy, the Merkaba spin, your energy is BEing REVERSED from the old human way, comes to a halt and then the spin begins again, but in the opposite direction than it was before when it was of a lower vibrational realm.

Judging the void only causes additional misery, for while still human, these are one step short of eternal suffering. The only place that we suffer more is when our human mind goes bonkers and takes over and CREATES more of a physical mess for us to then sift back through again. This is a very important place to BE. Understanding them allows you to ask for them to pass and then "do" what assists you in passing the discomfort with greater ease. I can share some of mine, that I can REMEMBER, for each one was different.

I had to pick something that would occupy my non-existent mind while not creating more for me to have to deal with after. Sometimes I had to physically get up and go move the energy. I would shower and go out to do something kind for another. This opened my heart quickly, no matter what space I was in. Other times I just went to bed, covered my head with pillows, screamed out loud to release the discomfort of it all and laid there looking at a wall. These were the times I "allowed" myself to watch movies or programs; always something "light", inspirational, and heart expanding like Avatar, Touch (Series), Fringe, Wayne Dyer "The Shift", Oprah Winfrey's "Soul Sunday", Eat Pray Love, etc. It doesn't matter, whatever feeds your heart and allows you to "zone out" with no thoughts present at all, while not introducing the old programming back in. Usually I would not pay attention, but the "distraction" of absent noise was what I needed more than anything, it seems; just a place to BE, with less discomfort present, while "nothingness" passed; for we DO what we need to at any given time.

Other times I would go into "review mode" and see everything that had occurred recently. I would just lay in a bed or walk in nature and observe. Sometimes this took too much energy, so I would resort back to the bed for some non-interactive anything.

As vibrations rise fast, these will be coming faster & faster as you "clear" dense thoughts and more. This is a very important space to be in and "when you have been here long enough", the energy will shift. You will awake with new energy and a new purpose. Appreciate this new space, for this is where you shall come to exist at all times again.

The higher you vibrate, the more you will actually "feel" time slow down and come to a halt. Eventually you will be aware of time energy reversing and going the "other way". You are moving further into a state of REMEMBERING here. This reverse spin is your Merkaba activating further. Once you have totally reversed your reality from human to your REMEMBERED SELF, voids will cease to exist. Here you will be walking, moving & traveling with an activated Merkaba and in a space where human does not exist, voids no longer do either, at least not any that you will care about; for these spaces allow you to expand further each time.

A VOID can also occur after a huge period of expended human thought energy. (Much of the time dense thoughts for an extended period of time). Your human brain went into overload, drove you crazy, expended tons of energy & now it "does not work", while you are BEing shifted by your Higher Self to your heart, once enough "time" in the void has occurred. Your "old" human you is dying so that it can be integrated within as a part of the whole again. This is magnificent, SO very uncomfortable, but HUGELY awesome! Eventually voids are a blip, while all shifts to reverse. A few moments and we are spinning in the opposite direction and unifying again! Wee-ha!

MINI-VERSIONS OF ALL REALMS WITHIN

You, as HUman Light BEings, ARE the projector of your own reality. All realms, absolutely all of them come to exist within you first and then "out there". The higher realms are accessible by opening portals as you increase in vibrational frequency. You then expand these open "pockets" of space from inside of you until you believe them and hold the frequency long enough for "out there" to come to materialize for you to actually physically see and exist in (again). Your own DNA activates further as you open your heart, while simultaneously your heart opens and activates your DNA. Your realities and consciousness expand as a part of the circle/spiral thingy again. It is not "one thing" but all things occurring simultaneously. It is the human that puts things into a box needing an order as how all things occur.

The lower realms also exist solely inside of you. Imagine a small version of your entire life inside of you and then the expanded version of the exact same thing "out there". One is visible by way of an internal viewer and the other by way of physically walking through it and interacting as if you are IN the play, rather than watching it inside. One version gives you the powers of observation, stretching your mind, clearing, releasing, and shifting into a higher frequency by "watching" the show in slow motion inside. The other gives you an actual physical tangible experience that you can touch, feel, and participate in, with your human body in order to observe, stretch, clear, release and shift. One cuts out the outside interferences, and lends clarity. The other has the chaos of the outside world thrown in for you to have to have stronger powers or abilities in order to "work" to transcend.

Now, as humans, we all originally chose an outer world experience. Our human minds blocked off, limited and small. Yet as our own Light Activations began in this ascension process, new DNA was activated, new pathways in our human minds were magnified and opened and the higher realm/self "viewer" was activated from within.

Now, your job, if you will, was to learn to utilize this new viewer, by going within to see what you could not see while participating and existing in your outside world. It gave you a place with no distractions to weed through the truths and untruths according to your own internal guidance system, instead of the human one you were "used to". It gave you the opportunity to choose to let go of the old realms inside of you, instead of needing an actual experience in the expanded physical world reality version "out there". Yet, the human says "I need a physical experience; I need tangible; I need an adjustment or something removed, actual proof, in order to get me to understand, for I do not like what I feel/see and I do not wish to honor the feelings inside, for that is not enough for me; I need something stronger to get my attention in order for me to let go of separation inside, brought to me by way of an actual physical experience "out there". And it is poof, like magic, we get what we ask for, for we ARE creators of our own reality, first inside and then "out there".

Imagine each realm existing in a mini-Merkaba inside of each of us, and inside is access to each realm "out there" As we go inside and release (transcend) the lower realms, we let go of them as the untruths that they were; we come to choose to let go of the anchors that held us "stuck" in the expanded version of the lower realms, and our LightBody /Merkaba spins faster, therefore expanding the other realms that exist inside of us to BE a part of us again. Now, these realms, these mini-Merkabas, these pockets inside are portals and gateways to the higher realms. As each one is activated, it starts to expand. The light activations give you access, for they have been locked away inside of you all of this time. YOU held the keys to unlock them by letting go of the old human that existed and kept you blocked from them to start with.

Each time you open your heart and let go of the old human way, the old human limiting belief systems, the old human separation, YOU unlock these pockets, spaces, realms (mini-Merkabas within). As you unlock them, much of the time, music or a song will be activated to let you know these have been accessed, or are present, until you fully exist AS them from inside again.

The "kicker" is, these realms cannot expand until you believe them and come to hold the frequency OF them inside. So until then, you are given a glimpse of what is accessible in them, by way of a "quick" experience to stretch your human mind and allow you time to go inside and reach the frequency OF them again. You, then, as humans, needed "time", as separated as you were inside, to adjust your human mind to comprehend these new things as even a possibility. Where there is much focus on an external reality, there is also more separation of time. Where one has released much separation and operates at an overall unified frequency of light, a faster spin, the less separation exists within, the more they live from within. It is this existence FROM WITHIN that allows you to BE a CREATOR again, but not by way of creating "new", but by way of existing as you REMEMBER inside, from your heart, as you have always truly been. The more you release, the faster you spin, the more mini-Merkabas (portals, realms, gateways, pockets, spaces) you open and expand; as you vibrate higher, as you unify inside, therefore so does "out there". And as this occurs, each realm/mini-Merkaba starts to expand from within. It continues with each expansion within until it is so large that you actually WALK and EXIST from inside your own Merkaba, where the bubble is no longer a little mini-realm, but now an entire realm that you walk in and exist AS again.

Your Merkaba your own vehicle of unified light that expands to connect with and AS All-That-Is, starts out as a little spot, a space, a pocket for you to explore from within. Simultaneously, the lower realms that existed inside of you, continue to dissolve and dissipate within. As they do, they also do so "out there"; for "out there" is the expanded version of those realms that you have always held within.

How you experience your journey, is entirely up to you. AS you become conscious, present and aware, and allow yourself to expand AS your higher BEing self, you have choice of how you experience the release of these lower realms. If you choose to go within, you have direct access views. Now, for awhile, this will be confusing, for there is so much and your human mind cannot comprehend everything that it sees. It "thinks" THAT is a dream, other realities, other places, experiences or memories of another time. It seeks to understand, whereas it is a "playing version" of something you have yet to REMEMBER or see. Absolutely everything you can see, both inside and "out there", is a memory of something, somewhere, some existence you have "been". You are seeing them because it is time for them to "go" as all is dismantled, collapse, comes forth and merges as one time now within. Some you will embrace as REMEMBERINGS and new knowledge or realities and bring them forth in your reality here. Where there are emotions to transcend, you will need to acknowledge these and allow them to be released as well. Human will get stuck in them, while the Higher Self BEing will observe and just allow them integrate. Where this discordant human energy is strong, it may take an actual physical response to assist the energy in releasing from your physical existence/BEing/vessel/suit. This can allow for energetic blockages to be released. Anything that has been held in your physical must also be integrated, if it does not hold the vibration of love, which is your version of you that already exists in these higher realms.

Now, each portal/pocket/space/Merkaba that you access and expand out from within, holds this higher vibration already and becomes a part of you as you vibrate higher again. Eventually, these mini-Merkabas are no longer mini, but have expanded for you to actually exist AS again. This is how you walk from realm to realm. You don't "go anywhere" for you are already here. You just expand AS these realms from within.

The realms all exist inside of you and it is up to you to choose to go in. In is where all is activated, IN is where ALL begins. Even your very human outside world existed first inside of you. The only difference was your viewer, your visibility, your own vibrational frequency you had limited yourself to. Your human mind expanded and these pathways & gateways opened simultaneously in your physical for you to be able to "see again". At first, you were limited by the small human mind, yet as you integrate these light activations and higher frequencies inside of you, new pathways to the entire universe are opened for you to again see. (Universal Mind). Unification inside of you, again, is how you access this. Your blocks, your veils, your partitions, you placed inside to block your own view. Your human experience the one you "needed" and chose as perfect just for you. These transmitted from inside of you to create the hologram, the play inside the matrix that you chose for you. Now, once you have released the barriers that existed in your own human mind, your heart will expand to BE your entire existence, not just the human heart you "thought" existed of inside of you. You are a walking heart, a walking light BEing, a walking everything that IS All-That-Is. You ARE source, your own creator UNIFIED AS ONE again. You were never separate; you just "thought" that you were. That thought was of a lower vibrational frequency that does not exist in these higher realms. You shall come to exist again, AS all realms from inside of you; then they shall also merge to no longer be separated realms either. For all realms are one, all spaces the same; the version of your reality is the one you project from within. The higher you vibrate, the faster you spin, the easier it is to move realm to realm from within. As you master this from inside, then moving between realms becomes possible "out there". You no longer need to move, for you have expanded them AS your reality and all you need is to shift in frequency and change frequency of your entire BEing to move between them instantly here.

THIS is what you have forgotten and locked deep inside of you. This you REMEMBER by letting go of separation and the limiting beliefs of how anything is, which was the lower realm, old human way.

IF you desire to exist in all realms again, you are the only one that can do this, and you do this by going within. "Out there" is your projection, so if you wish to change the frequency of the transmission, you must go inside and expand so that you can see there is another option. Your heart is how you shift frequencies, for your human mind does not have the ability to do this. Your heart, your universal mind, your own energy connected AS ONE again gives you the ability to "drive" your Merkaba, steer your ship, navigate your vessel and eventually exist as all realms at one time again.

Once you have existed OF and AS these realms long enough inside, then they shall materialize "out there" for you to exist in to reside. The more realms you expand and become again, the more you have to choose from, no longer limited to the reality of the human ONE that you "thought" was your only option.

So the next time you see something weird that just "could not be possible", yet it causes you to stop and think, know it is but a memory and if you desire it to exist, it is up to you to go inside and expand what you believe. It is up to you to "look" for that to actually become reality again.

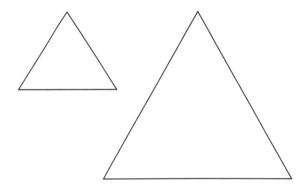

ENERGY AND FREQUENCY ACTIVATIONS: PARTICLE RESTRUCTURING: IN THEN OUT

Each time we acclimate to new frequencies of higher realms within us, WE actually SHIFT dimensionally, without ever appearing to move from the spot we are in. We feel the same, we look the same, but "things" are somehow a bit different, as we start to walk in the lucid dream. The only difference between the dimensional realms we exist in, is the amount of light or density that we hold. The more light, the more expansive; the more expansive, the more realms one can occupy at any given time. As you shift in consciousness (frequency), you are not the same version of you that you were before. With each vibrational activation and integration, you ARE a newer and LIGHT'er version of you. Your entire molecular structure is changing in every moment that you exist. Which dimensional version of you that you get, will be the one that you consciously choose from within. As you let go of the old human realities, your physical (inside and out) are re-structuring in light particles, without the denseness that once was. You need not do anything, you only have to let go, (sleep), believe, honor your heart, expand your view and choose a higher vibration in every moment. How your physical body will feel this will be relative to your own DNA, cellular make-up and the ratio of light & dense particles at any given time. In the higher realms, density continues to dissolve. One expedites molecular restructuring at a super high rate, for as density goes, we do literally LIGHT'en and hit a "point" where we are going crystalline and becoming HUMAN STAR BEINGS here. Physical realities become more bendable, flexible and just continue to re-shape in particle form. Particle materialization solidifies what used to be a dream. This is now visible and tangible, and tuning and reshaping is how we do things here. It is "real" here on NEW Earth NOW.

BREATHING COMPRESSION FOR A DIMENSIONAL SHIFT

Now there 3 specific times that I am aware where breathing is affected by dimensional shifts. These come from my own experiences and observations over the years. I will list these here:

3rd Dimensional Fear: (LightBody)

One is when light has been activated and fear is being pushed up and out for release. This is the unconscious human that will "think" panic attack and breathing will be affected by this. Breathe through it, shift back to your heart and observe the fear for the untruth that it is. For extreme experiences, do what you need to get through. Afterwards, go into observation mode and see what you can see. You are just trying to purge human density here. Assist it, do not fear it. Your soul is trying to emerge. This will occur to show you where separation exists within.

4th Dimensional Descension: (Merkaba)

The second is when we allow ourselves to drop in frequency to a lower dimensional version of us, therefore descending again (This will happen repeatedly until we no longer allow this to occur anymore and fully ascend inside). The more we allow this, the harder breathing will become, for we will feel like we are being suppressed. This is a sign that we need to shift and let go of whatever that is, go inside and come to peace again, and then out there comes into alignment after as well. Breathing will actually get hard. Go outside in nature, as Gaia and the Universe hold frequencies to assist you in re-tuning again. Again, you are transcending duality and any density within. Usually there is an old deep seated feeling remnant that has been suppressed and needing to go. We can't take these with us as we enter the 5th Dimensional Realm. This will occur repeatedly, until all separation is gone.

5th Dimensional Vortex: (Orbitron)

Later, breathing will compress substantially as you go to leave and move between OLD Earth and NEW earth and continue to walk in the higher realms. Your suit, vessel, carrier, will completely start to decompress, like you are being placed in a decompression chamber. Sound will go and your head will feel like it's in a vice grip. In a way you are. You are about to go through a vortex, a black hole, and come out in another dimensional version of the same place that you now sit. Your human mind cannot see the changes, unless you are aware this is what is occurring and you look for the subtle differences all around you. This is your version of teleporting, where particle matter reshapes to shift you between worlds, realities, and eventually other galaxies and more. There are no feelings here, just awareness that something huge is going on. Sometimes it feels like you are under water, and in a way, you are. When your frequencies are high enough, "out there" will appear for you to see what has truly been going on. Here your vessel is actually moving dimensionally and particles are being re-arranged for this. Your entire body is restructuring in particle form to "come out on the other side" of the vortex. In my experiences thus far, this can last up to a couple of hours. I have been awake much of the time this has occurred. Often I am in town and around others and the experience is pretty profound. I know I am not in the same reality that I was before the dimensional shift occurred. I look for the tiny differences and they are there if you really look. Things will be different in some subtle way and new is allowed to come forth. This occurs when you are unified and shifting dimensions already at will. You/WE are being prepared for Galactic Crossings with these.

Now, I am sure this will change as we go, for we are ever experiencing NEW every day. This is a guide for you to see what you see and to go from there.

THE
UPSIDE DOWN,
INSIDE-OUT,
IN-REVERSE,
BACKWARDS AND
OPPOSITE
WORLD OF THE SOUL

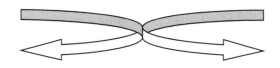

THE OPPOSITE WORLDS OF HUMAN & SOUL

As you come to expand more as your Soul self, the human part of you will continue to dissolve and fade away. You will start to see how everything was the "opposite" of the old human way. In order to shift out of the human reality and into one as an expanded Light BEing, we learn to completely reverse the old energy and then reverse it again to complete the circle that ever is spiraling up and out. For example, as humans we separated and became "I" and saw things as ours. We kept things for ourselves. We worked to obtain physical things, and to tie identities to everything "out there". Then we start to awaken and come to see this is not how it is. We spend all of our time letting go of everything as we came to "think" all to be. The walls we put up, must come down. We learn that protection is just another wall of surviving that which we perceived as a threat.

The human part was the one that was separated and forgot. The child that loved to laugh and play will return and the artistic dreamer will too. Your creativity will flourish, however you are inspired from inside.

As more come to move from a human reality to a Higher Self reality, ones entire world (reality) merges and flips. We slowly move from an outward focused world to an inner focused world. As we come to shift to the space in-between, we must learn the opposite of reality as it truly is. At first, it is somewhat of a cruel joke once one has the expanded view to actually see things how they are. Yet, absolutely everything was our own choice, as a Soul. Here, we are not victims anymore. We exist in utter and complete freedom, bliss, love, light, magic and peace from within. Then it radiates out to create the world that we live in; a world of unification, unity, commUNITY; one where we all reside together in love again. This can only be found by going within and releasing all that is not true. One will come to find that absolutely nothing was true that was not simply love that and Universal Love is not same as the old human love. This is a love that transcends all and is beyond the comprehension of the attached and expectation-driven-human. The entire human existence obliterated from the inside out to come to REMEMBER and EXIST in bliss and peace again.

I have found through observation, that there are many "opposites" that can be seen, when one wishes to expand. There is also the "space in-between". This is the entire 4th dimensional realm. The majority of "time" is spent in this "space in-between", awakening, sleeping, seeking, trying to understand and transcend duality, polarity, resistance within; ascending and descending repeatedly until one fully ascends. For this purpose, I have put together a "list" of opposites, to hopefully assist some in seeing "easier" how things can be. This does not say "how things are", just offers a broader perspective and view. It is up to you to go inside and see what is true for you. Each's reality is our own, yet there re common themes.

The human reality is the opposite of the Higher Self reality. The human sees only that an outer reality exists, while the awakened BEing has started to work from within. The fully Embodied Higher Self Light BEing, or Walking Soul, has come to fully exist as the higher realms, as the higher selves, as the entire universe from the inside again. They actually exist in the higher realms and interact with your reality, where it is meant to be. This one has the ability to walk between dimensions at will, and radiates light from within. Their entire reality is one of creation, yet creation only BEing again what was once veiled and forgotten. This is an Ascended Master now in your physical here, bringing forth the ancient REMEMBERINGS that all have waited for. This is you, when you allow yourself to REMEMBER again.

For those who desire a "cheat sheet", this may help a bit with identifying and shifting; yet these are only examples of observations. You must go within and see what you find is true for you. Cheating only gets more lessons, and was the old human way. This is more of a guide for you to recognize, consciously expand and create your own navigational tools!

EVERYTHING IS IN REVERSE/OPPOSITES

The human self works in the "direction" of separation. The "seeker" in the in-between realm (4th for the sake of this book), works towards oneness, releasing duality and transcendence. Another word for this oneness is unification. The Higher Self Light BEing is unified AS ONE, SOURCE, and CREATOR as ALL-THAT-IS again.

These alone are opposites and all things human must be totally reversed in order to come to BE a higher realm BEing of light again.

The human exists in an external world first and then goes within (by choice or tangible reality force). The "seeker" walks between the realms working to get footing and release the density that keeps it anchored in the lower realms. The "kicker" is, that one cannot hold on and let go at the same time. Forego, human suffering. The Higher Self BEing (HS) has completely reversed their entire reality to exist solely from within. Therefore outside is also an intentional creation just by BEing again.

So, for the sake of getting started, I will list some examples here. It's up to you to observe, see the opposite and reverse the energy when things start to get out of alignment ("out there" for the human and inside for the Higher Self aspect). See, that alone is one!

- ♥ The human sees the world "out there" first. The Higher Self (HS) exists solely from within.

- ♥ The human focuses on what others "think". The Higher Self does not care.

♥ The human changes according to "that out there". The HS shifts frequency inside and allows "out there" to then materialize to match.

♥ The human sees in boxes, linear, point to point, fixed realities. The HS sees in spirals, circles, geometric forms, frequencies, dimensions, vibrations and BEyond the limits of anything fixed.

♥ The human sees lack, and not enough, while the HS exists from a space of utter and complete appreciation and lacks for nothing anymore.

♥ One contracts and the other expands

♥ One operates from fear and the other from love

♥ One holds duality, the other exists AS Unity

♥ One holds density and the other exists in light

♥ One "needs and wants" and the other needs for nothing, therefore it has all that it needs at all times

♥ One lives in its head and the other from its heart

♥ One thinks thought and the other receives thought

♥ One sees "one way" and the other sees a multitude of ways by expanding

♥ One compares, the other doesn't care

♥ One has a small mind, the other has a universal mind

♥ One thinks and the other feels, sees, hears & speaks from its heart

♥ One judges (forms an opinion), the other just observes

♥ One is limited and the other is not

♥ One thinks of the "I"ndividual first, the other considers all as WE again

♥ One pulls energy from lack and the other transmits energy in light

♥ One procrastinates and makes excuses, the other one just "does it" if it truly feels that needs to be done

♥ One defends that which it has compromised, while the other does not compromise and has no need to defend that which it holds as true in its heart

- ♥ One speaks many words, the other is silent unless light words are necessary to assist in some way

- ♥ One needs external motivation to "do" something, while the other needs no motivation other than unity and what comes from the heart.

- ♥ One needs to know "who, what, when, where, why, how". The other knows all is exactly as it should be and draws all to it based upon that which it generates out (as love) from within.

- ♥ One studies and debates creation, while the other IS creation

- ♥ One feels restricted or pressured when opening to share. It needs to be asked and comes from a space that something is BEing taken from them. The other shares openly, with no need to be asked to do from compassion or love. This comes from within, and without thought.

- ♥ Human works alone while the HS brings all together to work in unity.

- ♥ Outer reality or inner reality? These are totally opposite.

- ♥ The human sees one focal point and then must expand out from there. The Higher Self is already expansive and works to bring all back to one again.

- ♥ The human places value on things. The Higher Self values everything as energy.

So, you try a few exercises now:

- ♥ If I am impatient, I am human. How do I reverse this energy?

- ♥ If I am greedy, selfish, stubborn or pushing others away, I am human. Why do I feel the need to be this way? What is going on?

- ♥ If I am judgmental, I am human. How do I observe and expand, instead of "shrinking" into judgment inside.

- ♥ If I am pulling to me, I am human. How do I reverse this and transmit love instead?

- ♥ If I am in fear, I am human. How do I shift to love and "do that" to dissolve the belief that I created to experience here?

- ♥ If I am in protection mode, I am human. Protection is a

perceived threat created by survival mode of the human. How do I dissolve this belief within me and take back my own power inside?

♥ If I am compromising, I am human. How do I maintain boundaries with love?

♥ If I feel resistance, I am human. How to I reverse flow and see this is my own energy creating this?

♥ If I take it personal, I am human. Can I shift to a higher view and see multiple perspectives and purposes and come to a place of appreciation inside?

♥ If I am focused "out there" on that" I am human. How do I shift focus and go inside and truly let that go?

There are a gazillion opposites and this may be a totally different book one day, but for now, hopefully this will get you started in observing when you are human and finding the opposite (which will always be love). Compassion, love, respect, integrity, honor and sacred are all Higher Self traits.

REMEMBERING
WHO YOU
TRULY
ARE AGAIN

YOU ARE
YOUR FUTURE
SELF NOW

HUMAN ASPECT VS. HIGHER SELF

There are so many variations of you, yet for the sake of this writing, we shall speak to the Human Aspect vs. the Higher Self/Soul/Light BEing Aspect. Any of these words will be used throughout this sharing, depending on which one feels appropriate for what is written here.

Your human you, has a limited view and focuses on "that out there". You came here for the human experience. You chose this, YOU as a Soul, as a Spirited BEing, as your Higher Self; you just have yet to fully REMEMBER. (or maybe you do!)

As your Higher Self, you are a Light BEing, a BEing of Light. This you will come to embody here in the physical. Until then, you exist in a space of "in-between", one where light activates to make density visible, "purging & release" occurs in every BODY (mental, physical, emotional), the merging of realities takes place within and the Crystalline LightBody DNA activates for integration as well. As you release all things dense and physical, you start to REMEMBER your other existences here.

Your Higher Self is your future you. It is all-knowing, holds the knowledge of all that you seek by way of the amount of light you hold within. For human reference, it is YOU from your future. Yet here, the future is just a higher vibrational frequency. Human created time (past/present/future). AS you come to release the separation of time within you, you again exist AS your Higher Self. You also do this every time you are present, conscious, aware and choosing love AS your higher-hearted self.

If you desire to BE your "future you", your unlimited and abundant you, you will make your vibrational frequency and journey your first priority. For here, separation does not exist. For you, in order to travel through "time", you must come to understand and exist vibrationally again. Here you have no limits and it is here that you "step" in & out of dimensions at will. It is here that you come to be multi-dimensional BEings. It is here that you REMEMBER that which you already are.

REMINDER: My Higher Self is me, from the future, just a higher vibration. Every time I raise my vibration and exist from my heart, I bring my Higher Self in and become this again.

REMINDER: I AM my Higher Self. I must set aside time for this. When I am silent I can hear.

REMINDER: If I wish to connect, all I need do is get silent and listen within.

REMINDER: Quiet time is a necessity, not a luxury. I must choose this and do this as often as I can.

REMINDER: Sleep is an awesome time to connect as my Higher Self. Meditation is as well. Either works. It is whatever I prefer and feel allows me to connect within.

REMINDER: When my heart is open and flowing out, I AM my Higher Self.

CREATING A RELATIONSHIP WITH YOUR HIGHER SELF

A relationship of love, honor, trust, respect, integrity and unity must be created for you to exist AS your Higher Self again. This is the most important relationship you will ever have. It is you and your future you, becoming ONE again.

Your Higher Self will give you tests and opportunities. What you choose to do, will determine the journey you get to experience. If you wish to ignore, you get an unconscious journey; while if you choose to listen and honor, you will get a conscious journey, which allows for greater ease and flow. It will usually be the opposite of what you've come to know, and to the human these are perceived as hard. This is because they bring up a feeling inside that is uncomfortable when they go against your higher-self-inner-hearted truth. Yet, they are not hard. They push you to let go of the human limits previously imposed by the external realities you created for your experience here.

You speak to your Higher Self, inside of you, through your heart. The more you do this, the more it will "talk back". It will be your own voice, for it is you from a future time. It will offer loving guidance, give you epiphanies, light bulb moments where the heart "catches on". Once you speak, then listen, observe and watch. Signs and messages will then become visible by way of things that transpire throughout your day, conversations you overhear or cool synchronicities and reminders that you are not alone. Your Higher Self welcomes every opportunity to assist you, yet you must ask, be present and honor what you receive.

Your Higher Self can be many selves, for you have been all things at all times. It can be an archangel or a Galactic BEing, for these are you as well. You will have many higher selves, some have names, some do not, for names are your own need. I never needed names, yet sometimes I got them, just to let me know "what I was dealing with", to learn to identify the different energies and basically "how serious" all of this was. When the Galactic High Council came from inside of me and spoke, I SO listened up! That got my attention and they did not play games either; straight to the point, no messing around. The message WAS the point. I also got "cracked on" by my Higher Self, for a sense of humor is always a plus. Ariel, yet another, gave me guidance and courage, while Jeshua and the Galactic Teams came through in LightBody Energy Sessions to assist and teach me that which I had yet to REMEMBER within. I had many many higher selves, yet eventually they all merge into one as well, for we evolve into one BEing, again to BE ONE. Separation was my own and for my own growth along the way. All now reside within and no longer separate at all. It was a "period" I expedited through. The faster I activated and integrated light, the faster they "moved inside" and I become one AS WE again.

REMINDER: *I must create a relationship with my Higher Self. This requires open two-way communication, and my honoring my agreements with "me" and listening to that which I am shown, especially when it is uncomfortable. Love, honor & integrity are my own.*

REMINDER: *As my Higher Self I am an observer. My Higher Self will teach me this, if I will be silent and open up to guidance from within.*

ALONE TIME WITH YOUR HIGHER SELF/SELVES

Your Higher Self is your future version of you. Plain and simple. "In the beginning" it was "out there", just hanging about in your energy field, yet as you activate and integrate higher frequencies, the more it will move "in".

It is important to give yourself alone time and honor the connection that will come to be your entire existence here. Your Higher Self will honor you as well. It waits for you to ask, so that you are in a receptive state to listen and observe. It so desires to guide you and be ONE with you again; to bring forth those REMEMBERINGS you have long forgotten. Those memories exist in the higher realms, where you will come to exist again. Yet you must CHOOSE to nurture you, set aside connection time, sit with your Higher Self in reflection and silence and honor that which you are shown through your heart, your connection AS your Higher Self within.

Speak openly, create dialogue and call "it" your best friend. Trust is a two way street here. For you will be "tested" to see if you will ask, listen and honor, while at the same time you are learning to trust what you hear, feel & see as well. All humans lack trust, especially where "that" cannot be seen. Trusting a voice inside our head or a feeling that makes no sense takes repeated "proving" to the human. As humans, we do not trust easily. Much of the time, as humans, we chose a journey of betrayal and disappointment, and reversing that takes a bit of time as well. Yet, the more you do this, the more you will trust. For YOU, as your future you, only have your best interest at heart. It may not always seem like it, but it will always be so. It will give you things that will keep you on path, teach you valuable universal lessons and reward you in the most awesome ways. It desires to be one with you as much as you desire to be one with it again too.

THE HIGHER SELF: AN OBSERVER THROUGH LOVE

The observer of the logical, will become the observer of what is no longer logical in order to transcend the limits of the logical mind. The observers of the Universe understand so far beyond what logic can comprehend. Observers can then translate and share based upon their own perceptions and relay for those who resonate at that same vibrational frequency. The level of access will be indicative of one's frequency and expansion of consciousness in any given moment. As one continues to expand, so does this.

In the beginning, all judge. It is part of human duality and the lower realms. (To me anything lower than 5th are the lower realms). Judgment is observing, but then taking that observation to a human level of forming an opinion or making it personal.

Consciousness allows for open-hearted observation and through this one learns to release judgment. With this release, one is able to the learn without forming an opinion and open up to amazing new possibilities of expansion.

DE-CLUTTERING OUR RECEIVERS:

In order to do this, one must be able to observe the density within and release it, without judgment. In stepping out of the "individual" self and into the Higher Self, one removes personal stories and individualism. By doing this one steps into a higher perspective and utilizes a view where nothing is personal anymore (and it never was).

Non-separation (unity/unification) must be applied on a personal level before one can actively participate in elevating to a higher level of observation. It is in these "higher" frequency perspectives of the Soul that one can clear & release with greater ease. Here, there is no personal, no separation, no right or wrong, blame, shame fear, guilt, etc. Those are all thoughts of a human mind. Things here just "are".

The observational heart-mind has the ability to expand what it observes. The clutter has to go before one has a view that is clear enough to see beyond the frequency of limits. In a space that exists beyond thinking, one can observe with expansiveness and tap into an infinite source of information. BEing able to access higher consciousness provides one with access to everything that exists. Learning to navigate allows one to see, and come to be, what the very limited human-thinking-mind cannot comprehend.

REMINDER: When I am observing without judgment and with love, I AM my Higher Self. When I form an opinion, I have "fallen" to a lower dimensional version again. (human)

REMINDER: Judgment is compressive and causes descension again. Release of judgment is expansive and is ascension from within.

EMBODYING YOUR HIGHER SELVES & ALL REALMS FROM WITHIN

Your Higher Self is within you, yet "in the beginning", it is "out there". This is because it "floats" in your energy field, bubble, aura (whatever you identify with here). All that you "gather" along the way, floats "out there", until you bring it inside, through your heart and truly "get it" and expand all from within. Until then, it is a thing you "connect to" from time to time. Now, that "out there" floating, is BEing "held in waiting" until you reach a vibrational frequency to hold it in memory inside of you. It is up to you to raise your vibrational frequency and speak to your Higher Self via your heart. If you wish to bring your Higher Self inside, you must shift your perception of "where" your Higher Self lives. It does not live "out there" or "up there", unless you believe it does. Shift your focus to your heart. Speak to your Higher Self IN YOUR HEART. This will assist you in focusing within instead of "out there". Close your eyes and imagine your Higher Self looking out from within you. Its viewer is your 3rd eye and it sees from there. You can imagine a visual and hold it there in your 3rd eye for your Higher Self to then see. This is how you communicate using visual imagery. Your Higher Self will communicate with you by way of the same.

Imagine your Higher Self as energy, sitting inside your body, with energetic hands where your hands are, energetic feet where your feet are, energetic hearing where your ears are and feeling all that you do from inside of you. When your fingers tingle, recognize that this is the energy of your Higher Self Light Being you trying to activate and expand. When there are heartbeats in your head, tummy, solar plexus, this too is your Higher Self (Crystalline LightBody) activating as well. Absolutely everything you feel inside is your Soul/Higher Self/Energy Body/Crystalline LightBody trying to emerge and expand from WITHIN you. When your 3rd eye gets full of pressure, your Higher Self/Soul has activated its light from inside and is working to release new visions, understandings and info that you did not previously REMEMBER. Astounding headaches are normal, in the beginning, while much work occurs in your now expanding head. You are activating your memories of ancient times and the projection of your new expansive and magical reality. Your human mind is in the way, so your Higher Self will shut you down for sleep. IT has integration work to do and needs your human to get out of the way and cooperate by allowing sleep. You can participate by going to sleep or napping any time you feel this need to rest or shut down. Absolutely everything going on inside of you IS your Soul, your Higher Self (as electrical ENERGY, sound frequency and pure LIGHT), moving in and pushing dense, old thoughts and stored human cellular memory up and out of the way. It is trying to activate your LightBody DNA, open your heart and fully emerge. Everything you take or put into your vessel that is not light, creates discord, suppression and pushes your Soul/Higher Self out of alignment. Every time you do not honor you, you will feel "out of balance" or "off" inside. Resistance is a great tool to feel when this is occurring. Your higher heart self is trying to tell you that something is not agreeable by creating resistance within. The more you ignore this, the more out of alignment you get. Eventually something will occur to force you to shift, if you do not learn to shift "quickly" on your own and come to alignment inside again. Listen to your higher heart. This is your Soul, your Higher Self, you FROM your FUTURE. Its job is to assist you, for you are it. Let it for all that you desire comes for when you do.

Now, AFTER your ascension, you have come to BE your 5th Dimensional Higher Self Light Being again, your additional strands of Crystalline, Human Star Being, Christed/Ascended Master, Ancient DNA (above the 12) that have been activating all along, really kick in. You go Galactic and are SOURCE INCARNATE and much changes even more dramatically here. And this, my loves, is the next book, as it is still coming forth!

REMINDER: I AM my Higher Self when I am existing AS my higher heart self from inside.

REMINDER: When I am present, aware, conscious, and existing from a space of utter and complete love, I AM my Higher Self again. I must hold this vibration until I never forget again.

SHIFT YOUR VIEW TO "ALL" FROM INSIDE OF YOU

All energies that I speak of exist within us all. Many have been under the perception that these come to us from "out there". It is the opposite as all previously perceived. There are many ways that you can practice this. My favorite was to tune to my heart and take my "viewer" up over my head as far as I could and look down at all from above. You can also shift to behind your 3rd eye, instead of trying to see only with your human eyes. This is a different viewer, one that you will come to merge with as you integrate to higher frequencies within.

The human sees all as "out there", downloads coming from "up there", activations coming from a source "out there" and the Higher Self "up there" too. And while, from one perspective, this could be viewed as true, this is not my perspective any more. It has not been for a long time. I write to you all to help you see FROM WITHIN. For the entire World, Universe, Cosmos, Star Systems that all see, is only a projector view of what exists within you.

All energies are activated from within us. The DNA activations, the dormant parts of your mind that were never utilized, all hold the "forgotten". This has been activated and all that you now come to be/feel/see, comes from within you, instead of the old human perception of "out there". Your Energy Body, fully activated, has capabilities beyond human. It exists AS ALL, without separation from anything anymore.

The journey was to come here to create a human body, a human existence, a human physical reality to experience, to gather material things, people, identities, separate into other times (lifetimes, dimensions, realities), to then come to "awaken" to the "truth" that none of that was ever you. That entire existence is what all must come to let go of, release and transcend. For what we all come to now move into, does not exist in 'human'. It exists in the beyond, that which human cannot believe or see. This is only available through an open heart and mind. And all shall come to realize this, in their own "time" within.

When I write of energy activations, every one of these are within you. When you tune to them, you are tuning to frequencies you hold within, yet have forgotten. Memories of the forgotten/other side/invisible, exist within you, deep beneath your human ones. As the human memories are allowed to leave, new memories are allowed to surface. "out there" changes as you REMEMBER through your heart.

You created those people, those experiences, those memories for your own experience here, both individually and collectively (as that is perceived to be). Yet the "time" has come where the human reality ends and a new phase begins. For this, many are led to leave absolutely everything behind in order to completely transcend their entire human existence here, which is where the magnificence begins. In "previous times" loss was necessary, for it was the only way to "reverse" the human existence to come to evolve as the higher self. Whether this shall change, remains to be seen and depends solely on how quick one embraces and finds their own humanity as ONE again. Letting go brings us to our soul essence inside. Hanging on created the suffering for the strong-minded-and-separated-human-soul.

The story, the play, is BEing re-written. It is BEing re-written by you and all who unify again. "out there" is a transmission from within and all create it with their new REMEMBERINGS and overall transmission. As you tune vibrationally, you transmit a new reality to come forth to exist in.

Your pineal gland must be activated with sunshine, and if you have not done so, decalcified. This is a huge part of the activation and integration process, expansion and what allows for your new physical reality to be transmitted to be felt, heard, seen and experienced again. This becomes your light transmitter and receiver. First it will transmit images in your mind, wait for you to believe them, then they "arrive" in frequency out there. Your integration of these higher frequencies bring you to exist where those images have materialized in physical form. This is your tuning mechanism, your light transmitter of your new reality that you seek. It works as one with your heart. They are directly connected to become one and the same, without separation of thought as well. Your new senses expand as your human senses diminish. Physical pain no longer exists for that too was a human thing.

All are evolving as energetic beings here. Now, there is discomfort in the physical, for your soul/higher self energy was not made to fit into dense human bodies, with the old separated organs and dilapidated carrier systems you once had. It needs room to move about freely, to float and the ability to expand and there are many dense particles that must fall away for this to occur. We work to integrate this light, so that the human body can LIGHT'en, evolve and transform, as we become Walking Souls, Ascended Masters, Human Star Beings, in newly configured bodies here. Much work is BEing done inside and out. Translucency, eradication, magnetization (and so very much more, are occurring within. Many are becoming more crystalline, starting to glitter and glow. Yes, we go so far beyond human now. Nothing is as it was before.

Over time, these things become more visible, shape-shifting, glowing and morphing becoming normal occurrence during LightBody Energy Sessions or in sacred magical energy vortex spots/places, where the frequencies were high and one was tuned AS their higher self and realms. I started "glowing" to others that I run into in public that walk up to me to "touch" me to see if I was real. Sometime we were invisible to others to all of a sudden appear. The most common BEing photographs or online webcasted events; for electronics tend to pick up on what the human eye-mind has yet to comprehend. Yet this is changing now as all become visible in the physical again!.

There is nothing typical, nothing normal, nothing rational here, according to human. Yet as energy, we get it, if we allow ourselves to believe everything as it transpires. Those crazy thoughts, lucid dreams and weird occurrences, yep, every one of them real. One just has to stretch in order to truly see.

All "out there" will be your own transmission. In order to change/activate/expand that which you desire to transmit, you must go totally within. WE can only assist you, by creating awareness that was not previously there. You are the key to your own existence, you always have been, you just were not consciously aware.

Together we all create a NEW reality. Yet this is not new, only forgotten. We have already entered the new, where "out there" is now visible once again.

IN
THE
BEGINNING…
THERE
WAS
UNCONSCIOUSNESS,
AND THEN
THERE WAS
LIGHT

THE BIRTH OF A SOUL

That first breath ignites the Soul within the physical form. The breath of light expands and with this expansion transmits all imprints and coding into the physical form. That first cry represents all tears that will occur for the Soul to emerge beyond the density within.

This imprint is in frequencies and all experiences are representative of those unique frequencies within. This imprint transmits and calls for all Souls to honor Soul contracts to respond. These responses fulfill Soul agreements of interaction to resolve their own duality within. All interactions are physical form of Soul agreements.

What occurs in the physical lifetime is in response to the unique Soul's imprint. Scenarios and experiences are created that are necessary in order to resolve perceived karmic debt (this exists only in the lower realms) and once the human ego (logical/reasoning/rational mind) is formed, to then provide opportunities of choice to reverse human energy to that of the higher self.

In the early years, those with extreme karma (discordant frequencies) may have experienced traumas in order to assist in the forming of the distorted ego. The more perceived trauma, usually the more distorted one's reality becomes. Yet, this was each soul's choice to endure, embrace, release and transcend from within. Only the human sees traumatic, for the soul understands this for what it is. Memories are holographic imprints that can be seen. The more karma imprinted, the more extremities one will endure. Memories are not stored in the physical, but do exist in the physical for one to access for the purpose of the experience. When that frequency is cleared, then one moves up in frequency and those memories are no longer necessary other than to "access energetically" in order to help another on their Soul journey. This is why so many experience "memory loss". It is not a loss, as there was never a memory to start with. Just a holographic scene created to bring forward those things necessary to play out a scenario or role.

Two frequencies are imprinted: fear and love. All other responses are created by the human mind (ego) to mask and create barriers for one to maneuver through for the sake of their human experiences. These are but the obstacle path of the Soul.

Every moment is a choice. What one chooses will determine one's path. That choice will reaffirm a frequency of fear (dense) or love (light). That choice triggers a frequency response. Fear will reinforce any density within. Love will allow in light in order to expand the light of the Soul. Each will reinforce karma dependent on the frequency chosen. Each choice will be to dim or brighten the light of the Soul. Each choice will transmit a frequency that the Soul will then experience in the physical reality.

What used to be Karma is now just conscious CHOICE from the higher heart-mind. Many cannot comprehend it is this simple and keep seeking other things. For those, they must continue to seek until they come back to this same space. Everything is PRESENT that one needs to see in order to choose. All "lives" are accessible now with the tools to understand them. The veils have been lifted to allow for consciousness and with consciousness one has choice. Choice is what will determine how much pain and suffering one endures.

Suffering served a multitude of purposes for the Soul. It opens hearts and allows one to choose differently, therefore resolving any lower realm karmic debt. In times of suffering, one will ask for help, where pride previously stood in the way. When strong masculine energy lets go of pride and finally asks for help, their heart opens to receive. A closed heart cannot receive. It cannot receive the abundance that is available, as there are too many blocks in the way. Blocks of "dense" energy are perceived as betrayal, hurt, pain, distrust, pride. These blocks maintain a victim mentality. A closed heart maintains separation, survival and protection of the "I" self. It allows the mind to think for it, so that it does not have to truly feel and let go. It says "I can do this myself" or "this is mine". It doesn't feel it can trust another, and it fears pain. Suffering takes away the strength of the human ego and choice to avoid. Suffering forces one into their heart and to DESIRE something different. This desire exists within the heart. Suffering opens the heart to receive light in order to allow lower frequencies to leave. Anger is a quick response to cover up the frequency of fear. Crying is the ultimate release of human separation from one's soul.

Here I will speak of Karma of the lower realms. In the higher realms, this no longer exists. Yet, for the unconscious or newly conscious human, it does. Re-wording to a "frequency loop", will assist in shifting one's understanding of this. Yet here, we address Karma as it is widely understood.

Then comes the test of karma. Karma is created or reversed in the moment of choice. It's not what one does when choice is taken away. Suffering is a symbol of karma. It symbolizes that there is an opportunity coming to choose. This opportunity is where one can change their entire reality and release that frequency that manifested that suffering. One chooses to maintain that same frequency or to step into a higher frequency of what is "right" according to the higher heart. One always has a choice to honor their Soul self. The rest of the scenario will be determined by that which you choose to do. Not doing is still a choice. What you receive shall be up to you.

The HUMAN REALITY perspective is present in the human thinking mind and exists in a limiting reality. "Life" happens TO it and one tries to "think" manifestation here. For the human BEing, the heart is subject to the mind. It operates in a linear format, seeing time as separation of moments like past, present, future. It observes and has an opinion, judges by seeing good & bad, right & wrong and duality in everything. In this reality, one is a victim and is its own biggest critic and abuser. This one tries to save, fix or change that which is not good enough by its own human learned standards. Things are personal here. Individuality & separation exist and decisions are made on an individual basis as well. One operates according to, or in conjunction with, the logical/reasoning/thinking mind. Growth & abundance are measured in things, comparisons, accomplishments. Age and knowledge are measured in time, years, experiences. I/me/my/he/she/they exist and one feels alone. When one is unconscious, they function here.

The SOUL PERSPECTIVE exists in the heart. The Soul CREATES their reality according to transmissions of the heart. The mind is subject to the heart and they work together. The mind is one of an observer in order to study & learn in order to REMEMBER again, yet there is no opinion or judgment attached. Every observation is for bringing in more light. There is no right, wrong, good, bad. Duality is acknowledged as a belief and separation of the lower realm human. It sees that there are a multitude of purposes in EVERY moment and here, one does not interfere in another's ability to choose. It understands perception of karma and the need to allow another to experience their own path of duality in order to resolve their own lessons necessary for growth.

The age & knowledge of a Walking Soul is according to the amount of light that they hold within and knowledge is "streamed" through light and the Universal Heart-Mind. Time is non-existent. One moment exists with versions of moments BEing acted out in a multitude of dimensional parallels. Parallels created with every choice one does or does not make in the physical realm.

In any given moment, one can raise or lower their vibrational frequency and step in and out of different realities. These realities will play out according to the transmission of frequencies from within. "Hidden" density materializes faster so one must bring up anything hidden, if they wish to participate in their own materialization process.

Everything on a Soul level is in reverse, backwards, opposite of the physical reality. Every moment is a test; a test to see if one chooses their own Soul and to bring (anchor) more light in. This choice transmits a vibrational frequency to the Soul that one is serious and they are ready. There will be continual tests to strengthen the heart so that one chooses on their own and not just when they are suffering. When one can maintain a certain frequency through repeated consistency in each test, more light is introduced for expansion and the vibrational frequency is elevated to maintain a new materializing reality.

Veils were placed for many upon their physical birth, so that one could not fully see. These veils lift for each who chooses the path of their higher Self Soul. WITH each choice, more light can be introduced by the Soul allowing for additional code activation and changes in cellular memory. Human cellular memories are only visible holograms of frequencies so that the physical eyes can see transmissions by the logical and limited human mind. As the dormant Crystalline LightBody DNA is activated, the higher heart and higher mind begin to merge and the transmission is one of higher frequencies powered by the energy of the higher heart. The human's purpose is to clear all low-vibrational "debris" from their energy field, so that what one now sees is the purity and exquisiteness through the frequencies transmitted by way of the unified higher mind-heart.

When one awakens, they are awakening to their own Soul which exists within them as light and sound frequency. These frequencies are felt through the heart and heard with the ears as tones that one cannot yet understand. This is where one starts to question things, as their heart knows one thing and their mind says another. Duality manifests as conflict within and one can "see" truth through feeling it in their physical human self. All duality within is manifested (materialized) in one's outward reality. Many have built a fortress of walls of protection around their hearts to drown out the frequencies of density within, represented by the conflict, chaos and never-ending chatter of their own human mind.

When it is time for the Soul to start to emerge, there are a certain set of codes that are activated. All things manifested in an outward reality, that block access to the frequencies existent within the heart, are removed for the individual's Soul to suffer to loss in order to open access to their higher (humanitarian) hearts. The harder one tries to maintain those walls of protection, the more suffering one is bound to endure. Manifestations of duality exist in anything that one values over any living Soul/thing (i.e. self, mother earth/nature, animals, etc.) Suffering will manifest in loss of finances, relationships, chronic health and more... everything that can get one's attention to make a change. Where one is already operating at a higher frequency with less low-vibrational karma to resolve, they may experience falling in love to open their otherwise closed off heart. For each Soul, this will be indicative of their own Soul's blueprint, which can be changed with conscious choice.

Frequency light codes are existent within, and are activated with each introduction of light (the Soul). The more one chooses their Soul, the more light will be introduced in for assimilation into the physical. Codes are continually activated as more light is introduced and integrated. The veils lift with every activation of ascension.

Every individual has choice. That choice is to choose their Soul. How "fast" one grows will be indicative of how much light one is willing to allow in, in order to release density previously held (suppressed) within. For the path of each Soul is unique. The only consistency is the choice of light. (This is why some grow "faster" than others. It is how much one is driven to choose their Soul and bring in more light. The more light one chooses, the faster they will grow INTO their own Soul and purpose. Every time one chooses something over someone (or life), they remain in a reality of duality for another experience to endure again. Every time one chooses LOVE, they maintain or access more light.

All Souls have the same access to unlimited resources and knowledge. This is not measured by age, time or even experience. This is accessed through the activation of light frequency, every time one lets go of the old belief systems or individualized human ways. When all bodies (mind/body/Soul) have integrated enough light, then a pivotal point is passed. When that occurs, the Soul steps in and complete peace and sense of home is felt within. There are no words to describe what one experiences here, and it is different for each according to their journey here. What you do have is this magnificent, vibrant energy that radiates out from the entire BEing and transmits out to all other BEings of light. Separation falls away and the Universe no longer exists anywhere other than within. One truly exists in-service of humanity. Every choice is then one of love and light and ONE again.

AWAKENING TO AWARENESS: IT BEGINS

Suffering was the old paradigm beliefs. That no longer exists here. Yet, if you identify with this in your current reality, then you still exist in an old belief system in your mind. Below was written under the old belief systems of suffering, as I started to understand more. It is shared for those who resonate, to show you this is no longer and that there is now another way. That way is love, REMEMBERED from inside again. Ego was used here and can be replaced with "the limited human mind".

In a world of duality, there is good & bad, failure and success, right vs. wrong and so on. Polar opposites to absolutely everything.

With the old human belief system that was created in a fixed physical world of expectation and duality, we learned to adhere to one perspective or thought system. In any given situation, we go "yes, I did it!" or "how could *that* happen to me?" or "I can't believe *this person/they* could do that to me" and so on & so on. *We* are taught to make everything personal. We are taught that we *have* to succeed in the eyes of others; that if we don't excel by others standards, including those who taught us, that we are not good enough. When we are old enough to start thinking for ourselves, when our intellect starts to form (5-6-7-8-9 years old, depending on individual growth), we carry over those teachings as our own thought/belief systems. We then spend the rest of our "lives" *thinking* the same way. We even *learn* to become experts at carrying those belief systems on & fine-tuning them into our own ego-based belief system. WE then take those things and we go "I can do better than that!" I can "think" those things and even more dysfunctional thoughts of my own! From there "lack" is abundant in whatever area is applicable to any given situation. Some have money but lack love. Others have love, but no money. There is always duality in the world of an ego/thought-based belief system.

In this time of awakening and ascension, everyone I have run across, something pivotal has happened to create a "what, wait a minute...", scratch our head... "but there is something more going on" experience. Something opens our eyes to other possibilities, but then the confusion sets in about "what" exactly that is. We feel it, but we don't quite understand it. Then our minds get involved and try to dissect it. Then the mind/heart duality experience starts on a whole new level than in the "past". In our previous state, we just ignored our intuition and our hearts much of the time. We gave into our thought processes because they just had to be right, as that is what we were told. How were we to think any differently? Confusion persists. The rest is a pathway that emerges, a new journey. A journey into beginning to merge dualities and trying to un-learn everything we have learned thus far. Death of the ego begins, which creates massive internal emotional suffering for many and minimally extreme discomfort for others, causes fears to run rampant, control issues to exacerbate, the list is endless. Our deepest fears and painful memories start to surface. But even through all of that, we still know there is something else. It is that knowing that keeps us going, hanging on. It is that knowing that is our heart overriding our mind. That knowing is what we feel and now come to understand and trust.

For me, I always had a very strong sense of knowing. I just knew. I knew things that others didn't. I don't think it was that I knew anymore than they did (although the ego would like to think that), but that I listened to it or trusted it more than many others. I knew things about people when I met them that others didn't "see" or desire to see. I knew "decisions." If there was a question, I knew the answer on how to do that. I didn't really question what I knew, I just knew. It was that knowing that gave me strength that others lacked in self. It was also that knowing that made me so "successful" in the business world and part of the reason why so many sought my advice on things.

That sense of knowing doesn't come from the mind, the ego-based, reasoning mind. That mind actually creates the chaos that we allow to interfere with our sense of knowing. We know or feel our truth. It is just instant. But when we don't get the answer we like, our reasoning, intellectual, ego-based mind decides it knows better and starts the "scenario" process. It is this scenario process that creates our fears, our doubt, our dis-trust and our self-created mind chaos that carries over into everything we do. So it is imperative on this new journey of awakening and realization, to start to be able to tell the difference so that we can move to a heart-based knowing that will remove the resistance and create a flow of ease. The resistance creates discomfort. The heart is comfortable with anything, as it understands the perfection in absolutely everything. In a heart-based world, we do not lack. Our focus shifts to one of caring, acceptance and gratitude. Judgment, blame, distrust start to fall away. We start to create a new world of balance; one of faith, love, honesty, respect and compassion for ourselves and others. We start to understand, as we grow, that we are all one BEing, one consciousness, one energy. In that moment that we "see" or "feel" that, our world opens to one of light, ease and promise. The denseness we have known in the past starts to dissipate. We start to accept ourselves and others and with the proper guidance of those who have experienced such things before us, we open up to learn about this "new world" with wide eyes of wonder and appreciation. We then begin our journey of awakening and ascension and awareness, as now "life" is a choice that we choose with a new purpose. One the reasoning mind can't comprehend.

HUMPTY DUMPTY E-MERGES AS A WHOLE SOUL

There comes a "moment" in your human "time" where you are activated "more" than in the past. This is indicative of when it is "your time" to start waking up. Here is where a new awareness of "something" occurs and one becomes a seeker of more, purpose & meaning in things that go BEyond the human physical world. How one does this will differ, based upon current belief systems, how logical and one's human past. Masculine energy will "hide" and try to research, whereas feminine energy will seek others to help them figure it out. Your universe may even send you someone (a relationship or job) that helps you open up to "more". The really logical mind will seek "proof" of what makes no logical sense. It is in the trying to prove, or satisfy a nagging thought or even trying to "prove wrong another" that one comes to see "BEyond". For me it was many things, but the first "notable thing" was BEing told I was an "Empath". "A what?" I asked. "An Empath" he replied. "This is where one feels and responds to others based upon energy that they feel." Well this just got me to researching relentlessly, for what was "wrong with me". And every bread crumb that I found, opened another door of seeking and soon, I was on a full-blown massive hunt, for that just blew open Pandora's Box, Pandora's Box BEing the journey into my own Soul. This took me through the world of intuition, psychics, energy, Metaphysics and everything Beyond the tangible physical world and what I had been suppressing was oozing out every orifice trying to get out. I had suppressed WAY TOO LONG (according to my human me), yet all is exactly as it was meant to be. You name it, I went through it, while the Berlin Walls inside came tumbling down. I had identities wrapped around everything "out there", and absolutely no idea of this, for this is of the human way. Ripped and stripped of everything and every wall broken down, I awoke to begin a "new way". This new way was with an open heart, tender and no idea of where to go.

Yet it did not matter, for I held love now and the sun outside was something to embrace instead of trying to block out. No longer in a dense cavern cave of my comfy apartment, my safety net haven that protected me, MY universe still removing things, to teach me what true appreciation, honor, integrity, humanity and sacred meant and to come to trust, expand and BE my Higher Self that I had been seeking to hear.

This seeking stage is what I lovingly call purgatory, which is the space in-between and the entire 4th Dimensional Realm. It's like BEing in a "sifter" and BEing shaken while all "out there" falls away. Stripped of all identities along the way, with our entire human existence being "wiped" so that we can start anew as "nothing" to become the profound essence of ALL-THAT-IS again.

As seekers, the interest may be quantum physics, others the psychic world, another fascination with synchronicities. Some will seek to master the Laws of Attraction, trying to learn the "trick" to manifesting more money or physical things, while others get interested in order to find a mate. Again it does not matter, for all bring you to energy & consciousness. All that matters is that you seek to understand more than makes sense in the tangible reality. All will eventually bring you to an inward journey, into your own Soul, which is the door we all have to walk through, to come to truly understand and expand into the BEyond. This is the beginning of opening the doors inside to come to exist again on NEW EARTH, the 5th Dimension and the higher realms.

Until one can release their identities to absolutely everything without hitting rock-bottom before they can see, rock-bottom is often the TURNING POINT (and reversal of human energy), where one actually totally gives up the fight to hang on and the soul is allowed to emerge. Hopefully with the expansion of light, new awakeners are less veiled and choose to shift without suffering the way that we did. That is why we even do this, to show there is another way (WayShower). For those embracing without losing all, feel blessed, for thus far, the only way back into the 5th Dimensional realm is the ripping away of your human self so that your Higher Self can emerge. Yet this is why all of us do what we do; to assist in eliminating suffering by creating awareness and sharing tools.

Eventually, we "shift" to become "Humpty Dumpty", while we are put back together again. Yet this time, it is without the density and the attachments to "that out there". This time it is the pieces of our Soul, purified as light and whole again.

For those embracing this journey and actually choosing to make this a priority, utilizing tools of bypassing the human need to suffer to REMEMBER again, hats off to you and thank you, for part of my job/mission is to assist in raising the light quotient, expanding consciousness, which ends suffering as we once knew it to be.

REMINDER: If I feel like I am at rock-bottom, my soul is trying to emerge. I can assist by letting go of that which is creating my internal suffering. Suffering is now a choice when one chooses to become conscious.

REMINDER: Rock-bottom is required for the strong —minded-masculine energy human. It is where my soul is allowed to come forth.

REMINDER: An identity is human. That is not me. I am so much more than that which I have tried to limit and attach myself to here.

REMINDER: Each time I let go, I REMEMBER more and more again.

THE LOWER REALM

THE 3RD DIMENSION

UNCONSCIOUS HUMAN

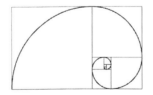

UNCONSCIOUS HUMAN, HELL ON EARTH, SLEEPWALKING IN A WAKING STATE

This realm is one of physical denseness and singularity. It is one is one of tangible existence, where one believes that which it can touch, feel and see and the way they have learned is the way "it must be". This is one where all things are individual, they are fixed and "that's just the way it is". There is no change here, there are no options or flexibility, and things are only believed if they are tangible and can be seen in the physical reality. Here "lies" (pun intended) the dense manifestations of the human experience one required for their experience here. A higher existence is a concept, rather than an understanding and there is no way one could even comprehend BEING their Higher Self. Now, the ego may try to claim this space, yet this too is of the human mind way. For the human, there is a "point A" to "point B" and nothing in-between. Things are just as they are, as that is how it is. There's no imagination, as that is not of the rationalizing human mind. Imagination, visualization and dreams are of the heart and that is the 5th dimensional higher self.

One sees their external reality as fixed and created for them. For this is all the human knows. It was the purpose. This is the physical manifestation of "Hell on Earth", yet this too exists inside and must be transcended. When one awakens, "hell within" is awakened as well. This is what many refer to as the within, the subconscious, the *Dark Night of the Soul,* the shadow selves or the "hidden". One's light is what has been veiled and forgotten and that is the self of a higher dimensional realm. This human is unaware they are traveling, for their journey is one that is unconscious, so they "get" the reality that was created from their own unconscious state.

Because all exist in all realms at all times, one does not just exist in this realm. The amount of consciousness determines how much "time" one spends here, yet all humans have hearts and that part of them shifts them into a higher realm, even when unconscious; they just do not get to navigate, participate or travel at will. Happiness is tied to external physical things, rather than an inner feeling.

Here, the physical manifestation (materialization) of one's physical reality is representative of the amount of density and light held within. The light part is not the issue, yet the dense reality is the one that will come up for review when shifting in vibrational frequency and the soul awakens to new truths. Where there has been greed, selfishness and individualizing, human "I" energy keeps one separated from SOURCE inside. This will surface and where there is separation, suffering will follow to show one where separation existed within. Where one can come to understand this, loss can be eliminated and sharing can be brought forth instead. Yet the unconscious human cannot comprehend this, for their human brain has not evolved to merge with their heart so that they can. That merging starts to occur as vibrational frequencies rise and that which has been dormant has been activated within. This shifts one into their 4th Dimensional existence, only to return here when their human mind is allowed to be in charge. In these times, the more one tries to return here, the more suffering they will now endure. One's attachment to physical things will determine which dimensional realm one is existent in as well.

Now, WE as the higher realm BEings are observing the deconstruction of the lower realms in a multitude of ways. This too is part of the process, for the souls that leave this plane chose to do so, before ever incarnating on the old earth that you once knew. Events shall occur to speed up this process as your human time continues to move forth. You only see the devastation, without understanding yet how all works. As you evolve and ascend, this will make more sense. You must allow yourself to see beyond your own limited human existence in order to understand this.

In this realm, the human calls it's higher self its conscience. This human may also "see" the devil/angel on the shoulders perception. Those represent duality and that is the 4th Dimensional Realm when one start to awaken and the battle of duality begins within. The human is asleep with their eyes open. They think their dream is when they are asleep. Yet it is the opposite of the higher realms, as the wake & sleep state completely flip. Yet before this can occur, one must enter the 4th Dimensional Realm, where realities are flip and merge while one sleeps to wake up.

THE HUMAN LIKES NEAT LITTLE BOXES, RESISTS AND HANGS ON

The human hangs on, fights, resists and does not like change. It likes "neat little boxes where all is in order and safe". Unfortunately, for the human, this is not how things truly are.

While the human hangs on, the Walking Soul, Higher Self BEing continues to let go. One comes from "safe", the other comes from an understanding that when *that* is let go, something awesome, and of a higher vibration, shall come to "fill that space".

For the human, it is continual "no no no, don't take that away from me" or "I need it this way, for this is the only way I can handle or I will fall apart." Really? Yep.

Human compartmentalizes, sections things off, loves bulleted lists, puts things in nice little rows and suffers from "don't touch that or do it that way, as I have it exactly the way I need it to be for me" syndrome.

Another favorite is "here, will you do this please?", to then criticize another completely for doing everything "wrong" or mumbling under their breath in a total resistant state of how it *should have been done differently*. One hair out of place, one can turn the "wrong" way, one dish left on the counter, and the whole inner world comes to an end. This one loves to argue and tell you how "that" should have been another way as well. It is opinionated and never happy. Pay attention to these key words "never happy". For this being has limited themselves so much and lives inside such a constricting box, that happy is a foreign language still. Be patient loves, for those hearts must be opened as well. This tightly wound human's reality that is strung so tightly, that if you pull a string, the entire reality starts to unravel and fall apart. This is in fact what shall occur, for the Higher Self will pull the string, when it gets to tightly wound and holding on is no longer an option and the perception of control must be removed as an obstacle to inner expansion. Look within, can you see any of this inside of you? If you can, this will resonate, you will feel it, and this will tell you much.

The Higher Self BEing could not care less about petty human details of any situation or what another is doing or did. It does not keep score, tally or worry about what another is doing or did, who did what to whom, or how many times. It takes that which needs to be done and just does it. It does not worry about another BEing, for our reality is our responsibility and when we no longer base our moments on another, we no longer have restrictions on "how" things need to be. Then we draw TO us others who also come from a place of honor and integrity to their own soul as well. Eventually, you have a bunch of Souls/Star Beings working together to make sure all things get done and work as they should. For, then you have the entire universe supporting each of you, for there is no lack, there is no struggle, there is no fight and there is no judgment or resistance to start with. Now how cool is that?

Resistance has an energy of a push/pull that can be felt by others and when it is present it causes others to respond the same. REMEMBER, you create this by BEing, so if you are resistant, then you create others to be resistant too. When you are in flow, easy, and LEADING with love, then those around you will come from love too.

This again is not about another, for all is created from within.

REMINDER: *When I have had enough of holding on, I will finally just let go. One is exhausting and the other again opens flow.*

REMINDER: *If I need things to be a certain way to be happy, I am human, for happiness exists first within.*

REMINDER: *A box is a limit and a bulleted list is too!*

THE HUMAN HOLDS "THAT" HOSTAGE

As I came to embody Christ Consciousness within, this one became a huge issue for me; for this was just an expanded version of "not sharing" that I had encountered on a smaller scale before. I could see the "hostage holding" collectively of absolutely everything that could help everyone, if "that" were just released. This was no longer tolerable in my own reality, so it caused me to go inward and find anything inside that I was not willing to share freely and shift that inside of myself first. Only then, can the limits on us be released "out there", after we have released them within. It is this way with everything on this journey, where we are still human and exist in separation within.

As your Higher Self, you know with your entire BEing, that you are here to reach many, teach many, and assist many with that which you hold inside of you. You may not know how, but you *will* know. How do you expect to do this, if you have limits on sharing that which you have access to in your own reality? Remember, your limits are your own.

In the beginning (lower realm), we have to learn to reverse the energy of "I/me/my/mine" to learn to ask for help, release the walls, the barriers, and learn how to open up to receive with our hearts. Pride, greed, selfishness and survival mode kept us separated. Focus on material things was a great representation of this.

In the middle realm, we spend all of our time learning balance. For with duality, there is always an opposite and the scales teeter-totter until we figure all out. There is balance in absolutely everything and in this realm; balance is a must before we can transcend duality within. We must learn balance with give (sharing) and take (receiving). Even the words shift in energy if you observe them.

Now, there is a time that we are "in between worlds" and we are trying to "learn" (REMEMBER) how to give and receive. Pride gets in the way, so that must be dissolved or broken. Value is the other one that is huge, while secrecy another. These are human things. In the beginning, as humans, we "work" to reverse the energy that restricts us within. If we cannot ask for help, we must. We must also learn how to receive. And where we are yet unable to share, whelp, yep, that one is a given for sure.

We can take anything and look at the one-on-one perspective, then we can span out to the masses. One is individual, the other collective. A great place to observe the microcosm (within) and the macrocosm (out there).

I observed others putting prices on things and refusing to share them when they did not sell. I see homes, rooms, offices sit empty, dormant and not benefiting anyone, all because of separation of the self and from wholeness as all again.

I hear in frequency, which means I hear the vibration of truth, regardless of the words being said. I would continually vibrationally hear and observe such separation as: "I worked hard for *that*, to achieve *that* and I expect monetary compensation for the value I have placed on *that*. I place more value on *that thing* sitting unused, than I do on all that "*that*" could help, *that* is "mine", I can't share *that* information for I need to charge money" or "I hold this hostage, so I can make a few bucks, and even if I don't make a dime, I still am not sharing, because it's about me and a reality that I have created in my mind about what is "fair", "I will share if I feel you truly need it, but I stand in judgment to decide that" or "oh, this was given to me it is mine and I come from a place of lack and can't share", "I have *this* and hold it hostage, when it could be freed to assist so many seeking "*that*", "oh this is meant only for me".

The list went on and on and it got overwhelming for awhile, until I observed the underlying theme. They had put a price on what they were willing to share. Now, of course, these are not the words that were spoken, but truth is visible in frequency, regardless of what is said. All completely human and Humanitarian SO got stomped on with this separation.

So, I wish to speak of this so that all can go inside and see where they have limits on sharing and what they hold out. For "out there" is only a representation of what we limit and hold hostage within.

Any time we put a price on something, we limit ourselves and restrict the flow. There are times we must, for we still exist in a physical world. There are times our higher selves will show us which is which, yet there are times we are confused and are not sure. And what we charge, if and when, will continually change as we raise in vibrational frequency. For the higher we vibrate, the more unified we become, the less this is necessary as we bring forth unity consciousness and sharing here.

The goal is not to hold onto more and sell more. It is to share more, in order to assist more, and in turn open up to receive more, from whatever the source. This is a huge spiral, for it takes creating a flow outward of sharing and allowing what we need to be received, from wherever/however it may come.

I share MY own with you, and hope to challenge you to go within. This is one you will have to see if you have limited and held hostage anything that could assist another, or many, the masses. Just another reason why we are here. To open up and share, and remove the barriers created by the human experience here.

Ask yourself some questions, and see what you get!

Where can I share with more for free in order to assist with creating change and uniting humanity?

REMINDER: Holding back was the old human way. The barriers and limits are my own.

REMINDER: The more I put out and share, the more opportunity I create to come to me. Letting go of my own limits allows me to also receive.

HOW MUCH WOULD YOU PAY FOR PEACE INSIDE?

Peace is an energy we become when every minute, every particle, every cell of us is in alignment inside again. It is an essence that we become when we breathe. It comes by slowing down our breath, slowing down our thoughts, removing obstacles and details of the human mind, existing from our hearts and REMEMBERING again. It is allowing ourselves to merge as all-that-is, no separation, no thought, no nothing… just presence and connection from inside again.

The old human would pay for things to fill a hole. That hole becomes so big, that nothing we obtain out there will fill it anymore. There comes a "time" when we desire more. Peace is a feeling that we must come to achieve inside again.

On this journey, the elusive peace, was something that we got momentarily by acquiring a "thing" to create this feeling inside. Now we have that feeling and do not *need* a thing. We found peace by letting go of all that was *not peace* within. Anything out of alignment, gone, to bring us back to peace again.

Many go on vacation to achieve that feeling of home inside. Once we have that feeling, ARE that frequency, we need not go anywhere anymore. Peace goes with us, no matter where we are. WE are peace and "out there" materializes to also be peace as well.

Money creates separation, and if we are trying to fill a hole, the separation keeps getting bigger until we connect with our Soul to again become whole. On this journey we are faced with paying for things that make no sense at all. We weigh peace against how much that costs, when peace is all we seek. We compromise our soul for money, so un-peace is what we get. When we decide to pay for that which assists us in connecting within, that which brings our soul forth in the physical, we find wholeness and peace again. Our souls, our higher selves, support us when we make this journey our priority, for unification and unity and bringing forth light is what we are here for.

So the next time you are challenged with paying for something or a service that will assist you in connecting with your true self inside again, ask yourself the question: "How much would I pay for peace"? And then do that. What you receive in return is bigger than you could ever imagine!

THE MIDDLE REALM

THE 4TH DIMENSION

SEMI-CONSCIOUS:
TWO SELVES

SLEEPING, AWAKENING, TRYING TO STAY CONSCIOUS, DUALITY, GOING WITHIN, BARDO, PURGATORY

This is a realm that I refer to as "the space in-between". I will expand on this at different times, for so very much occurs here and more than can be written in this book.

This is a place where all humans come to "work" to understand that which makes absolutely no sense in the physical, human world. It is one of duality, where dark (dense) and light (love) both exist. Here one exists in multiple spaces, and the head and heart are in direct conflict of each other. This realm is one of both visible and invisible, one where the physically tangible and invisible beliefs don't match up and much of the time, come into direct conflict. One opens up to the 5th dimensional realm here, when they start to hope and dream inside of something more than the tangible existence that no longer fulfills the heart. One's internal desire is either dormant, buried under un-truth's or not a first priority, as the human concept of tangible is "in the way".

This realm is where one will spend majority of their human time, while reversal, merging and integration occur. There will be a battle, if you will, a struggle, to come to understand the difference between the two worlds (inner vs. outer) and transcend duality altogether. Until this occurs, one bounces around between conscious & unconscious, in order to vibrate out of the frequency of separation within. This realm is where one feels bi-polar, for the ups and downs are dramatic when one is not yet conscious enough to participle and navigate their own journey. Even when one is conscious, bi-polar can be an understatement. We learn to shift quicker and create ease in this space. "All-over-the-place" can be somewhat tolerable when one understands and utilizes tools to navigate from within.

BELIEVING AND ACHIEVING "THAT": Here one believes, in some way, in the intangible, yet there is still enough of the human self present to "interfere", by continuing to still "need" tangible proof. One is "shown", through periodic higher realm openings, something "awesome and BEyond belief" to trigger a desires within. This also works to s-t-r-e-t-c-h the human mind in order to comprehend an extraordinary world that they have forgotten existed. It is this "new" belief and inspired desire for "that" intangible thing, which allows *that* to start to materialize in the physical. Yet it does not technically materialize, we "leave" the old frequency and come to exist in the frequency where materialization of that already exists.

We must embrace the desire to achieve or obtain "that" which is not yet tangible here in the physical. It is this determination and inner drive that shifts one out of the old human physical world and into the world of "believing" in the BEyond (forgotten) again.

This BEing "works" to achieve a higher frequency inside. This is done by embracing love, happiness, joy, gratitude and working with the light activations that occur within. The more one honors these, along with internal integrity, honor & respect, the easier one shall integrate and shift dimensionally into a higher frequency realm. There are a gazillion frequencies, spaces that one can occupy. Learning to bring these all together as one will eventually allow one to exist in the 5th Dimensional Realm where all exist as one.

Now, you will not hear me speak often of Karma, for from the higher realms, it does not exist. Yet for those BEings IN the lower realms (3rd & 4th), it still does, so at times I will speak to this. This too, is but a frequency loop, that has yet to be understood or cleared. There will be a moment that one will become aware that "their karma is clear". This occurs when one has totally consciously and intentionally reversed the spin of all human energy fields; the LightBody was activated with each heart opening release and is spinning as a unified field again. There still is much work to do "after this occurs", as while learning not to "create new karma" to have to endure or suffer to again. This is a space all occupy, while REMEMERING how to exist as integrity of their higher self heart at all times again.

From a higher realm, the entire open-eyed state here is seen as a "space of in-between" (the 4th Dimensional Realm), while to the one in this space, the closed-eyed state is the space of in-between where one can truly see, that which is not otherwise visible or tangible yet.

From the 5th Dimensional Realm (and higher), those here are still at times unconscious, yet consciously working to transcend this from within. It is the 4th Dimensional seeker that WE in the 5th Dimensional Realm (and higher) shall come to assist in the upcoming "times". Until one can come to exist as the higher realms again, from inside, the vastness of the realms in totality cannot yet be fully seen.

This realm is a combination of the earthly and Etheric realms. One starts to pay attention to energy here and get involved on a whole new "level". One begins to comprehend with their higher mind through their heart that which they already know. This is called REMEMBERING.

This is the realm where the Soul BEing begins to let go of all of the constructs that kept them "prisoner" "out there". They do this when they no longer believe it inside and just "let go" of that which created fear within them before. One must step into the fear to see that it truly never existed at all.

Continual re-birth occurs in this realm. The old is dissolved, the ego dies and a new you is continually re-born from within; pieces are recalled and the Soul wholes, in stages, according to the amount of separation over other times and existences, while simultaneously as this occurs, one comes to REMEMBER again.

REMINDER: *I do not need proof, that is my limited human me. All I need to do is listen to and come from integrity within my heart. Patience is of my higher self. Trust and honor are my keys.*

REMINDER: *I must believe and achieve and hold the frequency within where "that" already exists. It is already waiting for me; all I have to do is arrive in frequency again.*

REMINDER: *REMEMBERING comes when I close my eyes, tune to my higher heart and honor the peace and love that I hold inside of me.*

THE SPACE IN-BETWEEN

There are two spaces that I refer to when I speak of this. One is the space that you go when you close your eyes and connect, meditate, sleep or dream. The other is the entire 4th Dimensional Realm, for this entire realm IS the expanded view from "up here" in the higher realms.

ALL integrating, merging & flipping occurs in the "space in-between". Here I hope to explain a bit, so that one can further understand and utilize this space to work intentionally as well.

As an entire realm, one exists here as a "seeker of more", spinning and running around in "purgatory", releasing all human separation and beliefs of the old "fixed" human ways. One is always in this realm until "human" has been released, comes to exist again in a total state of REMEMBERING, and no longer forgets again inside. This is the realm of "purgatory" where pain and suffering reside. This is the realm where human beliefs are "exorcised" or "exercised". This is the realm that opens when one starts to question "who, what, when where, why" and "who am I". This is where the Star Seed, the Light BEing starts to wonder "why am I here"? This is where external realities start to fall apart when the Soul says it's "past time" to finally wake up. Here is where all starts to change and shift inside and out there. Yet it is not outside that is about to change. One is shifting from existing FROM an outside world, to CREATING it by moving inside. Here is where one shifts from an "outer to inner reality world" to an "inner to outer" reality world and all must be reversed. Here is where the fixed realities get bendable, flexible and outer realities completely dismantle, dissolve and fall apart, for the outer world will be completely rebuilt from the inside out.

Now, there are two ways to experience this realm. One is the open-eyed state (human) and the other is the closed-eyed state (Higher Self). One can actually choose the more direct route and choose to close their eyes and meditate or sleep. Yet the strong, masculine human energy form will resist this and choose to suffer to an actual physical world experience, for it is the strength of the experience that is necessary to "purge" the energy of the frequency inside. For one who desires to transcend, see, clear, purge by way of the "direct path", one will choose to shut down their human self, their human mind and sleep to activate, see, merge and integrate from within. The human feels they are missing out on the "physical world" somehow, so they will fight to stay awake and will actually NEED to participate in human experiences to learn the lessons they could see in the closed eyed state. The Higher Self, the spiritual BEing, the one who desires to reside from within, will choose to sleep, meditate and see from the inside first, which allows for the external reality to just "fall away".

One can actually utilize this closed-eyed-space. The heart is allowed to open here, and the Soul/Higher Self is allowed to emerge. Seeing is more visible here, yet the human self cannot comprehend that what they see is real. Absolutely everything seen in this space is true and real. It is of one of your gazillion parallels and existences that come forth as you active and integrate the higher frequencies from within.

Now, as all dimensional realms come to exist within you, you shall start see that which you could not previously see. Your dreams will act as clearings for your old human reality. They will present you with fears and karmic loops for you to actually participate in to reverse the energy without the need for an actual physical experience, unless you choose the old fear way again, then you shall invite a new experience to come forth, either in the physical or your closed-eyed state again.

Now, here is the fun part, for the entire 4th Dimensional Realm is also an illusion/dream. Not so funny, though right? You will understand, as you continue to embody the 5th Dimension and higher realms. Actually, all lower realms cease to exist here and you won't REMEMBER them anymore. You won't care either, for that was part of the illusion and you now exist outside of the matrix here.

The opened-eyed state gave you the physical experience you once required with tangible proof things to touch in order to believe. Yet the closed-eyed state shows you the entire realm in condensed form, so that you can choose to work with more ease from within.

That which comes forth in your closed-eyed state is for the purpose of observation (if even necessary) and quick release. The rest are REMEMBERINGS coming forth that were hidden far beneath your human existence that you were holding onto as safe.

Not getting stuck in trying to understand too much is imperative. Use what you see to dissolve any limiting beliefs. FEEL any emotional response present and if there are any, it is just coming up to observe (without judgment) and to leave. Getting stuck in it will keep one spinning in an energetic cycle here. The longer one gets stuck in this, the more "energy" they are needing to "burn". Staying conscious and understanding allows one to just see and release.

Now, other realities, parallels, dimensions and existences will also surface here. With all of the timelines collapsing, this can occur very fast. The higher one vibrates in frequency, the faster this shall seem. It is not faster, you spin at a higher vibrational rate.

There are two ways to "experience" absolutely everything here. One is the open-eyed-human way that requires an actual physical experience from "out there" to occur to "adjust" the physical reality and cause one to eventually go inside. This way is "slower and endures more suffering", yet it is the old chosen way of the fixed-human-mind. The other is to close your eyes and connect in a higher state. The experiences still occur, yet you are spared all of the physical world suffering. You can purge, interact and release limiting beliefs in this state. You can open your mind to believe all that you see as some form of reality. Whether it be of another "time", parallel or existence somewhere that you are just now able to see, all are true. All are your REMEMBERINGS of some reality of you. Much work occurs in each state, yet how you experience is now up to you.

REMINDER: The human needs an external experience with "proof" in order to understand. The Higher Self goes inside and cuts to the chase to see, hear, feel, know and REMEMBER again. The less one believes from inside, the more physical the experience is necessary to "shift" realities back to a SPACE of REMEMBERING again.

REMINDER: I can require an actual human experience to prove that to me, or I can go inside and honor that which I feel and see. "Doing" what I observe will instantly shift my external reality.

THE SLEEPY SEASON OF
AWAKENING TO REMEMBERING

There is a period that all go through during this process where all they can do is sleep. Sleep patterns are all over the place while the all of the dimensional realms of your higher soul self work to integrate into your BEing here. These are just a few examples of how sleeping patterns emerge: Many wake during odd hours (usually between 2-4 am), yet when they "need" to get up for "logical" things, they cannot. Oversleeping becomes an issue, and much of the time many feel the need to go straight home and go to bed. Late afternoon naps are almost a must, as one can barely stay awake during the hours of 2-4 pm in the afternoon. Here, usually a short nap will suffice, for sometimes this is just a re-boot time, while others sleeping for hours is necessary. Some will get up and go for an hour and immediately be so tired they cannot function and will feel the need to go back to bed again. Others just sleep all day, while at times several days are necessary as your soul light frequencies activate and integrate within you.

The human "thinks" something is wrong, yet things have never been more "right". These long sleep periods are pivotal in one's awakening. This is when much "work" is done, higher healing takes place, dense energy purges and mostly, realities are merging so that the old illusion can fall away. Lucid dreaming becomes apparent. Some have actual "weird" experiences that they do not understand and so many see things that make no sense. Some think they are hallucinating as the veils thin within of the dimensional realms.

The longer one suppresses the need to sleep, avoids the naps... the more they "prolong the inevitable". One can only prolong so long, then the Soul steps in and says "enough delaying", then things start to occur to "put one down". Just a couple ways are a long "depression", one's utilization of mind-altering substances to "escape", health issues exacerbating, or an injury interfering with ones mobility. As humans, we see these things as faults or extreme inconveniences. We do not understand they are a huge part of our waking up. I finally just did not care what others said and I just slept as much as I could. It became a joke, or huge conversation piece, at how much I slept; yet "after" I was the one awake, while everyone else was still asleep. Now they wake up and go through it in their way that their soul chose for them to experience here.

When one emerges from the "long sleep" (fog), things are different. More light will have been activated & integrated in the Soul, frequency impediments will have adjusted, Soul "holes" may have been healed, things actually look brighter and one has a whole new outlook, observations change and new "knowledge" starts to appear more and more. Synchronicities start to happen and one starts to notice signs everywhere that didn't seem to occur before. MUCH is occurring with these sleep states, as they are FOR you, if you will honor and allow them.

Many will attribute the need to sleep to anything other than what it is. The logical mind cannot comprehend this. One can suppress by seeking a physical reality "fix", yet to have it return with a vengeance another day.

Now, the groggy/foggy brain is also a part of your realities merging and flipping so that you can come to walk in a dream. Focusing is impossible here and memories, well, nope, those go too. Human will try to focus, yet if you can allow yourself to be groggy and just BE how you feel to be. You are not being lazy, your soul emerges and the higher dimensional realms come forth from within you and the outside world reshapes and materializes during this. You are about to be walking in a dream, yet it does not happen overnight. Your human mind is too separated and it takes "removing the ability" to control and focus away for this to occur.

REMINDER: When I feel to sleep, this is my higher self needing me to shut down. I can honor this as it is a necessary part of the journey.

THE UNIVERSE SENT ME A BIRD

It is through the stillness of thought and the observance of life, that I "learned" to lose myself in the flow of the Universe and become one again.

Little did I realize, at the time, that a family of birds building a nest outside my window would have such an impact on the next several years to come. Little do we actually realize at the time, how every moment is brought to us with a purpose of moving us in a direction of peace, love, kindness and utter and complete light.

I could never meditate. My mind was way too busy with thoughts that ran through my ever active head of "what about this, what about that"... thoughts of past or future that would come to no longer exist. But first, I had to LEARN to lose myself in stillness.

Every morning I would get up and take my notepad/computer to the living room, set up work for the day & open the blinds. This was after much of the heavy dense had dissipated, yet I had no direction within. Up until that time, I had withdrawn into denseness, while my own Soul pain surfaced for release. I would sit and work on designing websites, creating, organizing and thinking. What was the "future" to bring? Life as I had previously known it no longer existed. The Universe had seen fit to put me out of work, throw me into a barrage of addictions and emotional turmoil, while my Soul pain came up. I was experiencing chronic health problems that just kept surfacing, no matter how hard I "tried" to clear them... little did I know.

Loss provides for so many things. Those things we hold on to that are obstacles to finding our own inner self, the path to our own Soul, are often "taken away" and new things take their place. Things like loss of a job, loss of a relationship, loss of health... whatever makes us get stationary so we can go within. I REMEMBER saying to myself "well, I can't walk, so I might as well do my Metaphysical coursework"... and low and behold there was something that "I" needed in there. It took much to ground me, as I was extremely stubborn and refused to slow down. So choice, literally, got taken away from me.

Many do not understand why they lost that job, that marriage, that relationship, that material thing or why their health has failed. Absolutely everything that occurs is forcing one inside. Avoidance exacerbates the circumstances of how this occurs. The sooner one chooses to go inward, the sooner this will ease.

Much of the time we are even provided with the ways and means to accomplish "inner work" time. If one can realize the gift they are BEing given, they can choose to utilize it "quicker". Many are in situations where they have financial support, a place to stay, food to eat, yet they have "lost" what appears to be the very thing that occupied all of their time focused "outwardly". One isn't losing, but rather BEing given an opportunity that they would not have otherwise chosen on their own.

When there is buried treasure deep within, one must delve to the depths of the Soul to retrieve them and bring them to light. This only comes from inner reflection, inner observation and inner work. And this cannot be done by another. This requires that we learn to remove judgment of self and just dive in. We will always be provided oxygen (light) to breathe, but we must swim through it to get to that which will guide us to the utmost peace and love that one has ever experienced.

Every morning for hours, I would get "distracted" from my "work" to watch the little family of birds building a nest in a beautiful potted fern hanging from the overhead of the balcony. It started with ONE bird ONE day; then a few days later, BEing joined by another. The "bird show" got to be the highlight of my day. I started to look forward to going to greet my little birds and watch them create. And then one day, the nest was done, and there were little eggs in the nest. All of a sudden, how excited I was by the simplest things. I ran to grab the camera to take photos, as it was so cool! I would watch mama bird come and sit in the nest each day, while papa bird came & went throughout the day. One day I awoke to baby chirps and little heads popping up, and to my delight, I had a new phase of creation to watch while mama bird fed them with love. And finally, when I had been grounded enough to learn to sit still and observe and appreciate, one by one those little birds flew away to freedom and began their own journey to brighten another's day.

Recently I REMEMBERED my little family of birds and realized how that experience was part of teaching me presence and expanding my own consciousness. There are many things that contributed, but this one is the most present memory of yet.

Then one day, another emerging Soul of light said "There is this bird outside my window that I watch"... and I just smiled. And so it begins...

BEING CONSCIOUS

BEing conscious means BEing present, aware AND choosing something different than the old human way; one which now comes from love, honor, integrity, kindness and peace from inside your higher heart.

Many "think" that BEing aware is enough. I heard so many times along my journey "oh, I am very aware of that", yet nothing changed. There was no action, just awareness, usually with some judgment, blame, or expectation thrown in as well. Sometimes they saw, and chose to do nothing, because their stubbornness was stronger than their higher heart. These are so not being conscious, in any way, shape or form.

Consciousness starts out as a "new awareness", yet it eventually evolves into an entire way of BEING again. BEing conscious is not a "part time job". It is what you are as energy and how you allow yourself to BE in a REMEMBERED state.

The conscious BEing exists in a sacred space inside, where fear, lack, judgment and separation no longer exist. It honors all things as itself, for it understands that all are one. Any judgment or unkindness that comes out of us, comes back to us, for we ARE that.

WE come from a space of honor within. We do not have to be asked. We share from a space of love and we don't allow the limits and separation of others to cause us to "fall back". We hold the space of love and light, for if we do not, we have again become human and fallen, or descended, into separation and/or lack.

Consciousness applies to the foods we eat, the homes we live in, the activities that we participate in, the way we spend our money, the words we speak, the feelings we have, and the thoughts we think inside. Consciousness is not only what we do when others are looking, it is what we regardless of another's presence. It is what we ARE inside and out at all times here.

Consciousness does not hide, is not fake and it does not suppress or cover up. It does not fight "out there", for it understands that the fight is within.

Consciousness holds a certain vibration of love and light. It transmits by way of frequency, for all at their highest need no words to speak. To even speak means to drop down to human, so as physical BEings we must take care to observe that which we transmit with and without words. For there is no hiding in frequency as hiding is from our own selves.

REMINDER: When I "hide" something, it is not from anyone or anything "out there". My human me hides from my Higher Self (heart) and this is visible at all times. The only one who cannot see this is my human me.

REMINDER: I must be present and observant in order to be consciousness. Then I must DO that which exists in my higher heart.

REMINDER: Speak it out loud. This brings "it" up and out into the physical and allows me to SEE and HEAR that exists inside of me. If it is not true, I will hear the untruth in frequency. All is BEing created in my reality. Not speaking that which I do not yet understand exists inside, keeps it materialized in my reality until I no longer believe it anymore. Speak it, hear it, and release it if it does not transmit at a frequency of truth from within my heart.

REMINDER: BEing aware is not enough. I am conscious when I actually choose differently than my human self and shift to horning from my Higher Self heart.

YOUR SOUL SPEAKS THROUGH YOUR BODY

Your Soul will speak with every fiber of your BEing, if you know how to listen and choose to do so until you don't have to try anymore.

It will speak in soft voices, as you, from inside your head. It will come across as "other BEings" when it is "outside" in your energy field, waiting for you to let go of enough human, so it can "fit IN" instead of BEing "out there", separated.

It will show you when something is out of alignment in your physical, out of tune. For there will be physical pain or dis-ease that occurs to get your attention, that density is in the way. It will try to expand and push UP and OUT from every orifice of your body when something is too dense and is in the way. There is nothing "wrong" with it, for "that" is trying to leave. You Soul is trying to "move in" from "out there", where it has thus far been.

Your Energy Body used to be outside of you, and this was your Higher Self/Soul. Yet it is "time" for it to fully come to BE EMBODIED from within you. It wishes to drive now and your human you must step aside.

All density must go. All thoughts, emotions, memories, foods, and physical world things that interfere with your inner journey expansion to become ALL-THAT-IS again. You are to become ONE again, AS the entire Universe and Gaia from within. When, is up to you and your specific journey of choice set forth by your own Soul/Higher Self. NOW would be the appropriate response, for this is your ultimate purpose here. How is dependent on how conscious you are and how much to choose to suffer by trying to not be conscious and let go.

You hear in frequency, for you are but a frequency yourself. So when you hear something "not right" "out there", this is an "out of tune frequency" within you.

You orchestrated your entire journey, long before you arrived here. You set forth every moment and how it would occur. You, as your Higher Self is guiding you, for it knows what your journey is. It will drop bread crumbs, to see if you will pay attention and wander off to see where they go. It will send you little gifts, to encourage you along the way. It will show you some amazing things "from your future" to keep you motivated and desiring "that". It will do all that it can to assist you in shifting from your human mind to come to exist with it as one again, which starts by opening your mind and heart.

Your physical body will continue to tune, as the frequencies continue to rise here on your Earth. This is your perception, for while they do this out there", they only do so as a projection of what is going on inside of you "for real".

You will FEEL truth from inside of you now, whereas before you might not have understood this. You are a Soul walking in a physical body vessel, but before your "suit" did not fit. There is absolutely everything going on to get all of your bodies to integrate and merge. Whew, you are a full-time job!

As your energy activates and expands you will feel energetic movement in the spin points of your entire body; Chakra vortexes, meridians, (fingers, toes, solar plexus, your 3rd eye, your crown, your heart and more. Your entire body will start to feel things it has never felt. It will "eject" anything right back on "out" that it doesn't like anymore. Anything you have used as a suppressant in the past will no longer work. You will know when to let go of these things, for you will feel this inside. You suppressed because it was your journey, yet your journey now shifts into love.

There are many of you who have always been connected, yet "out there" just made no sense. These tools can assist you as well, in making sense of a backwards, inside out, upside-down world that reverses from human, then reverses to become ONE again.

Now, in the beginning, so many of us "become" Empaths, because we become aware that we feel "others' stuff". As we evolve, we come to realize that we only felt their stuff, because it was our stuff and they were showing us where we were out of tune within. Eventually, we feel all things, yet without the emotional triggers or responses. We become one with/as the Universe again and this always existed within. This is why we could feel all of "that", for that was always inside and never "out there". "Out there" was our projection, or projector's view, and now we create that, instead of responding to that, like we did when we were human.

REMINDER: *Absolutely everything that occurs within me is my Soul expanding and trying to communicate and emerge. I can assist, listen and honor to "expedite" this journey of embodying my own Soul.*

REMINDER: *The human is an empath, the Soul is the entire universe again.*

THE OPEN HEART VS. THE CLOSED HEART

The key to REMEMBERING is coming to exist AS love again. In the 5th Dimension, you are a BEing with a totally open heart. You have no blocks, veils, or walls anymore. You only did when you separated and became human. Your ascension is so that you can find your way home from inside again. This will occur as your Soul becomes whole, as you release the limiting belief systems you learned and acquired and as you come to REMEMBER BEyond your separated human self and unify again within. All of this was held in your old human DNA and transmitted out in frequency from within.

As humans, the human heart is a "house" for all human experiences and memories necessary for your human experience. This house has many walls, partitions and blinds to keep you from seeing your true you and all untruths that were held inside.

Humans have been conditioned to think instead of to feel; to suppress instead of express; to hold on instead of let go; to hide and compromise, where judgments were formed; to protect from some perceived threat and to expect disappointment and betrayal from others "out there". This is not always the case, for there are many beautiful open hearts. Yet, this is a list of some of the common blocks that one might encounter along the human-journey-way. All of this must be reversed, released, and re-aligned from within. Your Higher Self memories exist beneath all of "that". As you release these blocks, new memories will come forth. All that you have attached to, is not you. It never was.

As humans our human hearts became blocked, walled off, separated

112

into a million pieces, over a million existences and "times". These are energetic blocks that manifest in the physical reality in a multitude of ways. Some might present as medical problems, others as emotional/physical ailments or pain. All, just an out of tune frequency, that can be released with tuning or energy work, in addition to the work one does by going within and becoming totally conscious again.

Now, lack in the heart is a "hole" in the Soul, yet only a discordant frequency to be tuned. This you "heal" yourself, by reclaiming that which you have attached yourself to "out there". You see where you have compromised your own spirit for anything less than inspirational love.

You have a human heart and a higher heart. Your higher heart holds no lack or separation within. It is connected AS the entire Universe, Gaia and your Higher Self from within you. This is the one you access, every time you shift from a place of thinking with the human mind. This one lets go of all that does not inspire, unify and transmit pure light and expansive love.

An open heart transmits love from the inside out. This is an energy that can be felt radiating out from your entire BEing. The human heart that is blocked or holds lack or fear, pulls energy in, or puts up a wall, that stops all energy flow all-together. This can actually be felt. It is this flow of energy that determines your entire existence here.

An open heart has no attachment and no expectation of return. It just does, no reason, just because. This heart needs no result or response. It does not "give" more than it has, for it shares that which it already is.

Exercise: Close your eyes and go into your heart. Now think of something you absolutely love, something that inspires you and causes you to expand from inside. Maybe it is a visual or maybe it is a word alone. What matters is that you connect to a feeling. Not the word or the thing. The feeling is what you transmit. Notice how you feel and imagine energy flowing OUT of you, from inside.

Now, think of something you fear or something that is a lack in your mind (money, loss, BEing alone, not good enough, etc.) Now FEEL the energy shift. Can you feel it stop flowing out? Did it pull in and reverse or stop? This will tell you much.

REMINDER: I am love. I am an open heart, flowing out from within. When I feel this flow stop, I must go inside to reverse the energy again.

GETTING OKAY IN YOUR CURRENT REALTY

What is not okay in your reality? Anything that is not, is you out of balance and alignment inside.

BEing okay is peace within and it is something we come to exist AS and resides inside. Yet, a common human mindset is "if I had *that (or more)*, all would be okay." I need this or I want that, not realizing or truly appreciating what they already have, as for this BEing, what they have is never quite enough. It is "I am thankful, but.... ". This is a discordant frequency, again needing to be adjusted or tuned. Usually an adjustment or experience will come along to make one appreciate (and share) again.

As usual, there are a multitude of perspectives to choose from!

Can you lay or sit in any space and be at complete peace within you? Can you FEEL and KNOW that exactly what you have, right here, right now is perfection? Can you appreciate what you have or do you always want for something else? Is your "happy" based on anything outside of you or something that you don't already have?

Happy and okay is not anything "out there". It exists within and RADIATES OUT. WE create our happy and peace from within.

All that represents happy "out there" that is not in alignment with your Divine Essence and BEing, usually get "adjusted" to show where something is "backwards" or "off". If things are not working, there is a reason and falling victim to it is the "old" way. Observing it, going within, finding it, owning it & CHANGING IT are all aspects of the Higher Self.

All things are "reversed" in this process. All have spent their entire "lifetime" acquiring things, controlling, achieving; for all of that to fall away. Identities have been created around others & things. One has no idea who they truly are. When it is time for one to come to REMEMBER their own true self, as an energetic BEing, all things "out there" will away until this has occurred. One can choose to participate or allow it to occur for them. The latter is a whole lot less "fun".

Stop for a moment and breathe, get in a space where you can get quiet and go within. Now remind yourself that, in this moment, you are okay. You have everything you need. Re-focus your energy. Get out of "another time". The "future" is BEing created by that which you FEEL right now and visualize in your mind's eye. If that is anything less than bliss & perfection, YOU ARE CREATING that which you do not desire. If you do not want it you have to stop focusing on it and start to focus on transmitting out that which you DO desire. Desire comes from your heart, not your rational-thinking mind. If you wish to create, you must first get okay and come to peace inside. Otherwise, all you are creating is that which is not okay according to your own mind. BEing okay is not in your head, it is always deep within your heart. Now the question is, can you exist, in every moment, from your heart? If you can, then you can start to create that which you truly desire. And this will ALWAYS be a FEELING which then creates the thought rather than a thought that creates a feeling. This will cause a dimensional shift, first inside and then "out there".

Now, there is an additional step to this. If you can get "okay" inside with letting go of *that*, not having *that*, or whatever it is, see what you would DO once you no longer "have *that*" obstacle in your way. What different thing would you do? Then go ahead and do that, as this may be the entire point. If you have a wall or block in place, this may be what your higher self is trying to get you to see. What, from your heart, would you try to attempt when you have nothing left to lose? Fear, pride or judgment are usually in our way, so something will occur to shift us to that space of "having to". So, use your higher-heart-mind to see what you are not otherwise willing to see and go ahead and "do" that which your higher hearted self is trying to get you to do from within. Much of the time you can bypass the need to lose, if you will go ahead and do *that* which is uncomfortable, yet that which you already know deep down inside. You will have to observe and see, as it is YOUR reality!

This world is backwards. Welcome to the inside-out world of the Soul. Embrace crazy and you will do just fine here!

GETTING PRESENT TO GET "UNSTUCK"

You are your Higher Self when you are present and in a space of love. This is no longer your future you, this is your present you, your NOW you. You must REMEMBER this, if you wish to exist as your Higher Self/future you. In this space, you are your future version of you.

In the beginning, we must practice BEing in present moment, and as we integrate the higher light frequencies within, we find that we are always in present moment. Stepping out of present moment is very uncomfortable and we do not like it there!

So, if you find yourself needing to shift. Try this!

Imagine if you will, that in THIS MOMENT, all time stands still.... in THIS MOMENT, you only have THIS MOMENT. GET present.

With the ability to get so very present that one can raise their level of consciousness, then one can CHOOSE to manipulate "time" as it is perceived to be. Soooo, STOP EVERYTHING and pull your thoughts and the situation INTO the present moment you are in. Do not leave to go "over there" in a time that does not exist. This takes much practice to master this one!

Now, observe it. Take the faces off of all of those involved. It is no longer personal. Examine what energy exists (responses or actions allowed this to occur... and if a karmic loop, the repeated actions, etc.).

Now, own it. Say so what... it no longer matters and in order to release it from my energy, I have to let it go. There is no right, wrong, good, bad, fault or judgment. It was a lesson and a test. The only one judging the situation is you. You are responsible and in control of what you think in your head and choosing to participate (human) or observe (higher self).

Now, let it go.... be done... and say thank you. Thank you for YOU making the choice to choose this amazing opportunity to learn from and REMEMBER again. Move to a place of gratitude for all of those souls that fulfilled their part in the contract that YOU agreed to, before ever incarnating here in the physical.

Now, if a decision is necessary, choose the one that is dictated by the heart, not the individual human mind. Self-created chaos exists in the mind. The illusion exists in your mind. When you put your hand on your heart & close your eyes, you know what is important and what to do. Details no longer matter and everything unimportant falls away.

Step INTO it. Breaking a frequency loop requires that one DO what is necessary according to the heart, according to the Universe inside, no longer according to that of the human-thinking and holding-on mind. Whatever you do, must be done with love and compassion for all, always, always, always while honoring you. They are your mirror here to show you what existed inside.

Now, if you choose to suffer, to a thought, you will. This is your fearful and individualized human mind and your heart must be stronger in order to stop the old programs running, belief systems, frequency loops. If you allow your mind to run rampant, then you are not present or conscious.

YOU HAVE THE ABILITY TO CUT, RELEASE, CLEAR, LET GO AND TOTALLY BE FINISHED, yet this is a choice of choosing your heart over your mind; and that cannot be done when one's head is in the perceived past or future, that technically do not exist.

REMINDER: *The past is gone. I am the one holding on. Cut the thought, let it go. I am not a creator when I am stuck there. I am getting the repeat version of the lower realms if I continue to try to hang on.*

REMINDER: *The future has not yet occurred and my thoughts right now are creating that!*

REMINDER: *In-This-Moment,* _____ *(you fill it in). This is what I am creating, and presence gives me the power of creation again.*

IGNORING OUR OWN HEARTS:
THE ULTIMATE BETRAYAL

In watching the chaos transpire all around, there is one underlying theme; that chaos is self-created in the mind.

When we choose to go against what we "feel" in our hearts, when we choose to give way to the "thoughts or belief systems" learned or acquired, we betray ourselves and what we "know" deep within our soul. As humans, we then look at everyone else as the ones who have betrayed us, when in fact the betrayal lies within. This is why we have such trust issues, as we place trust in another when in fact trust is to honoring our own divine essence, our own heart and humanity within. We don't need another to betray us, we manage that all on our own. And from this stems the inability to trust anything at all until we learn to honor our higher heart and all as one again.

Now, not listening will bring forth another energy to have to deal with later (usually anger). To avoid the frequency loop that this creates, we can choose to listen and honor at all times. In order to do this, one must be present, conscious and choose from the higher heart until all existing loops have been diminished energetically.

REMINDER: *When I honor the truth within me, no one can ever betray me again. Betrayal is my own, when I choose not to listen to my heart within. Even if I do not listen, there is something I needed to show me this, so that I release the need to ignore my heart again.*

CHALLENGES EXISTENT WITHIN

Everything that is challenging is to show us either what still exists inside as a belief or where we have come to see it as no longer a part of our fixed reality so that it can finally go and we can exist in a space where that no longer exists.

At first, a challenge presents because we believe it, are limited and feel bound by it. Once we truly challenge IT, we come to see the energy of why it even exists to begin with.

Each time a challenge is presented, if we embrace it, challenge the belief and release it as "no longer true" in our now "flexible reality", the "shorter the amount of time" it hangs around (exists inside). The more we observe this, the "faster" we see it "each time", the quicker it is allowed to go. Eventually it comes back around and we see it "in advance". We say "I no longer believe that; that is no longer a part of my reality inside" and we allow it to "float on by". Each time "this scenario" occurs, when we choose consciously, we shift up vibrationally and out of the old lower dimensional frequency. Eventually, WE come to exist in a frequency where *that* no longer exists at all and we do not even see it or encounter it anymore. It is not because THAT no longer exists, for it still does in a lower dimensional realm, yet WE have shifted in frequency to exist in a dimensional realm where that no longer exists. So, it does and doesn't exist. Both are true. The realm you exist in determines the reality and experience that you transmit and receive. It is up to each to face each "challenge", each time we feel or notice resistance inside. This is a key to choosing to shift OUT of that frequency, so that we no longer have to "try" to do this anymore. It just happens, for shifting at will is what we now do.

How long this "process" takes, depends on how present we are, how conscious we are, how aware we are and how quickly we embrace from inside. The longer we "see it "out there"", the longer it exists for us to have to shift and go within. If we choose to go inside "faster" then it can start to dissipate once we step into the discomfort of the energy presented to bring "that" to our attention. WE put that there. WE have the power inside to completely obliterate and dissolve that. WE have to REMEMBER and "do" what is held in our heart. If we allow our human mind to interfere, we get a physical experience (tangible proof), and much of the time an uncomfortable one, to cause us to go back inside to REMEMBER again.

The bigger the challenge, the stronger the human belief inside. These hold the most energy and will require "many experiences" to no longer "believe that" anymore. The "faster" we see it and embrace it, the faster we transmute, transform and transcend.

The more discomfort, the more awesome and magical we get to receive, see and experience AFTER we shift.

INTENTIONALLY DISSOLVING SEPARATION WITHIN

If you wish to integrate at a "higher rate", you will intentionally work to dissolve any separation that you hold within you. This will apply to absolutely everything there is. If you do not feel completely whole and at peace within, then you exist in separation. If you look to another "time", you are separated. If you exist in fear, doubt, blame, shame, or lack then you are separated within. Connect AS your Higher Self inside to come to center, back into your heart, to align and find peace again.

If you do not know how to do this, there are plenty of Lightworkers & WayShowers (including myself) "out there" that have created tools to assist you with this. Find a program that resonates with you, that directs you inside yourself to find answers and you make this your priority. Your entire existence here is for this journey. The longer you "avoid it", the harder it will come to be. Embracing the journey within allows for one to learn to navigate and avoid the suffering that those before you had to endure in order to show the way for all others seeking existence as a Christed and Sovereign BEing existing AS the 5th Dimensional Realm from within.

THE ILLUSION AND SEPARATION OF MONEY

A money system was created by all of you to create separation within. This one represents separation to the extreme. Yet, when one can truly come to understand the purpose, one can then create change within. Then, and only then, will it change, "out there".

Separation is in your human DNA; therefore the illusion of money is too. It is another tangible thing that can be used as a crutch for an existence of BEing or as a tool to reach and assist more in Ascension and unification again. When money is no longer about you, but how you can utilize it to bring forth ONENESS, CREATE the NEW, share it to create unity, rather than separate, gain material things and make your own life more comfortable, while others "out there" suffer, then you shall no longer live within the confines that money creates. Until then, your existence will be controlled by money, for you believe it to be this way.

There are many things you can do to "shift" your reality, so that loss is not the "lesson" you receive in order to "teach you this". You have complete power just by shifting in frequency, from a state of separation into love.

You will have to make this an internal journey as well. For money only represents what is still separated within you and where you have forgotten humanity and unity inside.

First, ask yourself what money represents to you. Your answer will tell you much. For the human, the focus will be on what they "need". For the Light BEing, it will be first on their mission and how they can assist others.

Money is a form of energy and when you can see it as energy coming to you to assist you on your journey of becoming one again inside, how you use money will change, and the lack of money will then too. As the entire money system continues to dissolve, how you experience your material world will be up to you.

The human works relentlessly to make money in order to acquire things and "survive". This is an instinct exacerbated by the belief that one *needs* to survive at all. You don't *need* to survive. You never did. This was a human belief.

There are many tools and ways of shifting. You will need to create ones that work for you. I can only share mine, as guided by my Higher Self along the way.

When you look at money, what are your thoughts? Do you go into fear or love? Do you see how you do not have enough or do you see where you have more than another and plenty in "this moment"? Do you see how this can help only you or do you see where this can help all? Do you feel lack or do you feel abundance? One separates, one unifies. And what you DO with money determines whether you ever have enough.

When I first started to understand this, I was in lack. I would get "down to my last dollar" and panic. "Oh no, I might not have enough". I realized that when I looked at that dollar, my subconscious belief was "this was my last dollar", and therefore BECAUSE that was my belief system, then it was true. So I created a way to change my own internal belief system, from one of lack to abundance. When I was "done", I no longer looked at that dollar and thought lack. I was in gratitude that I had a dollar and felt my heart swell in appreciation and abundance.

I also came to understand that I needed to reverse, flip and completely transcend my belief system about what money meant.

To the human, money means "more for me". To the Higher Self (the unified being, the humanitarian), money is only a way to help, assist and reach more in love, light and unity again.

One operates from fear, lack, a closed heart, separation, survival and "me" mode. The other operates from an open heart, creation, unity consciousness. There is no "me" in WE.

Again, my Higher Self guided me, as I heard the words "If your rent is paid, you can work for free". Really universe? I have to work for free? "Yes, until you understand and DO for no reason to help many without needing anything in return, when you already have enough".

Wow, THAT put things in perspective. I had lowered to a human frequency of "I need to worry about that time in a future that doesn't technically exist", instead my higher realm version of "what can I do right now, in this moment, to create and share?".

So, every day I would get up and share information freely, and my Higher Self would deliver that which could assist all. Information is free, yet the human has decided to put a price on this. The human puts a value on "the work they did" and expects something in return. It puts restrictions of how much to give, when to give, who to give for it believes that "giving" takes from them in some way. This is the "backwards" reality of the human- mind-way.

Now, as long as you still exist in a money society, then some money will be necessary for you to have what you need in order to exist to fulfill a purpose of assisting others, creation and unification. Where the human gets *stuck*, is when they focus on money instead of how many they can reach and assist with their *free time*. Yes, TIME is FREE, and it is the human that has put an amount on how valuable this is. Now, when you are in creation mode, time does not exist. So BEing in creation mode all of the "time", allows you to do more, to reach more, to assist more, while not existing in the human separation of time. The more you create, the more you have to share. Yep, it's that spiral thingy again.

Another "tool", if you will, is that we learn along the way is to minimize waste and to stop spending money on material things that are unnecessary. I used to ask myself, which energy am I feeding when I desire to buy (or pay for) this? Is it lack, is it necessary, is it wasteful, can I use this money to help more instead? Am I supporting this journey and change for all with this? Can this buy me opportunity to reach more? Then I made a conscious choice and by doing this, learned to live on little of nothing, compared to the old human way. And once I had done without long enough to become conscious, I never had to do without again. And if we look at it all, we never truly have done without. We just didn't have what we had come to "expect" as humans. I also stopped looking at what *that* was costing me and I looked at what I was getting by way of opportunity to reach others in return. This shift in perspective was huge. For with this, I was no longer victim to money, as I was using money as a part of my Light Mission here to reach and assist more.

Now, the human will work for money and have to buy opportunity. Yet the Higher Self BEing will see money as a way to create opportunity to come to it. We "flip" everything into opposites and reverse of the old human way. And money is a huge one, since separation can be so huge here as well.

Now as humans, we do not like to pay for things that don't give us something tangible in return. Even vacations are a necessity, as they bring that feeling that all should already exist from inside at all times. This is how it works for the human. I pay for this because it makes me "feel" a certain way. This feeling alone is an activation of peaceful "home" energies one is seeking to start with. This is why so many will pay top dollar to go to the mountains, a power spot or beach. It represents a frequency they need to activate and integrate to hold within.

For me, I would come to a place of peace inside *and THEN*, I would shift my view on "that". I would expand my perspectives and "see it" from every purpose that I could. If the purposes were all about "me", then I knew which mode I was in. If the purposes were how it would assist me as to "why I was here", then I knew I was existing AS my Higher Self and that "this" would allow me to further serve. We are not meant to lack so that we can serve; only for awhile, until WE no longer hold that frequency of lack belief inside anymore.

I created "exchange" from the Universe for all that I did. I took the need to receive from a specific individual off anything, and only when I was guided to place a value on a specific thing, did I do this. For there were certain things that my Higher Self assisted me in creating that would bring me income so that I could continue to reach more along the way.

Now in "BEing of Service", we have many ways that we do this. The goal is to have so many options for one to choose from, that they can pick from free or choose to pay you for your individualized and personalized attention that we so abundantly share. Yet, the human will also put this in a box, for they will set "guidelines" for everyone to adhere to. This is no longer a reality of guidelines. That alone is human.

I started to notice the difference, along the way, of how I got paid and the "theme" of human or Higher Self BEing. The human placed no value on their own Soul and did not wish to pay for any of this at all. They wanted the easy answer, the quick fix, "that thing for free", and then they did not appreciate the amount of my time that I put into assisting them. Instead of placing more boxes and restrictions on "them", I created ways to maintain my own energetic boundaries within and not compromise myself for one who lacked integrity within. I learned that when *I* compromised myself for one who lacked integrity, it was me that lacked integrity to me. After awhile, we no longer draw these experiences to us, for we no longer operate at the frequency where we need this.

I started finding that the more I shared freely, the more I assisted others, the more others identified with me. They came to trust me and resonated with that which I shared in frequency. The more I did this, the more I drew "Souls" to work with. Walking Souls come from a place of honor inside, for true integrity exists in the heart. These were offering to pay me, for they did appreciate that which I shared to assist them. This created flow WITHIN the exchange that allowed me to continue to assist more/all. For these, I did not require payment, and I came to exist on complete honor and trust. I was there to assist when requested, and they supported my work and free sharings, from their heart, just because.

Ask yourself for a moment, if your entire foundation is built on money and things, then what will you do when this is gone? It IS going, technically it already has. Will you have already created a commUNITY that is there to support each other, share and exist in unity and love together again?

When you can see money as the illusion that it is, you will come to use money as unifying energy, rather than of separation.

When it is *your time,* the money structures within you will start to fall and dissolve. You built your money/belief system as a human, and as a Walking Soul, human separation must fall for all to rise up to become one again.

REMINDER: *Quick fixes are of the human way and will require a lesson so that will learn to go inside, which is where I should have gone to start with.*

REMINDER: *The human pays to achieve a feeling, whereas the Higher Self BEing achieves the feeling inside first, and then pays if it truly serves a purpose.*

REMINDER: *When I focus on money first, I separate within and drop to a lower vibrational frequency and become human again.*

REMINDER: *WE do not need money, if we can all learn to share*

REMINDER: I have more than enough, therefore I can share with others too. It is up to me to BE the one who "starts" this, rather than waiting for others to do this first.

REMINDER: When the focus is money, I limit myself. When the focus is all as one, I open up to unlimited possibilities and opportunities to be brought to me.

REMINDER: In this moment, I have enough, therefore I can DO for others without any expectation of return. I am limited in receiving as long as I am limited on giving/sharing that which I already have or is freely received by me. Sharing is of the open heart and receiving comes TO me dependent on how much I OUTPUT energetically. The more I share freely, the more I am open to receive.

REMINDER: Money is a representation of energy, that is all. Am I supporting change and that which I truly believe inside? Or am I supporting an old belief system that I allowed myself to believe? That which I support shall be my reality.

WE MUST DO IT FIRST; THERE IS NO WAITING

The human will make that which it does dependant on someone, or something occurring, "out there". This one will wait until something happens to make a decision. It will passively place an expectation on another/thing, wait until it is "let down" or another substantiates it's expectation of "BEing let down" or "that occurring like it knew would happen". This human then forms a reaction to "that". This is passive aggressive human behavior and it is a "game" that the human plays. This one acts from (and even creates an experience) to have an emotional response to in order to keep up the human ego drama game. This one feeds and breeds fear and separation from within.

The Higher Self BEing observes what it truly desires and it takes action and does not wait. From a space of love, it "jumps" into that and through action says "I am not waiting, for this is what truly exists within my heart". It does not wait for another to come from honor, integrity, respect and love, for these are our own inner BEingness that radiate from the inside out. This higher self being is supported by their Universe, for they are following that which is of their higher heart.

Here there is no fear, for that was an illusion to keep all imprisoned. Love, honor, respect, integrity from within and DOING that which unifies Humanity and all as ONE again, is all there is NOW. As WayShowers and Light BEings, we do not wait. That was fear, and the illusion of the old human way.

Reminder: I get exactly what I expect inside. When I release expectations and open my heart, that too is what I shall receive in return.

HUMANS REQUIRE BOUNDARIES

In the beginning (the lower realms), we had no "healthy boundaries", for this was not of the human way. As we come to embody our higher selves, we come to REMEMBER how to create boundaries for ourselves. This is a very necessary part of the process, for it teaches us to stand in our own strength, where we did not before. It also teaches us, if we are present, about the energy of honorable exchange.

Now this one is "tricky", for while we must learn boundaries in the "space in-between" (the middle realm/4th Dimension), in the higher realms we no longer need them anymore. So this is one of the paradoxes. First we learn them, then the need for them just fades away.

Boundaries are walls, they are limits and they keep us separated inside. But before we can come to a place where they are no longer necessary, we must learn to utilize them to create a sacred space that WE honor for ourselves. We must learn the energy of give and take, push & pull, too much and not enough. Yet this too is never about another, for they only honor a contract to show us where we lack or have walls. Once we see what they came to show us, their "role" (or contract) changes. We can choose to keep them in our reality in another capacity or release them all-together.

REMINDER: *When boundaries are an issue, then I must go within to see where I have overstepped or allowed another in my energetic space. It is not about what they do, it is about what I allow and what I do (from love). Note: "No thank you" with love, works really well here.*

EXERCISE: ENERGETIC BOUNDARIES

Stand in a room and draw and imaginary circle around you on the floor. Arm's length is good, bigger if you desire, it does not matter, for the circle is the point. Now imagine another human (or get one to actually do this with you) standing 10-20 feet away. Have them draw the same imaginary circle around them on the floor.

Now, observe your circle and then observe theirs over there. Notice how far apart yours is from theirs. Now, everything that happens inside your circle is your energy, your responsibility, your concern and everything "way" over there in their circle is theirs. The moment you "step out" of your circle to "impose" on their energetic circle, you have overstepped your boundaries. Every time you allow another to "come into yours", you have allowed them to over step theirs.

Practicing staying inside the circle will help you establish and maintain honorable boundaries, if you have never had any before. Then you can turn around and let them go when you have established enough boundaries to not need them anymore.

REMINDER: I am responsible for what occurs in my energetic bubble and what I transmit out from within. I am also responsible for what I allow into mine. "That is no longer acceptable in my reality" (said with the strength of love) works well here.

THE HUMAN COMPROMISES

This one is another HUGE one and takes repeated experiences to learn to navigate with ease. This one starts out where the human compromises in every aspect, the awakened one seeks to master this and the Higher Self BEing no longer compromises at all.

Now, compromise is not as most would see this one. Compromise is what we do, JUST BY BEING HUMAN. For it is the human mind itself that creates all compromise to begin with.

The higher heart does not compromise, for it is conscious and acting from choice in every moment. Here, one is creating with every thought, for thought of the Higher Self BEing comes through the heart.

Others are sent to us, answering a call, to show us where we will compromise inside. Our "job", if you will, is to see it and shift out of this space from within.

If another comes to you and asks you to do something you are not comfortable with, your first "clue" is the discomfort that you feel. And it is up to you not to compromise and to honor that which your Higher Self is showing you by way of "giving you a feeling" inside. FEAR of another's reaction stops one from honoring their heart.

Now, eventually, when you come to exist AS your Higher Self again, compromise will no longer be an issue. You will have practiced enough to no longer hold this frequency inside and eventually all of your responses will be from the heart and your human mind will not enter the equation.

Until then, you must intentionally remain conscious and do this intentionally until you have shifted inside to come to exist AS this again.

Which frequency you hold (compromise or not) will determine which dimensional realm you exist in.

REMINDER: I created this situation, asked for this contract, this Soul to come and "test" me. My test is to see if I will come from honor and integrity from within me to that which I feel in my heart. If I do not, I will call another Soul (or many) to me, to test me again, until I no longer compromise inside.

REMINDER: Compromise is what we as humans do, when another triggers our own lack of honor and integrity within. We are the ones that allow. They are the ones that just show us how.

REMINDER: Discomfort shows what I must do, when I have avoided standing in my own integrity and truth as a normal response before.

CHALLENGE YOUR OWN MIND: THOUGHTS

As a human, your thoughts are not your own. They have been learned and acquired along your human existence here. This was the PURPOSE. No one is victim here. Yet, until this is understood fully, victim is what all are and were, for we were ALL victim to our own human mind along our unconscious way. When one starts to awaken to this (wakes up), confusion, anger and lots of tears also then must come up; for the human mind is a suppressant to our Soul awakening from deep within. When you REMEMBER this, you will not listen to anything that it says. You will just listen instead.

Now, as vibrational frequencies rise and the photonic light activations continue to occur, human thoughts get louder and louder inside until that is all that one can hear. This is why so many cannot sleep, meditate or be alone, for their human mind drives them crazy, sometimes literally, and off the deep end we go. Yet it is this "deep end" that assists us in purging deep seated energy that needed to come up and be released all along.

As a Higher Self BEing, we start to question our own thoughts. We ask "where did that come from" or "why do I think that"? We pay attention to whose voice we hear in our head and when we do this, we start to understand that that isn't even our own thought. Then the "weeding" starts. This is a long and relentless 24/7 job. It is exhausting and we just want it all to "shut up". Yet it only shuts up when we have listened to, transformed them, and released them, so as not to hold any energy anymore. Giving them energy causes us to fall into a loop of arguing with ourselves, and if you feel to do this, go for it. The best thing is to go out in nature or off to yourself and talk out loud. That which is no longer true will sound ridiculous and if you are conscious and present you will choose to shift into a productive thought that completely changes "that".

This is where expansion occurs. We observe our thoughts, without judgment, and we expand BEyond the previous belief that thought represented. We find something, anything, to be grateful for. It does not matter how small, as the purpose is to shift. The gratitude for purposes will expand as we do inside, as we continue to open our magnificent heart.

What will happen, is eventually the mind will start to quiet down and go silent, and even this space is uncomfortable at first. At first, the mind will usually try (very strongly) to interfere and create "busy work" to keep you from enjoying the silence inside, for it knows that "death" is imminent and it will fight to hang on. Figure out a way to recognize this, so that you can shift on your own quicker from your head to your heart.

Your Higher Self is patient and will wait until you are silent to speak or "move in". It will give you the opportunity of choosing this, until waiting is no longer an option. Then it will start "removing distractions" from your reality to force you to have to go inward and listen to what's really been going on. The stronger the masculine energy, the more the "loss" is experienced here. Stubborn requires very uncomfortable lessons, yet these are the ones we REMEMBER (and asked for) the most. Now, it is important to mention, that loss too is just a human perception. From the higher self view, no loss ever occurred, for everything was choice and happened exactly as it was set forth to.

HAND-ON-HEART EXERCISE: Close your eyes anytime you desire to bypass your human-thinking-mind. Put your hand on your heart and shift focus to inside of you there. Breathe slowly and allow your mind to quiet down. It usually takes the human mind about 15 minutes to calm down. Practice this daily, or even more often, until it becomes natural for you. Shifting becomes easy when you REMEMBER this.

REMINDER: *This is my head and I can think any way I want!*

REMINDER: *It is my human mind's job to keep me distracted. It is my job to be conscious of this and shift.*

REMINDER: *I must challenge my own mind if I wish a different reality.*

REMINDER: *I cannot exist in my head and my heart at the same time; therefore I choose my heart.* ♥

134

QUANTUM CLEARING: IN-THIS-MOMENT

This is about releasing all other moments of a "past", that is perceived as the past. When focused on BEing conscious, one must start to let go of all other "times" that do not exist in present moment. This takes observing the "past" to know that it served a purpose, yet it no longer does. The past and the future are timelines that have yet to clear, and while they are BEing "wiped" from your template for you, your need to hang onto the "need" for them will keep you in a space of suffering that is no longer necessary at all. It was your lower realm perception that these existed. Yet here, they never did. This was a creation to accommodate your need for a very human experience. As you vibrate higher, timelines cease to exist.

One way to "let go" of other moments and get present is to use the words "In-this moment" and to focus your mind only on what is present right now. It shifts perspective "back" to where you are, instead of allowing your human mind to wander off into times that do not exist. Your need to be in those times, diminishes your capability to exist in present moment. It also eliminates your ability to be an alchemist, a creator, which exist only in present moment. Here, now, all other moments are created. Your thoughts, desires and transmissions occur in present moment. When you step outside of present moment inside, you step out of your own field and leave. BEing present reverses this, an allows you to expand your field from within. The more present you are, the more expansive you are, until other moments no longer exist. Creation of all occurs in present moment and "materializes" in another "time". The less separated you are inside, the higher you vibrate, the less "delay" in materialization as well. No separation, no delay. As a MASTER again, this is instant here.

Now, the human will want to hang on to "that which happened" in another time, the details of "that", and it will continually focus on future times that have yet to be created, not comprehending (or REMEMBERING) that the present moment thoughts are creating this.

There came a time where I too realized that the illusory past had kept me imprisoned and it was "time" to just let go. In one fell swoop, all that I had been holding onto, I just let it all go. I let go of all of those that I perceived had hurt me, all who I had "held onto" that needed to come to some atonement that I held out for on my end. I had "thought" that "they" did something wrong and I was owed or wronged in some way. This had ruled my reality, and then I "got it", and that *I* was the one holding on. *I* was the one suffering and *I* was the one focused on BEing wronged. *I* was holding out for something to occur that never would. This was because all the "wronged" was in my mind and *they* did not live in the reality I did. They saw reality according to their own mind. Some had refused to "see" anything wrong, sweep it under the rug, ignore those things ever occurred, pretend all was okay, not own up to responsibility, and so on. I had a HUGE list of "wrongs" that kept me stuck in a prison of thought energy tied up in times that did not exist. Then all of a sudden, one day, after holding on to being a "survivor to all that", and all of the identities these traumas brought to me, I finally decided I wanted to be free. I no longer needed the prison of time inside my mind.

Now, this is where one can QUANTUM CLEAR all by releasing or shifting their own perception of another time. This was my first quantum clearing, and not only did I clear my past and present, but I QUANTUM CHANGED my future too. I let go of all perceived wrongs, all holding out for "that to occur" as it did not matter anymore. I needed to focus on me, be happy and come to exist in a space of peace INSIDE of me. In that moment, my entire world/reality shifted and changed. I was free for I was the one who had imprisoned me. Not them, that too was yet another perception and perception is huge. It can imprison us or free us. It can cause us to contract or expand. It can keep us in low (dense) vibrational space of judgment and fear or it can release us and allow us to expand in love. In this moment of letting go, I allowed my heart to open and my own soul to expand. I was able to start loving me the way I needed, something that I forgot how to do in a space of BEing unconscious. This was the beginning of a huge turning point for me, and it allowed me to assist others in learning to quantum clear and create as well.

QUESTION: Can you think of another moment while never leaving this one? Sit on the floor or a bed and look at one spot in front of you and focus. Get present, in this moment, and do not allow your mind to wander off to another time. Now, pull another "time" into this moment, without leaving the present moment you are in. When you leave present moment, your energy shifts. Yet when you pull time to you and work in present moment, you become a CREATOR again. The more you practice with this, the more powerful this is. It takes much awareness and mastery to be able to do this. As masters, we create in present moment, without ever leaving "here".

REMINDER: There is no wrong or right. Everything is exactly as it was created to be. It is my perception and this is a part of duality. Duality only exists "out there", if it exists within me.

REMINDER: Forgiveness is a thing the human holds onto, with a perception that something wrong was done. The heart holds no wrong, therefore there is nothing to forgive.

SO WHAT, WHO CARES, WHO SAYS?

These are the questions you ask yourself inside, for the only one that does is you. "They out there" are to show you what exists within you, and if compromise is there, this will show you that too.

These questions are for you to release yourself from the beliefs inside of having to do anything a certain way. Anytime you feel conflict within, it will be because your Higher Self and your human self are in direct opposition. One holds the human created belief system, of things having to be a certain way, while the other holds the truth of your Soul and truly does not care. One is in your head and the other is in your higher-self heart.

So, the next time you feel conflict within, ask yourself the question "Who says?" Then try to listen to the voice you hear in your head. Whose is it? It is the kind loving voice of your Higher Self inspiring you to listen to something that comes from within your heart? Or is it a pre-programmed belief system that you no longer believe anymore? Close your eyes and listen. The truth will emerge from within.

When I found myself worrying about what "another would think or say", or better yet, something I had limited myself to "that" not BEing "good enough", I would say "So what, who cares?". I had to break the energy inside of me and give myself permission not to care what anther I perceived another thought, for I was not in their head, I was in mine. It was my head focused on changing or doing something I did not desire to do, yet I needed "permission" not to worry about those things anymore. So I gave myself permission to let go of the constraints I had placed on myself inside. I gave me permission "not to care" about conforming anymore. And wow, the freedom this one gives us once we allow ourselves to actually honor and listen to our heart.

There is another thing called PERFECTION and this too does not exist. This is a thing created to keep us stuck on how things "should be" too. This was another hard one for me and I had to REMIND myself over and over along the way, all throughout each day, as I found myself needing for anything to BE a specific way. I had to release me from the perception of perfection that only existed in my own human-thinking-mind.

Your Higher Self is your inner voice that inspires you with something new. This is your future version of you. Your human self is your inner critic and presents with doubt or fear. This is your lower realm you.

REMINDER: I am perfect just the way I am. That is perfect if I perceive it is. All is perfect, when I believe it to be.

REMINDER: I release me from the perception of perfection. I am perfect just as I am.

REMINDER: I must give myself permission "not to care" about changing my true hearted self for anything I perceive to be "out there" anymore. This comes from a space of love and honor to me AS my Soul self.

REMINDER: All is perfect, I am perfect, in this moment of perfection, just as it is. If it is not, then I must go inside to FEEL perfect again.

REMINDER: Perfect is a perception. All things are always perfect, it is my perception that is out of alignment from within.

REMINDER: The need for perfection is a human creation. The heart is always perfect just as it is.

REMINDER: If I am holding on, I am human. If I am letting go, I am my higher self heart.

WHO, WHAT, WHEN, WHERE, WHY, HOW?

These words are all human, nothing less. The human self wants to know FIRST, and this is not how it works here in the world of the Soul/Higher Self. We understand AFTER, sometimes long after, until we come to REMEMBER again inside. Eventually, WE do not need to know such things, for we already KNOW all *already is*. WE also see so expansively, WE CREATE just by BEing vibrationally again.

Needing to know is a tough one, until we come to understand and break the pattern of this. It is our human-thinking-mind that needs tangible things that "make sense". Until one has connected again inside, created a trust and honor system with/as their Higher Self again, then much of the time we do not get to know. Every *once in awhile* we get a "blip" of what's to come, but mostly we just have to trust and "do" that which we feel and observe AS the Higher Self (through the higher heart). By doing this, we start to see how all things are connected, how the "dots" are connected and the puzzle pieces all fit together to create this "geometric" thing that actually does make sense. (And it is usually soooo very simple, we can't not even believe it then!)

Sense in the world of the Soul is a twisted thing. We contort the old beliefs, bend, twist and stretchhhhhhhhhhhhhhhh them so far BEyond what the human mind can comprehend. We actually make up our own rules here. Our rules are "there are no more rules". We do not conform to "need" any longer and we seem to fly by the seat of our pants. This is because, as Souls, we do actually fly, float and flow. Realities are fluid like water and bendable as well. Eventually realities are AS we create them from within. But first we must let go of the need for anything human. We must break away from the barriers we created to start with to start to understand THROUGH the heart, rather than the head.

REMINDER: If I "need" to know, I am human. I must honor my heart with integrity within, then observe all the pieces to actually see through the eyes of my heart and come to truly understand from inside again.

REMINDER: I will recognize when I NEED to know anything. I must create something that releases me from this human cycle and allows me to trust what is in my heart.

REMINDER: I will know after, for needing to know first keeps me stuck in a moment that is not present here.

REMINDER: Needing to know is my way of trying to control that which lack trust in my higher self inside. My higher self IS me, so do I trust me to look out for me, to provide for me and to bring me that which I always truly need? Listen to my heart. That is all I need to know.

"YES, BUT...", IS "NO" TO THE UNIVERSE

The human will hear or feel truth, yet it will make every excuse not to listen to *that*. It will argue and defend, while there is only one truth and this exists within.

When your Higher Self tries to assist you with guidance by giving you a feeling or answer you do not like, the human you will rationalize and "yes but" is a human response. This is like slapping the Universe back and saying "I hear you but I refuse to honor your assistance in trying to give me the answer that will make thing easier for me". The universe hears this loud and clear and getting slapped back is sooooooo not fun at all.

So listen to your words and pay attention when you hear the word "but". This will be a tell-tell and this will tell you much. Listen to your inner voice (heart), as this is your Higher Self. It is trying to assist you and always does with love. Until you don't listen repeatedly, then the love comes strapped to a Mack truck.

REMINDER: Universal 2x4 anyone? Not me! I am listening and honoring!

MEDIATATION VS. SACRED SPACE

Mediation is a joke to those who are of strong human minds. That thing (the human mind) will not shut up long enough for us to sit still for this. So, we get creative and we find ways to OBSERVE OUR THOUGHTS without sitting in a group of other people humming "OHM" and feeling silly in those uncomfortable positions. Yet, you will find later, how important this truly is… for now, wander with me into a crop circle if you will.

Now, the one who can meditate, has a one-up on those of us who cannot. So this is written for those who struggle with meditation due to strong-human minds. Those who can meditate won't even need this section, because you "get it" already.

Meditation is the human word, whereas *sacred space* is of the Higher Self. They are the same, just a different focal view vibrationally from within. For the purpose here, I use the word mediation when I speak of human.

Meditation is anything that allows us to observe our human thoughts and to create a connection with our higher self, and our entire universe from within. We learn the difference between "thoughts we think" and "thoughts we receive", and they are SO very different indeed. One comes from our human mind and the other through our creative heart while listening to our higher self mind; One is created in our head and the other is received AS SOURCE. Both are our own voice, which is why so many get confused. (I speak of other voices/energies elsewhere in this book).

Now, your head is like an antennae and it is a both a transmitter and receiver of light and sound frequencies by way of thought, hearing, while accompanied by the images that you envision and see as well.

You are always transmitting and receiving, dependent on the space you occupy at any given time. Now your human you has unconscious individual thoughts and these transmit at a lower frequency than the ones of your higher self heart-mind ones that you receive. These come through your heart and are audible in frequency, yet you cannot hear if you are not quiet enough to listen.

If you do not listen, you will not be aware of what your subconscious, unconscious human mind is transmitting for you to materialize to come to exist in physically. When you are silent, you are aware, yet the fearful human will avoid listening, for often they do not like that which they hear. Meditation gives you a space where you can get silent and hear what is inside. If it is human thoughts, it is your job to listen and become aware. For before you can become a transmitter, an alchemist and a creator of your reality in unison with/as your higher self, you must first learn to listen and release that which is not true from inside.

Your higher self waits, in your own voice, to speak to you. First sometimes, in a soft voice it whispers, so you must listen close, for it is subtle and there to assist you.

If you have trouble meditating, get creative. For the strong minded human, something that keeps the body distracted allows one to listen to thoughts, while DOING something else. This is very important to learn to do, so that you can connect TO/AS your Higher Self at all times. First in the "busy" ones, and then eventually, at all times.

This is the fun part, so get as creative as you can. The more ways you can find to do this, the more you can connect and observe!

I will share some of the ways that I used along the way. Many utilize these opportunities to listen and observe. It doesn't matter "how", just that you do.

Washing dishes, cleaning, vacuuming, driving, mowing grass, walking in nature, BEing artistic (drawing, painting, writing, etc.), hanging up clothes, sitting anywhere in silence and watching nature or something quiet where your mind can wander off, or sitting at a window looking out.

Mine were usually driving the car, doing dishes or cleaning, and then one day MY Universe sent me a bird. Eventually I learned to go back to bed each day for a few hours and take a journal to write all that I heard. This is how I started channeling, automatic writing and a flooding it did come. So, create a way to listen, for it can be so easy and fun when you do!

Now, creating a *sacred space* where you have crystals and a specific place where you dedicate silent time for connection is an awesome tool too. I did this in my room and my bed became my writing spot and connection spot as well. Some will create altars, with crystals, flowers, essential oils, sage and more to raise the vibrational frequency of the space for connecting. Now, anywhere you place your body for an extended period in sacred connection and honor time, you will create an energy vortex that will hold these higher vibrations. At times, when light energy activations begin, this space will be too intense for some. Just remove your body from that space and go outside or in another room until it passes. For those who can handle the intensity, this will speed up your own LightBody activations. Just do what is comfortable for you, and you will know inside, if you listen.

Additionally, anywhere you can drift off into thought and dream is productive. The human mind will say this is a "waste of time". Yet, this is what the human mind is for, to convince you of the opposite of how things truly are. I used to drift off in every meditation and worry that I had "messed up". It wasn't until much later that I understood that I got everything I needed, even better, when I was asleep!

Eventually we CRAVE this *sacred space*. For we eventually come to exist in a walking meditative space inside to exist AS a *sacred space* at all times.

Note: The photonic light activations, solar winds & more activate inside of you to drop your brainwave and entire overall energy body state in frequency, so you are walking meditative space at all times. This is part of why things feel like they are slowing down and you feel such need to sleep more. Your actual functioning brainwave state is much lower than it used to be. We drop to gamma over time to allow us to exist as the higher realms and more again.

REMINDER: Anytime I can observe my thoughts and listen, I am in meditation. The more I ALLOW myself to do this, the more I am connected AS my Higher Self inside. (Judgment not allowed, but definitely should be observed and recognized as well!)

SOUL CONTRACTS

Understanding and utilizing Soul Contracts allows the human much more leeway in working with that which is not logical. This is a magnificent tool for one who really desires to let go of that which keeps them bound to human attachments, blame, shame, guilt and more. IF we truly, truly, truly desire to be free inside, this is the way we do this. If not, even this won't help. For one who really desires to hang on and suffer will not even desire to hear this. There will come a "time" that this will change. Usually this occurs when one has suffered enough and desires something different inside. This difference is known by the human as "happy and free". Until then, hanging on, is what WE respectfully understand as "personal hell" or "prison".

I prefer simple on everything; cut to the chase, cut out all of the details to honor what feels right in our heart. But, it was not always this way. I was one of the extremely masculine energy, stubborn humans that chose to suffer, having to experience all, *needing* and abundance of tangible proof, for *this world* logically did not make sense. Hence, part of my purpose. To hopefully reach others by cutting out the "extra stuff", yet for those who hold strong masculine energy like me, feel free to read a ton of books on Soul contracts. The simple version is: "as a Soul, we all chose everything that occurs". There are no exceptions to this one. Yes, it is that simple, yet the where the human mind cannot accept this, more is necessary to get the point across.

As a Soul, you asked for that to occur. As a Soul, "they" are answering your call for an experience that you need(ed). The purpose of a Soul Contract is to show us something, by bringing up suppressed and hidden energy in order to see. This can be a strong low-vibrational thing or this can be the most exquisite love of all. You can tell the purpose of a Soul Contract by that which it causes to occur within you. It will either trigger human pain, conflict and fear or the most blissful peace, inspiration and love. This will also tell you much. One causes you to suppress your Soul and the other inspires your heart and Soul to expand magnificently from within.

Now, those closest to us hold many Soul Contracts (purposes), and there will never be "just one". They hold the biggest contracts to trigger the most human emotions within you (and you them). When we REMEMBER this, we begin to see them as part of the purpose of showing us about ourselves, what has been hidden inside, what we suppressed within out of fear, where we lack boundaries, where we compromise, where they inspire us to BE our higher selves. We do have to be careful with this one for the one who holds "lacks inside" will become dependent on this other to inspire them, so that they can feel good inside. This is a different energy. A contract shows us where there is the frequency of lack or balance that exists within us.

Have gratitude (without an attitude) for those who have/do honor their contracts to show you YOU. The attitude is victim. The gratitude is the Higher Self Soul.

REMINDER: As a Soul I asked for and created this. As a Soul there is nothing to forgive. (This includes them and ME!)

YOU MUST GIVE YOURSELF PERMISSION

As humans, we are taught to hang on, don't do this, don't do that, do it this way, this is right, this is wrong, you shouldn't feel this or express this, be perfect, don't cry, getting angry is wrong, you are not good enough and the list goes on and on. We have come to listen to "all "out there" to exist in a box, with constraints and opinions of other humans on "how all should be" according to their perception. We took those perceptions on as our own, to come to realize as we wake up, that absolutely none of these things were our truth and that these were separated, judgmental, limited and learned views. Yet, until we realize this, we do not know any other way.

This journey is the "opposite" of what we are taught or came to believe, according to the adult human reality that ASSISTED US COLLECTIVELY to form our human experience that we ASKED FOR here.

For releasing (transcending) discordant human frequencies brought forth within our own soul, anger and tears are not only okay, they are required. Yet "how" we do this changes, for we do not cry or get angry as a victim anymore. We do this to release the energy that suppressed our Soul within the confines of a human box, and our suit, for way too long. We let out the lack and the pain of the Soul, and we understand it for what it is. This takes away the "affect" of the drama at which the human used to go on and on with never-ending drama around "that" that had occurred. We don't care anymore why, we just recognize that *that* is an out-of-tune frequency wishing to be released and transcended from within. We know that in order to do this, we have to tune our own frequency again. Sometimes we do this with the moans (sound) of the cries that we let out.

For the release alone IS TUNING, and necessary, if we wish to "find our way back"; back to HOME inside, where peace and love exist. For without this release, we are blocking ourselves, from REMEMBERING truth again.

So the next time you feel the need to cry or get angry, or any other emotion that you feel, find a safe way to express it and let it go from deep within. It is just a discordant energy, that held in creates dis-ease. Nature is the perfect place (or a bed with your head covered with a pillow to mute the noise), and give yourself permission to release that which was never you inside.

You will find that as soon as you start ALLOWING yourself to let go, that the "magnitude" of the emotional release that you feared will get less and less in "volume" each time. Your allowing it, takes away the strength, so that you are able to release with greater ease. Soon you will find that you are releasing so fast, that there is nothing left physically to experience. You will bring up the emotion, recognize it, ask for it to be released and "poof" it is gone. For that was all you needed. Eventually there is no emotional charge to "that" anymore. You just watch it float on by, until it completely disappears completely from your reality. While in all truth, you shifted to a whole new dimensional realm. It IS SO very cool indeed!

REMINDER: I honor however I feel as the way I need to be. Expressing this (safely) is a necessity of my Soul's journey here. I release judgment, for this is of the human mind. I release this discordant energy and re-tune to love inside.

REMINDER: Anger and tears are the point and suppression is what got me here. I must safely release these to the universe, so that I can move forward and shift up into a higher vibrational frequency (dimensional version) of me.

DEPRESSION IS HUMAN'S WORD FOR SEPARATION FROM THE SOUL

You will find that everything "human" has one term and yet, from the Soul's awareness, all serves a very important purpose in the evolution of merging the Higher Self within. What is viewed as "something wrong" in human is always quite the opposite here. It is important to note that this is not a psychological or medical perspective. This is a view from the higher realms.

Depression and bi-polar spaces serve a multitude of very important purposes as well. SO much occurs in this space of "separation", where one comes to awaken to their own truth from within. For a star being on Earth, much of the time, the transition is "too much" and so very overwhelming to the Star Beings system. Withdrawing and suppression is the chose path for many until enough time has passed for the human experience energy to purge and their true self can start to emerge. Many beings have no idea this is what "this is", for they too are very veiled, they just know "things are not right" and go so deep inside in order to cope as best as they can. (This occurs with substance abuse as well. Many resort to this to also try to make it through until they can wake up.) Much of this is beyond human comprehension, yet that too is changing as well.

First, depression is a human term "label" that keeps one even further separated than they already feel inside. While inside is where we all must go to awaken, what this represents is so very opposite than what the small and very limited human mind can comprehend. Perception is everything, for everything is exactly how you perceive it to be, yet nothing is as you perceive it. Your perception will determine how you experience all.

Depression is many things. It is all things simultaneously, rather than one or another. The human mind separates this. Depression is separation from SOURC. It also is:

♥ Separation from one's own Soul, as Source, Higher Self. This can be mild to extreme, depending on how much separation energy one holds in out-of-tune frequencies inside.

♥ Out-of-tune discordant frequencies in one's Soul. With energetic tunings, combined with the integration and expansion of one's consciousness, this possibly can be totally eliminated from within. The amount of deterioration will determine the amount of "time" necessary to allow for system repair.

♥ It is the human experiencing themselves "stuck" between the 3rd and 5th Dimensional Realms. In a closed-eyed state (or any observation mode), one can "see" their 3rd Dimensional self and desire to BE their 5th Dimensional self, yet will be lost and confused as to how to accomplish this. The human gets stuck in human emotions of lack, judgment, not-good enough, blame, shame, guilt, and more. It is a horrible feeling inside that one cannot shake and "rock-bottom" can very present here. This is where many "end up" so that realities can be challenged as "not true" and where all must come to "see", before a huge shift can occur. Rock-bottom for each shall be different. It doesn't matter, for it is the complete stripping of identities and belief systems before "reversal" can occur.

♥ One's "waking up" to the fact that they have become separated from "home" inside. This is extreme purgatory and time to connect inside through love, compassion and unification again.

♥ Where one's Soul has been dormant and is trying to emerge from within. All things dense will surface to become visible to be seen. Where one does not understand, there may be fear and judgment keeping them stuck in a never-ending loop here. New awareness and understanding from a different perspective can assist one in emerging from this space and for the suppression phase to end.

♥ The human's identity crisis and the disconnect from the Soul while "new" is getting ready to be birthed from within.

♥ A space where the Higher Self is trying to integrate within, as you, so you are never alone again. Alone was your human you *trying* to do your experience all by yourself, separated and possibly not understanding. That time is over. Here you now merge as you sleep and the old continues to fall away. Any fight to hang on to the old will cause suffering. Letting go will allow the REMEMBERED to start to come through again.

♥ It is who you are no longer, as your separation (I self) surfaces for review.

♥ The masculine and feminine, good bad, right wrong, duality come front and center to be visible. The human is forced inside to see this, yet "out there" is the focus until "rock-bottom" creates a shift.

Now, I only speak of "rock-bottom" for all who do not understand this, have to "end up here". Those who understand, may still "visit", yet their stay here is a "short vacation" in hell vs. the long commitment that many of us endured. The unconscious BEing stays here, the conscious one can actually shift, just by BEing aware and seeking to do something to assist.

Energetically, these are void spaces where energy does not appear to move. It can be very dense here and "stuck" is a very prevalent feeling. The denser the energy, the more separated one has allowed themselves to become, the "longer" one feels they are here. This too is perception, for the amount of time is only indicative of density or separation. Again, unification tuning can assist greatly with this.

The 3rd Density Realm holds the most separation, which is represented by the energy of selfishness, greed, savior complex (too much "let me fix/save you" energy, lack resulting from focus on the material world reality.

Identity crisis is a huge importance of this space, for it makes us question who we are and why we are here. It is these questions that opens the door for old human programming to become visible and for new to begin to surface from within.

For one to have an understanding of the purpose of this, the amount of time spent here can be negated, to some extent. The sleep that is necessary for one to awaken must still occur, yet it does not have to be out of "victim and separation" rather than one embracing the purpose and intentionally sleeping instead of suffering to this.

Entire realms are visible in one's sleep state. Until one comes to exist fully in the 5th Dimensional realm at all times within, the higher realms and the lower realms are available here. One can sleep and see what they are not willing to see in an open-eyed state. For some, this is why we slept for 20 years. We had a lot to transcend and sleep was the only way we could accomplish this. Yet, with new tools of understanding and navigation, this does not have to BE like this anymore. The strong-minded human will still have to suffer. The open-hearted Soul can bypass the suffering that the rest of us came here to endure, to then teach and share to assist with NEW EARTH transitions from within.

Much of what can be experienced here is feeling stuck, rock-bottom, confusion, questioning one's existence, how things "got like this" and why we are even here. The paradox is that it is these very questions that cause one to shift out of the old human belief systems and programming, and into their heart (and Soul) again.

What one experiences "here" is also imperative. For if one is suffering loss of some sort, they tend to go into "if THIS will just happen, I swear I will do THIS". What they do not realize is that the Higher Self is listening and was waiting for that "bargaining" so as to be able to step in and for things to reverse from inside now. Yet, one must be honorable and keep the "bargain" and honor their word to their own Higher Self that they made. For this is the chance for humanity to surface from within. This is the time for greed, selfishness, pride and inability to share to fall away. This is the time where you "do" what you said you would do, without BEing forced to out of necessity or desperation. This is the "test", if you will, to see if you hold honor and integrity within. For if you do, you will shift out of your lower self and into your Higher Self of love, sharing and compassion here. If you do not, you will be asking for a universal 2x4 to grow into a universal 12x12 to come back around and slap you down until you learn to come from integrity to all again.

The key is to be conscious and aware and honor all that you "saw" when you were in the state of desperation and separation inside. If you saw to change something, you must change that. If you saw to ask for help, then you must do this as well. If you saw to share and give more, then this is what you must do. It is not about what you do, but reversing the energy of your old human you. The doing is necessary for the human to get the point. The "pain" of loss is what causes us to get the point. When we can choose to "do that" instead of BEing forced, the lessons cease to come as fast or as strong. When we do this on our own and always from our heart, we no longer need "lessons" anymore.

Now, suffering was a human belief. We do not have to suffer. If one believes that they do, then they do. As one comes to realize that even suffering is not truth, then suffering ceases to exist as it once did.

Anytime you experience this, there is something of the lower dense realms that is surfacing to challenge you with realizing that is no longer true. If you are conscious, you can "wait it out" and use it to observe the untruths finally leaving, as you are vibrating out of where it used to exist.

I rename things from the human word (depression) to other words that shift my view to something productive and having purpose. So, you find a word or phrase that works for you. Some examples would be "sleeping to see untruths", "void of observation" or "stuck energy space before new birth comes forth". You decide, for it is your space to understand for you. It doesn't matter what you call it, as long as you understand it and shift out of a victim mentality and utilize it in ways that assist you in integrating your Soul inside. Embrace it, sleep, and awake to "new" another day. Find someone who understands Soul separation and points you within. Those who truly understand can assist you in seeing what never was true and the magnificence that was hiding inside of you.

No one technically is depressed, for that is a human word. They are separated from their own Soul as a star being and just need to unify within again.

THE IMPORTANCE OF ANGER

This one is so misunderstood and not understanding this one, while holding onto judgment, keeps one stuck in holding onto anger as well.

The human sees anger as a fault or "bad thing", while to the Soul this is just an old suppressed energy that is just in need of BEing transcended within. The lower dimensional unconscious human will work to suppress anger, while the middle realm human will work to purge, release, transform. The evolved middle realm being will just bring it up and let it go. And the higher realm version has no anger at all. Yes, it is that simple.

Now, all humans have anger, yet how it materializes is as individual as we all are. It starts out as one BEing angry at something outside (a person, situation or occurrence), while these are just the triggers of the discordant beliefs and frequencies held within.

Anger is never at another, it is always at ourselves. Until we understand it, and then we no longer need to be angry at anyone anymore.

Anger is based upon a belief that something wrong was done. Yet if you look beneath the anger, it will be because we are looking "out there" and holding onto something from the human perspective. We have not allowed our self to utilize soul contracts to let go and once we were of a mindset to make a choice, we compromised ourselves in some way. Much of the time, we got "stuck in a situation, because of a hunch, sixth sense or gut feeling we did not listen to. We just "knew" not to, and we did anyways. Now, where we repeatedly did this (not listening), we build up a lot of anger over "time". This energy has to go somewhere, for it just doesn't disappear (yet).

First, the higher we vibrate the less anger we have. Then dualism goes and anger goes as well. But until then, we learn to use the anger for the purpose it serves; going within and letting it go. We learned the lesson and we don't need that anymore.

One, get through the situation with love as best as you can. If you are lacking boundaries, then you will have to establish boundaries or maintain them, whichever is true for you. If you have compromised, then you will be faced with no longer compromising yourself and reversing the energy flow that you have created in the "past". Figure out why you are truly angry and let it go. Anger is a judgment and causes us to be prisoner to a belief that is untrue inside.

Now, all humans have anger, because when we start to awaken, we realize that our entire human existence is untrue. We realize that WE have lived our entire existence based upon the beliefs we acquired from all others along the way. We realize our thoughts have never been our own. All part of the human experience, as part of the experiment that we chose. Talk about angry, yep, it is definitely coming up.

If you find yourself in a situation, deal with whatever it is as consciously as you can and then go off to yourself and safely get the energy out of you. Go out and yell out to the Universe until you have no more anger left. This is not about suppressing the way you feel. This is about allowing yourself to feel however you need to feel and letting it go, so you do not have to feel that way anymore. Nature offers a wide open space where one can do this. I used be respectful if I was with others and then excused myself to go talk to myself in a mirror to "get straight" before I would allow myself to interact with others again. I knew "this was my energy", so I would go deal with my need for whatever it was, with myself. Soon, I could just recognize it and let it go immediately, without having to do this. You figure out what works for you. The expression is necessary for suppression was the old human way. This world is opposite. We no longer suppress the way we feel. We understand it, it is transmuted in strength and we shift to our hearts and out of our heads in order to be okay inside again.

REMINDER: If I am feeling anger, it is important to safely FEEL it and safely let it go. Otherwise I am suppressing and creating additional pain and discord within. I tune when I release, without judgment. The feeling and release ARE the purpose and I appreciate the opportunity to allow this density to leave so that my soul can further expand.

REMINDER: Anger is a human expression of something that is no longer true.

CONTROL: A HUMAN UNTRUTH

Wow, this one was one of my huge ones too. (Yes, I had many, for I was super human! LOL)

I was a total control freak, obsessive compulsive to the extreme. So, I had to do a lot of inner work to get through this one. I came to pay attention to the energy and resistance in myself every time I needed something to be a certain way. I would go inside and REMIND myself that it MY own out-of-balance need and to let it go. I found that I was unconsciously constantly putting "that thing" over another soul's feelings or needs, even my own, and this was my own lack of humanity inside. Everything had to be in a certain place, done a certain way, or it would drive me absolutely bonkers inside. I seriously about went insane with control issues getting super extreme.

So, I would again, come to recognize my own "need for that to be a certain way" and then I would make myself "deal with it" until the energy dissipated inside. This one, I just had to suck it and deal with it. I forced myself to sit and go through the false internal suffering feeling all of this created, knowing it was not true and it needed to be "pushed" until it dissipated to leave. I was constantly confronting myself here for awhile. Then it eventually was just gone; just a discordant energy waiting to be tuned by me!

One example was that I wanted my kitchen to be all in the same order, no mess, clean up after yourself, don't destroy it or it would be harder to clean up after. A previous roommate really wanted to learn how to cook, yet had no respect for "stuff", and I had a lot of expensive stuff. So, I would not allow him in my kitchen. My answer was always that I'd rather cook for him instead, rather than have him mess it all up. (My issue, my perception, my out-of-tune frequency that I had to deal with inside).

One day, he really wanted to learn to cook. Nope, not in MY kitchen. Then I felt his heart. I felt the disappointment inside and how he just really wanted to learn to cook. He did not want me to teach him and he wanted to do it himself. My very controlled-reality ME even tried to tell him that he could learn to cook, yet only if he would let me teach him (my way again). Nope, wasn't having it, which sent me into even a bigger fit inside. Then, right in the middle of the "tug-of-war", my Higher Self stepped in and showed me how "all of this was me". My need to control had overridden another's need to just do something to be happy. I saw myself putting "things" over another human's heart. Not acceptable, and I "got it", I realized that I had to go deal with myself and suffer through the discordant energy that needed to go. So, I said to myself "what's the worst that can happen? He could burn the place down. So what, that is not realistic and if he does, then it is mean to be. It won't kill me, I will live and it's more important to honor another human than to worry about a thing such as this. OR he could destroy the kitchen. So what, I'll clean it up, for it is only time, and time is free. It is not more important than him BEing happy inside." So, I gathered my ego up and I went into the living room and I forced myself to sit there and allow him to cook, forced myself to suffer to the feelings that arose while I watched him destroy the kitchen, the entire him observing him with the biggest smile on his face having the grandest time just doing something that made him happy. When he was finished, he was so proud of that food that he had made. I realized how selfish I was BEing and how it was my issue and energetic frequency loop to break. This was never about him or the kitchen, this was the controlling energy I had inside; the controlling energy of everything having to be a certain way, which caused me to place "stuff" over another, never intentional, for it was "just my way". Yet when the Soul awakens, the old ways do not work anymore. And we start to recognize how "out of alignment" we are inside and that another is only our trigger, honoring a Soul contract to show us what we could not have seen before.

Now, I had many angry fits as I learned to understand my human me. I had so much hidden deep within; I was amazed each time anger surfaced, for we do not know "all of that" is "in there". It came out when I least expected it and I had to learn to understand it for the purpose that it served. Soon I welcomed it and let it go, just as fast as it could surface. I learned to use others to show me what I could not see. They were a magnificent mirror that I placed in front of me.

This is not about anger; this is about the flow of energy, the frequency of it and the lower dimension we exit in while we hold onto it. This is about restoring love, compassion and humanity inside and then "out there" again.

Now, the paradox is that we get control as we learn to let go of the need to control. This is one of those "backwards" things that is the opposite of how it truly is. As we come into alignment inside, flow is restored again. Here we have absolute control by doing absolutely nothing but BEing our true selves again.

Control is a perception of something you don't "think" you already have.

REMINDER: Control is a discordant frequency. It is my need for things to be a certain way.

REMINDER: If I need control as a human, this means I do not trust my Higher Self, which is my future me. It means I am not listening, honoring or coming from love inside. Control is human, letting go is the 5th Dimensional Higher Self version of me.

THE IMPORTANT SPACE OF CONFUSION

Confusion is a space we come to when we start to realize things do not make sense and as humans we try to "match" all up again. Our human logical mind has much to play with here. This is where stretching goes on (mind-wise). This is where we become observers of every perspective. Where one gets "stuck", if you will, is when they focus on "that out there" trying to make sense of why another does what they do, or why that does not work anymore. The more logical (masculine energy), the longer one will "visit" this space of confusion while continually trying to put the puzzle pieces together, fit the square peg in a round hole and connect the dots. I too spent much time here, for I too was a very logical human mind. I "suffered" torment relentlessly while I tried to measure, compare and squeeze all into a space where *that* made sense again. The key is not to try to "fix" the old human world "out there", not to try to make it conform to your old beliefs. The key is to stretch your belief system BEyond the previous limits, BEyond that which you are used to, to see what you could not previously see. This is not about a specific human "out there". This is about what adversity, what response, what beliefs that human brings up in you. This is not about a car or a house or a very special coveted thing. This is about your perspectives, how you value that thing, how you have identities attached to that memory, time or thing, how you won't share that thing, how you "need" that thing to function, etc. This is about everything outside of you that you focus on in order to find your truth. Truth is bendable, flexible and no longer fixed. Truth is what your heart and Higher Self together guide you to feel, see, and do. Truth is inside of you, not "out there".

WE know when one is confused, that they are trying (in human) to figure it out, to understand and that something has occurred to kick them into observation mode to try to fit all of the puzzle pieces together (while sooooo many are still hidden beneath the internal veils). The key is to switch inward, for answers come much faster here. The logical mind will focus "out there" until they "get it". More and more, one will eventually understand that all they have to do is close their eyes, open their heart and allow their Higher Self to speak, then listen and honor with conscious choice. Go into a receptive state if you wish to go to "Soul School" and truly learn (REMEMBER). Observe with your eyes closed and work it out "in there". The answers you get will make more sense, for you can remove the faces, detach and observe. The longer one stays focused "out there" seeking answers, the more they use others give them answers instead of listening to their future self. Both will bring you answers. One requires lessons, physical exchanges or experiences in order to learn (the human learns). The other goes inward or talks to the Universe and listens for the subtle answers of guidance that come through the Universal-Mind-Heart. This is part of REMEMBERING again. The masculine human energy does not like to listen. It will seek "proof" and spin in a circle endlessly until something happens to bring me tangible proof. Maybe it is by way of finding 100 people, videos, writings "out there" that say the same thing to convince them that there is a different way to view "that" and that they always had the answer inside. They just didn't know how to listen yet.

Masculine energy will get stuck in the mind and focus "out there". The entire exterior experience could be viewed as masculine. For this entire inner journey is one of feminine energy which is just listening and honoring through the heart. This is The Divine Feminine emerging from within you again. The Divine Masculine occurs as you release separation and then a new strength emerges from within. Then "New" is born. Each time you release a huge chunk of the old exterior reality, you will go through a "re-birth" from inside of you. The "Divine Child" is then birthed from inside as well. Literally, for this is part of what the "air babies" are! (Explained in the Evolution of the LightBody).

REMINDER: The more confused I am the better, for this means I am waking up to the truth that I hold inside of me. I must use this confusion to go within, to find my own truth instead of the old beliefs I acquired here. That was an old belief system that I no longer believe. Only that which exists within my higher heart is now truly me.

REMINDER: WE do not argue, for the need to defend is what the human does when they are trying to convince themselves of something that they don't truly believe. That is discordant energy and we go inside, validate our own truth and tune our own frequencies from within.

OBLIGATION VS. INSPIRATION

The human does things out of obligation, fear, or guilt according to the limiting mind of how things should be or what has been imposed within the human mind to force the Walking Soul to compromise itself. This is an energy, nothing else; A frequency in need of tuning. That is all.

Anytime you "do" anything, the energy that which you do it is creating the reality that you get.

Do you "do" that because you think that you must? Or do you "do" that because you are inspired from inside? Inspiration does not have energetic cords attached.

When you are inspired, all comes from within your BEing-ness and flows out. When it is done for a human reason, there are "emotions" attached to the doing. These are usually expectation or a need of some kind. Inspiration has no attachment. It has an energetic flow OUT from the heart and just floats to touch all that it can touch in light and love.

Where one does out of obligation, the energy feels like it is BEing "pulled" from within you. This is depleting. This is a "giving away" of your own energy and we do not compromise our energy anymore. We also are enabling the other person by re-enforcing their own lack. We come to realize we are not helping the other and in turn the same goes for us. This is OUR own discordant energy to be tuned; our lack feeding theirs. Every different perspective gives us a whole new choice. Now, where there has been obligation, we break this frequency loop by either do it without the attachment of emotion and "be done", so that "next time" we can make a conscious choice, or we step into the fear that exists beneath the doing and we negate the "need" for another experience to shift this inside and "out there".

When we actually look at the energy of WHY we do thing, we can start to understand where we are out of tune or holding discordant frequencies within. When we no longer do anything because it is expected, release the attachment to the doing and just do it and let go, energy of the LightBody/Merkaba starts to spin again. We get lighter and our LightBody raises in frequency again.

Pay attention to the energy of everything. You are energy, and you are a master of energy, when you are connected, listening and honoring through love from within.

REMINDER: I am them and they are me, for we are just one energy. If I wish to understand, I must pay attention to the energy that I feed. When I feed love, I feel light. When I feed anything less, I feel dense again. One creates flow and spin. The other keeps me in a lower dimension.

THE IMPORTANT SPACE OF INTOLERANCE

When one becomes intolerant, they are about to the point of BEing done. This is an important space as well, for intolerance means you are shifting out of that frequency within. It also means that are shifting out of the limiting human space that you used to exist in. You are expanding into another dimension!

The key is to be conscious, figure out if you are intolerant because you are unconscious and focused on the other BEing the "problem", or if this is something you have cleared recently within and that "that out there" is an irritation because you no longer accept that in your reality any more. Which it is, will determine whether you are moving out of it or if you are stuck in it. One will have an inner focus and the other will have an outer focus. This will tell you much.

Now, there is a space we "hit" as we evolve, where we start to realize how small the human mind is. BEing around small and limiting minds, means BEing around those who are unconscious, whether intentional or not. BEing around one who chooses to be unconscious is even harder and will get less tolerable as we expand our own consciousness from within. You have become more conscious and you have expanded your own reality so much that you can no longer tolerate those who exist in the small constricting space of judgment, fear and lack. Lack comes by way of many things, such as lack of consideration, compassion, openness and love. It is selfish, greedy and oblivious to the reality of sharing and love. Your inability to be around these limiting BEings will cause you to start "purging" dense things in your outer reality; for you cannot shift dimensionally and stay in the same limiting space that you once were.

You are expanding and for you to expand, that which is in your way of expansion must be allowed to "go". It does not go; you expand out of the reality *that* existed in. You are shifting to a higher dimensional realm where you are more conscious and where others who are more conscious exist too!

REMINDER: When I am intolerant, I will know "that is going", once I finally decide inside that I am "done". Then a reversal of energy will occur and "out there" will (eventually) catch up too.

REMINDER: Intolerance represents something I have recently cleared inside of me. All that I am intolerant to, has a change for me to see it and for me to allow it to leave my reality, as I shift into a higher dimensional version of me. The longer I no longer need this in my reality, the quicker I will let it go so that I can shift. Participation keeps me anchored in the lower realm. Letting go allows me to navigate and shift at will.

THE IMPORTANT SPACE OF "BEING DONE"

We all have to "be done with that" before it can leave our energy field. Until we are "done", we still exist in the realm where that frequency exists. It does not leave our field though; we expand BEyond the space where that existed within. Letting go of "that" allows for all that represents that to "leave" as well. This will be humans, things and situations that were a part of that frequency. In the beginning, this spans out to huge things, for we were so very separated in other times, people, things. As we simplify and lighten inside, come to exist spread out in others places and times, this gets much faster and affects less. There is a "zero point" where everything in our human existence must go, so that our new existence can emerge to exist in. How this occurs, will be dependent on how much you allow yourself to live from your heart. The less conscious, the more abrupt and "forced on us" this is. The more we participate, the less we have to lose in order to shift.

BEing done is not about "that out there". It is about the energy we allow (and hold in frequency) inside. BEing done first starts with "that out there" then moves inside to not be tolerable any longer within. Then it moves outside again, while that which represented "that" is allowed to fall away (dematerialize). It was dense. And yes, it is that spiral thingy again.

REMINDER: I must be totally "done" inside with that lower dimensional thing, (and DO whatever is necessary by way of actual action, with as much love as I can) before I can shift into a higher dimensional version of me.

REMINDER: When I am "done", I no longer operate at that frequency inside of me. There may be a void or delay space where that "out there" materializes in response to my shift inside. I must REMEMBER to hold this frequency until my new physical reality arrives.

REMINDER: "No thank you" (with love), is necessary to shift away from the old, lower vibrations that I used to entertain as a human.

REMINDER: "That is no longer acceptable in my reality anymore" is a kind way to maintain boundaries and remove yourself from a space of human compromise and lack.

REMINDER: It is not what I say, yet the frequency at which I speak it. I can transmit my words with love, anger, or fear. My transmission is my creation of that which I receive in return. A dimension is just a switching in frequency. That which I create with my thoughts, words and actions, is the one I get.

REMINDER: "Being Done" kicks in a necessary masculine energy (with love) that we need to shift us out of the lower realm version of us and into a higher realm where that no longer exists. This stubbornness we utilize for this is beneficial in actually making a dimensional shift. It will "push" us quicker into a higher realm if we will embrace it and utilize it as the navigational tool that it is.

HUMAN GETS SICK WHILE THE SOUL TUNES

The human's first response to anything that is out of balance with any of the "bodies" (physical, emotional, mental), is "sick", when it fact it is quite the opposite. The LightBody has activated and your physical is trying to tune to higher frequencies. Anything dense is of the old programming and is trying so very hard to leave, but the human tries so very hard to hold on, take the easy way, take medicine, go to the doctor, fix it, when nothing is broken other than the programmed human belief system mind.

Now, this is not to tell you that you should not go to a doctor, take your medicine, or whatever you deem necessary in your world. This is to tell you that there is an alternative option that is the opposite of what you have come to believe. This is to stretch your limited and conditioned human mind beyond that which you have learned and been told. This is to assist you with awareness and choice, something all have in the evolution of the higher self/soul.

The human does not respect the physical vessel that will carry you dimensionally from realm to realm. It does not have this understanding yet and that which it "feeds" itself has caused great depletion and must be repaired. Cellular restructuring will occur once the dense human wakes up and the Light of the Soul starts to expand. If the human can adjust their mind to understand that their soul seeks their assistance in this great overhaul and repair, they will choose to assist, rather than to continue to suppress and deplete, as they once did in the past.

"Sick" to the human is discordant frequencies to the soul. That is all. When you "think" sick, something is out of energetic balance and in need of tuning. Now, one who has suppressed much, they will have much discord, be energetically out of balance and much tuning will be necessary to assist with this. We speak overall, rather than to a specific thing.

Anything leaving the body (air, gas, excrement, fluid, etc.) is representative of density leaving. This is a good thing. Yet why it is leaving may be what you wish to observe, for if it is a continual process, then there is something that continues to lend to this need.

Chronic issues mean much suppression has occurred; both by way of emotions and anything "taken/used" to push it back inside. The longer one was in discord, the more the physical had time to dis-integrate. More time must be honored to allow for cellular repair and re-generation to now occur with light and alternative LightBody Crystalline loving care.

The physical body is continually tuning, so the more duality and density one holds within, the more they will continually have things resurface again. It is important to REMEMBER, *that* is not coming up again, it is *trying to leave again*. Your action will determine if it exacerbates by BEing pushed back inside again, or if you assist it in coming up and out to leave. It will continue until every last remnant of that discordant energy is finely tuned in alignment with the light of your soul/higher self as a light BEing here. Now technically, it is not leaving; Your body is trying to release the density that kept it anchored in lower realm. It is trying to shift "up" dimensionally, into a higher frequency, and *that* is in the way. It needs it to go, so that you can shift. Your human suppression keeps you held and anchored in lower dimensional realm. The longer you try to hold onto the lower realm, the harder and more uncomfortable all will get. Sleep and feed your body light to assist with cellular restructuring and repair.

Every huge energetic shift and dimensional change will cause the head to be tuned again. Head clearing (sinuses, upper chest, nose, ears, throat, etc.) will continue to be affected as you ascend into the higher frequencies. Light headedness, dizziness, disorientation and loss of memory are just a few of the affects of bringing the higher realms into your physical vessel there.

You are going to Heaven, Paradise, and other galaxies when you choose, and you cannot take "sick" and discord with you. It has to stay, SORRY, let it go, for there is no sickness here. Your old thought systems, your old beliefs that you are sick, as they don't get to come with you either. Those were the old lower dimensions and those have to go as well. Now, after heaven, after paradise, we go galactic and become crystalline again. Now this, is a whole new ballgame, and you must get go if you desire to play!

Density is an out of tune frequency and it anchors in your physical to "tell" you where you are out of alignment within. A medical intuitive/energy worker/naturopath who is familiar with this could also be of assistance here as well. There are natural herbs, live foods, crystals, sound healing, and more. You would have to know how to administer and use these, as you just don't "jump" without BEing aware of what you are jumping into. So consult your higher self and ask around or do some internet searches. There are an abundance of books on natural medicine that can assist as well. What used to be "alternative", becomes mainstream, and the only way to exist.

There are so many things that could be covered here, yet that would be another book. Just know that an ailment is not an ailment, it is your physical trying to get you to listen and your higher self waits to show you another alternative way.

So, can you be conscious enough to say "Wow, I am out of tune, what could be going on and trying to leave?". Don't get stuck in needing to know, for the purpose IS the question and its ability to shift one out of BEing a "sick victim" to one miraculously evolving and activating/integrating more light. Now, the more disconnected you are from your bodies (separated), the more physical and emotional pain you actually feel. The higher the realm you exist in, physical and emotional pain no longer exist. As you unify inside, pain of all kinds will start to go. In the beginning, it can be painful, and from time to time as you shift dimensionally and from realm to realm. Your perception and own unification will determine this. Eventually there is no pain anymore. That too was a belief and goes when your new DNA is activated and the LightBody/Merkaba are fully integrated and you come to exist in the higher realms again.

Any emotion held inside and not allowed to be released, creates discord within. The purpose is to safely let that emotion surface (with love) and leave. If you are angry, dismiss yourself and go vent. Release it to the Universe, for that is why it is there. If you need to cry, then cry consciously. How do you do this? Be aware that the purpose is the tears. Here you are not a victim, but the one assisting as well. When you shift to assist the energy needing to "go", the "time" spent here will greatly diminish. Tears are a Soul's release of all that has been held in over all existences of all times. Let them go. You have held on long enough.

Note here that one must be able to connect to their Higher Self in order to get true clarity as to that which is going on. Where one has established communication, all is needed is to ask and pay attention to what is felt inside. If one feels to seek outside assistance, this will be the feeling and we must honor this at all times. This is to create the opportunity to understand more and expand perspectives to see through the frequency of love, rather than the human frequency of old belief systems, old responses and fear.

Now, once you hit the 5th Dimension fully, with access to a multitude of higher dimensions, other worlds, galaxies and more, your Human Star Being Crystalline DNA activations kick in, and the body takes on a whole new meaning for its purpose as a vessel for the Dimensional Traveler, the Human Star Being here. The crystals within you are activated, and light particles are visibly reforming in front of your eyes. Your entire sub-atomic molecular structure starts to change and your nano-bodies wake up within. You just thought it was fun before. Becoming a HUman Star Being... well that is an upcoming course and book!

REMINDER: If it does not feed light, it depletes it and I need sunlight!

REMINDER: "Sick" is a mindset, a belief. I must change my own perception, if I wish to shift.

REMINDER: My Soul is pure light and my physical human vessel is dense. In order for me to "house" my Soul, the denseness must be pushed up and out, from the inside out. My Soul wishes to expand into a LIGHTBODY. I can assist by just REMEMBERING (and visualizing) this.

REMINDER: The human works to "fix", heal or repair a perceived physical problem. The Higher Self BEing allows for tuning, adding light, removing density, and works to transcend the density within.

REMINDER: I am not sick. I am tuning and coming into alignment again. That is leaving. It is up to me to allow and assist, without the need to suppress it again.

REMINDER: My body will repair, if I do not allow my human me to interfere. Utilize my higher self if I wish to assist and transcend the physical restrictions I once had.

REMINDER: I am a Crystalline Star Being, OF COURSE my human body was all out of whack! It was never meant to carry this much light, so reversal and repair are necessary now. Feed myself love, respect and honor this vessel for it shall carry me between dimensional realms. I keep myself stuck here when I do not.

REALITY ADJUSTMENTS: THE HUMAN SEES LOSS

This human thinks it is losing out, missing out, has to have that, do that, be that or that something has been missed out on or lost. It works to keep things the same, and when something changes to remove a distraction (thing or identity), it views "that" as a loss.

Sleep, connecting with nature, BEing creative and spending time alone or with others in love, are the things that we, as humans, treat as "inconveniences" to the fast pace human reality that WE created to keep us all in an unconscious state.

ALL THINGS THAT ARE IN THE WAY OF ONE'S AWAKENEING shall be removed to get your attention, make you listen up and chose differently than you did before. These are meant to OPEN your heart, by taking the thing away from you that means the most to show you how that was not a part of you.

That person, situation or material thing you had your identity wrapped around to feel safe, secure and "as something", had nothing to do with you. That car, that job, that title, not you. That relationship, not you. That house, not you. They were what you defined yourself by, created an identity around, and they will continue to be removed as long as they stand in the way of your own humanity and unification inside.

One's health is much of the time the "last thing" to go (it is perceived this way, yet they are simultaneous as well). For this is the one thing that will force one in a bed, on a couch and in such fear of dying that they will change "that" out of desperation and "hope or pray" for another "chance".

This is when the human bargains with the "higher whatever" they speak to for "help". This moment of breaking creates a shift inside that will start a different energetic flow.

You do not "lose that". It is removed by your Higher Self (YOU) because it was blocking your view. Your view of who you truly are inside and who you never were.

All things are removed to shift you to a space inside. It also causes energy wrapped around "that" to have to come up and purge.

REMINDER: If something is BEing taken away "out there", there is a bigger message that I am meant to see. Where am I focused, separated and lost in a physical reality. I am BEing REMINDED that is not me and to go within again.

REMINDER: Loss is my perception, for "I" as my higher self did that FOR me so I could REMEMBER again.

REMINDER: If I focus on that material thing too much, it may be removed as an adjustment to my physical reality.

REMINDER: The human sees loss and the higher self sees a part of the soul regained.

MEMORY LOSS: YOUR TRUE MEMORIES ARE BURIED UNDER YOUR HUMAN ONES THAT MUST BE RELEASED

You came to earth for a human experience to turn around and let go of your entire human existence to come home again. This journey will be as hard or as easy as you perceive it to be. Your cooperating (navigating through consciousness) will allow you to participate rather than BEing a perceived victim.

All occurs for you, by you, as you set it forth to be. You are only a victim when you allow yourself to be human.

Memories were borrowed for the human experience. When you are "done", you put them back, in the Akashic records, and for a time you can "pull from them" anytime you are in "assist another as light" mode. Eventually these are gone, for you do not need them anymore.

For this purpose, we will address "memory loss", for there are many reasons for this. The purposes are vast, and this is just an introduction, as we offer a condensed version here.

Human memories span over human time and lend to the separation experience you hold within. Your Etheric cords of attachment are what keep you in suffering and unable to ascend again. YOU must choose to release your attachment for it is YOU that created them. As you let go of the need to hold on (to everyone and everything), you literally start to "float" inside. This is because the denseness of that attachment kept you weighted gravitationally to the lower realms. Each release allows you to become LIGHT'er, literally. Now follow the spiral thingy here, for there is not beginning and no end. It just keeps going as you release all and let go inside and then "out there".

You had an attachment to "that", you cried, mourned and suffered inside to the "loss" as you perceived it to be. Then when you are "done", a vibrational shift will occur within. You will come into alignment and "know" that was meant to be. All will be "okay" and then more light will enter in. This light will start to expand and your heart will expand as well. The more you do this, the more you leave the vibration where that existed to begin with. You are happy and you float and are free again inside. This is because you had "lost yourself" in something that existed OUTSIDE, which was not true, was not you, and you have found your *true you* again.

Now, "big things" of attachment have lots of cords attached. These cords are obvious by the amount of "thought energy" that you have. The more thoughts you have "of that", the more cords you still have attached. It is up to you to say "enough", for I no longer NEED to THINK of THAT. Here you CHOOSE to go inside and let go of the hold that THAT has on you. You REMEMBER what you are inside and not attached to THAT "OUT THERE". You focus on your heart and you remind your mind that THAT IS NOT TRUE; That *that* has nothing to do with you. When you shift TO your heart and allow love to expand from within, all pain and suffering shall diminish and you will REMEMBER your true essence from inside of you again.

I created (brought forth) numerous "tools" of letting go and expanding, some of which I will share here with you.

I would first RECOGNIZE that my mind was occupied with the energy of something or someone else. I would say "no, that is no longer my reality and I do not desire this anymore". I would close my eyes and use my right arm as Archangel Michael's sword, and I would actually see the energetic cords coming out from my head to "that". I would use my arm of light to cut the cords coming out of my head and going to "that". The light would cauterize the ends, so that they could not re-attach. The super strong "issues", I would have to do repeatedly for there were cords that I could not see until it surfaced again in me. I also would see a lotus flower inside my heart opening up and emitting light from within my heart. This would allow any constricting "hold" that had to be released to just fall away. Some will image pink light of love and expand this from within. They envelop the other with this love too, to raise the vibration of all at once. Whatever works for you is the point, for it does not matter how, just that you do.

Now, once you release the attachment inside, where *that* was anchoring you in that dense reality (lower dimension) will also come up to go. So anything materialize in your human body or represented by a thing that you held onto, will also start to go; the discordant frequency in your human vessel, now allowed to come up and purge. The coffee cup, the couch, the car, the job, no longer important, for they no longer represent who you truly are.

Fear will keep you stuck, attached and anchored in the lower dimensional realms. Letting go will bring in a newer and higher dimensional version of you; the one that is happy, free and full of love again, for this is who you have forgotten yourself to be. Eventually you will "leave" that entire realm and lower version of you behind (by merging all back inside) in order to exist in a space of love at all times again.

Each release allows you to bring more of your Higher Self inside, for there was not enough space inside of you before. It was cluttered with outer things, taking up precious space that your Higher Self needed in order to come to BE inside AS you again. Until you choose this, your Higher Self "waits" in your energy field and "floats" "out there" to try to assist you in letting go of your own accord. Yet there comes a "time" when your Higher Self gets tired of waiting and providing you with chances to give it its rightful place again inside. This is when things started BEing adjusted and things start BEing removed. You can participate or be "forced" as you perceive it to be. Yet there is no "force", as these are human words to get you to see. Your Higher Self IS you, and you are also it. You have become separated into dualistic BEings and it only desires (and is time) to become ONE inside again.

Human memories are a human need and do not exist "up" here on New Earth, the 5th Dimension and Higher Realms). Here you exist in one moment and your heart is all you need. Your memories of ancient times are also within you and not "out there". They will surface as you let go of your human ones blocking you from REMEMBERING again.

The fuzzy head is part of this, bringing the inability to focus or recall another time. Human will "think" there is something "wrong", when things have never been more "right".

REMINDER: If I cannot REMEMBER another time, this is a good thing, as those were of a lower dimensional realm. I am preparing to REMEMBER more soon!

PURGING, RELEASING, TRANSCENDING

The human words are purging and releasing, when in fact you do no purge or release anything, other than in your mind. You do transcend that vibration where it used to exist inside. AS you transcend this, your physical will be adjusted to TUNE to the new frequency inside. Denseness will be pushed out of your reality so that it can dissipate and "leave". You leave it, you let it go and then it just dissolves, dissipates and ceases to exist at all, and the space that it once occupied will come to be filled with light and love. Light holds no density and there is no place to hide. Love floats and has no attachments, cords or anchors, so you "leave" the dimension that existed at rather than the human view of it leaves you.

REMINDER: As I release, I get lighter as all in my reality of fear, judgment and attachment was dense. This anchored me to a reality that I no longer exist. As I let go, my physical will be adjusted to allow me to float and fly. I will experience this inside as my LightBody forms and my Merkaba spins to take me to another dimensional version or parallel reality that I now desire to reside.

THE HUMAN CONTRACTS, THE SOUL EXPANDS

Now, this one is "tricky" for there is a paradox to all things. The human is small and the Soul is expansive, vast and so totally encompasses ALL-THAT-IS within. It is not bound by space or time; these are human perceptions and are created to keep the human limited and confined to a space (or box) that only exists inside the human mind to start with.

You start out with a spark in your heart and your Higher Self, your Soul "dangling" in your energy field "out there". Those downloads you get, from your own energy field. Your belief is that they come from a source from another place, time or outside of you. Some may believe they come from "space", other dimensions or more. They in fact do not, as they have been with you all along. You have yet to integrate the frequencies inside of you, so technically they do "exist "out there"", yet floating and waiting for you to achieve and HOLD the frequency that they exist AT, just "out there".
The spark is ignited repeatedly by events that open your heart. It may be loss or something awesome and new, for it does not matter, for the purpose is for "it" to expand from inside of you. Love opens your heart freely and allows your essence to expand. Yet if it is of a discordant frequency, it will leave and cause you to have to open your heart further to release the Soul pain that you have always carried within.

Crop circle out in left field: Relationships are a whole different book, for they serve so many purposes of understand that which exists within, so I will only briefly mention it and allow you to find other resources that will assist you in going within for this, rather than focusing on anything "out there". I do this in private sessions and workshops, when one truly desires to understand from a higher realm perspective rather than who did what to who and when. Now, back to YOU!

Anything that opens your heart is your Higher Self purpose. Each time this occurs you release something dense that no longer serves a purpose in your new reality coming forth. It was dense energy. That was all. You make it more than that with your human focus on needing to create "what that was" or focus on the human details that have no importance as all. Details keep you distracted from truly seeing within.

If you value ANYTHING over human lift, humanity, human heart and unification of all, it can be removed to bring you back into alignment inside.

When you are in alignment, all things are bliss, peace and exquisiteness BEyond. Anything that shifts your focus to "out there" that is not higher love and unity, is a distraction from who you are and why you are here. You can come to understand it or risk losing "that" to be able to truly see again. Resistance, conflict and an uneasy feelings are tell-tell signs that you are not listening or honoring your Higher Self and that an adjustment to your reality may be coming.

REMINDER: When that "out there" is not working, it means I am out of alignment somewhere inside. It requires going IN first, making my own adjustment to coming back to a space of peace and balance within for that "OUT THERE" to adjust AFTER I have re-aligned again inside.

FREQUENCY LOOPS

This is anything one gets stuck in, repeats, and can't seem to shift out of. These are what the human calls karma, spin or repeat cycles. This is just a repetitive frequency that one has yet to recognize, understand or shift out of fear into love. That is all.

How to break the frequency loop? Get conscious, get present, observe it and make a different choice. Much of the time, it will be the one thing you have previously avoided out of fear. The belief of fear creates the loop, while no longer believing is key.

Staying in the frequency loop creates an abundance of parallels, ripples and fractal selves and times. Breaking the loop and shifting to a higher frequency, a higher dimensional version of me, allows for all condensed times to purge, parallels to collapse and unification to begin again within.

REMINDER: If I find myself stuck in a "loop", I must get present and make a different choice. One from the heart, instead of avoidance, compromise or fear.

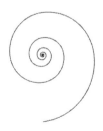

LACK ENERGY: MAKE IT YOUR PURPOSE

Lack was programmed in our old DNA, our old template, our old belief systems. It was a human creation that was not true. It was all of our journeys to experience it, release it, transcend it and unify, to never lack again.

It is brought forth in human thoughts and experiences to show us it existed, so that we could become conscious, identify it within and release it as the untruth that it was.

Lack is an energy, carries a multitude of frequencies, represented in the human as "not enough", and can be identified if one is present, aware and honest with themselves. If one sees it as just a discordant frequency, as an untruth, then one can release it by confronting it and refusing to believe it anymore.

The goal is to identify it, make it the purpose to see. It is not a fault, there is no judgment, there are no victims and it is not a necessity. It is not set in stone as the human would believe. It is not a way of living, not a punishment, not a fixed anything. It is a belief, an old programmed frequency that was anchored deep deep deep within. Our job, if you will, is to be present in every moment, to recognize it, change the frequency and to no longer believe this untruth.

We now have the power to believe and to not believe, to say "No, I do not believe that anymore" and to hold that new belief, regardless of what we "think". We can override the old programming, just by holding a frequency long enough that is higher, that does not break down and give in.

We hold onto that knowing inside of us, SO STRONGLY, that the old belief can no longer "get in". We do not "listen" to our head anymore. We hold onto what is within our hearts, inside of us, no matter what it says.

There are tests, and strong ones at times, to see what we really truly listen to inside, our head or our heart. If we believe our head, we give in. If we believe our heart, our soul, our higher self, we know that we do not lack, that we do not do without, that we are not alone, but it is up to us not to believe it and to actually listen to that which we feel inside. WE have the ability to shift out of that old untruth, that old programmed frequency. REMEMBERING this is what our higher dimensional version of us does.

Out there materializes based upon our own internal beliefs. Challenge your beliefs and refuse to listen to the old human programming. Hold fast to that which you know and don't take it anymore. DO something to hold onto the new frequency of what you truly believe. That you are an abundant and unified being of light and as this version of you, you lack for nothing and you never did. You must let go of any perception that tells you otherwise. You do have choice. You have to choose what you wish to believe now. No one can do this but you. Your higher realm version of you.

REMINDER: I do not lack. I never did. This was an untruth I believed. I no longer believe this. I must hold the new belief inside long enough for "out there "to shift.

REMINDER: If I fall back into lack, I can REMIND myself with the words: "I am pretending again".

TEACHING VS. GUIDING

To the human, we are teachers. To the awakening Soul, we are a guide. The human seeks to learn, while the Soul seeks to REMEMBER from inside.

Now, when I am "dealing" with humans, I actually use the word teacher, for this is what they understand and identify with. I also use the word guide, for the Soul-BEing knows that they need not a teacher, but another who resonates in frequency and has expanded to embody the information that will activate them within. This is not always conscious, for much of the time the seeker has yet to understand.

Both seek information. One activates the human mind to stretch and the other opens the heart.

Now, REMEMBERING (MEMORIES) of the Soul are buried deep within. There are many ways to activate them and what one "needs", will be up to which "space" they are in. Here is but one way:

IF YOU WISH TO LEARN (REMEMBER), BECOME A TEACHER:

You need others to teach you what you already know inside. When you speak to teach, that which you hold within you will surface to be heard. It is through sharing of this, that you will start to actually hear the spoken words. For the words you speak are there for you to see.

If it is untrue, you will feel it within you. It will be harder to speak untruths in this way. One does not quite understand that which is held inside that is untrue, until they try to teach another. One's language shall change, as they seek the words to describe what they feel and know inside. This will expand "new" vocabulary. It will also allow for any coding within to activate, along with presenting you with others as activators for you too. One huge room of activators.

The "old human" is set in a certain way. It takes another to "challenge that" to show the human self that this may not be the only way to see. Your perspectives shall shift as you do this, and expand with every challenge that you observe with an open mind.

Fear is able to surface here, and that is the hugest truth of all. Fear of saying the wrong thing, looking like an idiot, not knowing the "right" answer, and even, according to the human mind, failure. For one to come to see that none of these are true, one must first bring them forth in order to "do".

What is "no longer", will be allowed to surface and fall away. Any energy held in lack, will also surface to leave. Any "fixed" ways will be challenged to expand and any untruths that need to shift, shall be able to do this too. Then, the "new" truth inside of you shall be allowed to emerge. Besides, you have a gazillion Souls "out there" waiting to fulfill their contracts, to bring up everything hidden inside for you to see! Step it up and hold up your end of the contract by allowing it to BE!

REMINDER: If I wish to REMEMBER, teach. It is the quickest way to hear that which is no longer true to me and that which I had no idea I already knew inside.

ENERGY OF GIVING VS. SHARING

Changing the context of words in our mind assists us with expanding our perceptions BEyond the previous associations. One that is important is the ENERGY of these two words. The word "giving" usually comes from a place of attachment and lack (separation), while the energy of the word "sharing" creates unity again.

Giving is what the human MIND does and then expects something in return. It indicates that we are "giving" something of ourselves, and that something is expected in return. Much of the time, it is hard to detect, for the human is seeking acknowledgment or a certain feeling, and nothing one does can "fix" that. The response from another might be appropriate (or not), for one's response will be their own and may never appease the human mind. The human mind distorts things, and attaches to everything that it gives. Even if it is acknowledgement, that is still expectation of something, and that is of the human mind.

The confusing energy is when one gives of their mind and "waits" for a response with their human mind-heart. They give, and then get hurt or disappointed when they do not receive that which they "attached" by way of expectation to "that". This was never about the "thing given" but instead about what the seeker needed in return. Sometimes they are even seeking BEing let down or disappointed, for this is also an energy of lack that they hold within.

The human has also not learned to share, and attaches "mine" to that. It keeps for itself out of lack, survival and the perception that there is not enough.

Take the phrase "if you need help ask". The question is, if someone has something that can assist, and they know the other could benefit, why would they hold out for the other to ask? This goes back to the attachments to sharing again, the me/me/me that is "mine" mindset and the value one has placed on some*thing* over some*one*. The pure hearted soul offers that which they have to share and receives that which they need (even later) from wherever it is meant to come from.

The Soul gives and seeks nothing in return; it "does" just because. There are no cords attached and no reason for the giving. For to the Soul, the Higher Self BEing, this comes completely from the heart.

Sharing is what the Walking Soul does. It says "Here, let me share, for I always have enough". It already holds the feeling of wholeness inside, which allows it to truly give. The Soul knows that whatever it needs, will always be provided, BECAUSE it is able to share. It also attaches no feelings to any "thing", so giving "that" does not deplete anything within. Sharing creates a "flow" without restriction.

When one can see the energetic cords, one will no longer "take" from one who gives like this. WE, as Light BEings, can see the energy of attachment with that which is given, shared, and received.

Giving and receiving are an energy of "back and forth". Sharing creates a circle that never ends. Yep, it's that spiral thingy again.

REMINDER: I can reverse the energy of lack by REMEMBERING to share again.

REMINDER: Sharing starts with me. There is enough for everyone. Human created selfishness through separation within. When I am human, I am a part of creating the same and am separated within too.

REMINDER: Giving depletes, sharing expands and creates light that rejuvenates within. When I have given too much, I will feel depleted. Rest, nurture and then start sharing from within.

I ALLOW

I allow: Two very powerful words in reclaiming your own power again from within. These two words can change your entire mentality of where responsibility exists, and it is not "out there", it is within.

I used these words to shift ALL back to me, so I would stop focusing on another who I had given my power away to, by focusing on them and what "they" were doing.

I realized that it did not matter what they did, for *they* did exactly what I allowed them to. So, I used to say over and over "It's not what they do, it's what I allow". I had to put this up on my wall to see every day, until I stopped allowing "that" anymore. This was a huge one for me. They cannot do anything TO you. As a Soul, created that to occur, so that you could learn (REMEMBER) love, honor and integrity within. When you hear yourself say these words out loud, they make a huge impact. You will stop allowing that which you used to and shift to love for yourself, which you can then share towards those who honored their Soul contract to come to show you where an out of tune frequency (lack) existed within.

REMINDER: It's not what they do, it's what I allow. AS love, I no longer allow that in my reality anymore. I love me and them and "no, with love" is a boundary that we all must learn at some time along the way. Love for me is required; for I am the one that created this reality for me to see.

GAIA & THE UNIVERSE: TUNING, HEALING, TEACHING IN FREQUENCY

I awoke one morning to seeing a "contract", if you will, between Gaia and the Universe to assist in healing and teaching. It was quite interesting to observe from this perspective. So I share with those who may resonate.

Gaia holds all frequencies that one needs to "heal" on every level, vibrationally. This is why so many are BEing "moved" to connect in this way more. There comes a "time" in each's journey of re-evolving as energetic BEings that one's entire BEing shall be tuned, taught & healed from within. Every "body" shall be "tuned up" here, to the perfect vibrational frequency to allow for oneness with/as All-That-Is.

The higher selves are present here to communicate freely, without the disruption of the external reality. The elementals come out to play. The heavenly realms are open for all who allow themselves to connect as this very sacred space inside.

All bodies of consciousness are supported here. The mental, physical, emotional & spiritual are allowed to heal and whole again. All can be observed here. One can be at one with their own thoughts, in supporting frequencies, to hear that which otherwise would be dismissed, cluttered or suppressed. The Higher Self can guide and assist with releasing judgment and gaining clarity, for the simplicity of nature puts things into a new perspective, one where appreciation and gratitude exist. "Weeding" is easier here.

As the physical body moves, physical denseness is allowed to be released. When one allows their self to just "be" in nature, the emotional body shall also heal, as lower dense vibrations are able to surface on every level in order to be able to see. Any feelings suppressed can surface and be released to the Universe, the ground or trees. Yet this is in reverse here, for the human goes to nature to release, it is the other way around. We go to nature to BREATHE IT INTO our BEing, to raise our vibrational frequency inside so that the untruths can surface and go. We do not go to "get rid" of anything, the BEing in this, brings the higher calming truthful vibrations in and in exchange transmutes and transforms that which was within us that was not okay. The part of us that was human and allowed ourselves to forget. We bring that which REMINDS us and allows us to connect in vibration again.

Gaia and the Universe are an external view of what is true and real. They exist inside of each of us, and are tools we placed "out there" They are here to assist us when we need clarity, to help us re-align to love and go within. They bring us calming and gentle reminders that we are unable to find otherwise inside. The help us remove ourselves from the chaos and separation of the exterior world. They show us how to go inside and become ONE as All-That-Is once again. They ARE reminders, just by BEing present with them. That connection is what all have forgotten and they put all into perspective again.

Along my journey, they were pivotal and I had to be forced to get out into nature for I was an "inside" girl. I had to have my apartment taken away to cause me to move near a lake. I had to have my relationship end to cause me to "need" to go outside and breathe, think, cry and get air. It was in my own re-connection with nature, that I came to understand and REMEMBER inside again. It was in conversing with my Higher Self and BEing shown the true purpose in things that didn't make sense in human. It allowed me to see BEyond the veils I had put in place and to choose love over fear in order to come to finally transcend duality within.

In nature, the Soul is allowed to be "free" here, and it is here that one can come to a place of unity. For unity exists within us, yet the spaces within appear to the human to have holes or lack, if you will. In this place with nature, these spaces are allowed to "fill" energetically to be tuned each time, so that one can come to maintain this within. For you see, once you become one inside your entire BEing, you can maintain this vibration internally.

Gaia and the external Universe, also teach about energy, for it is that connection with energy that one can truly hear, feel and see. For me, I received clarity, messages and learned to "know" when certain things were present (animals usually) before even stepping outside to connect and "heal" me. I came to tune to "that" frequency (snakes, birds, deer & more). I came to see energy with my physical eyes in the air and water. I came to feel it, hear it, know it, yet not "out there", but internally. I eventually knew before arriving at the lake, what was present for me to experience and see. I allowed myself to wander off into the woods, on paths, to venture into places I would not normally have gone to see. I allowed myself to listen to those weird messages that made no human sense, but made sense to me and offered crazy clarity. I learned to dissipate clouds with my entire BEing connected AS ENERGY. I learned to tune to the energy of Gaia and her to me. I also learned to look up and speak to the Universe "out there" and allow it to guide me from within.

It was here that I learned about the separation of time and where we are physically looking with our head & eyes are what "time" we are in. This was pivotal in showing me how simple things really are. I found that when I was looking at the ground while I walked, I was stuck in another time. Usually a thought of a past that no longer existed and "holding on" or a "worry" of a future that had yet to occur. As I came to understand the power of thought, this was pivotal. For the only moment was the present one and that one "got missed" as long as I was walking, looking at the ground and "thinking in my head". I found that when I looked straight ahead, I was present, looking at what was directly in front of me. Meeting the eyes of others, speaking, smiling, appreciating the nature and life that came into my sight here. Once I learned how to be present, I then started to look up. Here is where I found my Higher Self connection as the entire universe "out there". Here is where I asked questions and allowed myself to dream and desire and create. I was astonished at how something as simple as walking could completely change one's reality from outside to within, then to also assist with bringing the higher realms in.

In nature, I was able to release my thoughts, my tears, my anger and my own lack there in that space of free. I talked to the Elementals, my Higher Self and the higher realms, not even realizing that all of that was inside of me. For I was healing, whole-ing and learning BEyond that which anything else could offer me. I was tuning my own frequencies, as the Universe that I would come to know myself to be.

I spent an entire year in this "cycle" before a completion took place inside of me. For I then held these frequencies and I no longer "needed" to go to Gaia, for Gaia had become one with me. I had expanded my own Universe and wherever I came to be in the physical, as an Energy Body,

Gaia and the Universe were now me. I connect from within, in frequency, and now I can go anywhere I desire to be. For now I need not go to the ocean, for the ocean is inside of me. If I desire to connect to a tree, I just tune to it and allow myself to be. For the Universe is no longer "out there", it exists within and is accessible any time we choose to connect energetically.

So when you feel the need to go to nature, know you are BEing summoned for tuning in frequency. There is a message for you, that only you can receive vibrationally.

There may also come a time that you are "called" to assist with Ascension, Gaia and the Universe. The Light that you hold inside, the frequencies you have achieved within now are a part of your purpose in assisting all of humanity. It may be as an incarnated angel, an enchanted elemental, as a Galactic Emissary of Light, as the cosmic portal that you are. It does not matter how, just that you honor and "do". You need not worry how or where, for you will be shown and "directed" when it is time. All you "do" is listen, honor and arrive.

SPIRITUAL HIERARCHY IS JUDGEMENT AND THEIR JOURNEY IS NONE OF YOUR BUSINESS

WE all hold the same magnificent, beautiful energy within us. How and when we come to expand that is according to our own "time" to awaken and grow how WE chose to do so, for our own journey here. Yet, there are moments when we forget this.

Spiritual Hierarchy is where we "judge" another's journey, observe another's journey and "get stuck" in focusing on how another is choosing (conscious or unconscious) to have their own journey.

Maybe it comes from love for them or maybe it comes from differences inside. It does not matter where it comes from, for when we "worry" about another's journey, we have stepped out of our "circle of responsibility or right". Our responsibility is our energetic field and what goes on inside. That "out there" is not your concern, unless it affects your actual energetic field and it can only do this if you allow it.

Usually we see something that triggers us about "honor or integrity" in another. Sometimes we even go so far as to take something on that had nothing to do with us in the first place. WE decided to get involved in "that". Or maybe we didn't. Maybe we got "challenged" in some way. Regardless, we get on the "high and mighty" about how "they are not BEing honest" or "how they are doing their journey". Question: If you stand in utter and complete integrity, respect, love and honor, what business is it of yours?

Their integrity is their own, and the only time it is yours is when you drop in frequency to participate. They only honor a Soul contract to show you something about yourself. Usually it is where you are compromising inside. If it were not, then you would not even notice or give it any attention at all.

So, ask yourself, who says your way is better than theirs? Who says you have all the answers and are sovereign over them? Stop for a moment and observe. Who says that their own beliefs are any less valid than yours? Who says that they are not entitled to choose to be conscious or not? And when one stands in judgment and get all wrapped up in another's world, who is the unconscious one? Judging them assists no one. It separates again. When we focus on them, we are not BEing a light. We are BEing a dimly lit bulb. Our job is to love them. That is all.

We all "slip" and do this along the way, until we can stay in total alignment again inside. Recognizing when this starts to occur is key to becoming conscious, moving back into our sacred space within and honoring all as a part of the whole. Besides, as humans, we already have our hands full with observing, shifting, activating, tuning, integrating and expanding our selves in every moment. When focus is on that "out there", we are not present. When we are not present, we are not aware, when we are not aware, we are not conscious. Now, who needs to get back into alignment inside? Besides, when we stand in judgment, this shows that we need (expect) something different from them. Who is in lack (need) when this occurs? Notice the energy of the entire thing. This will tell you much. When we stand in integrity INSIDE of us, "out there" no longer causes us to get out of alignment inside. THEN "out there" shifts in response TO us again.

You chose your journey, just as all others chose theirs too. The sooner you understand this, the sooner you will come to honor their choice. Until you do, you are the one in judgment and the lack of integrity is yours.

REMINDER: Their journey is none of my business, and I am a full-time job. When I judge them (participate), I am the one unconscious. My job is to love them and to continue to BE my 5th Dimensional Self and to transmit light at all times.

REMINDER: My lower realm version of me judged and lacked integrity. My higher realm version of me stays focused in love, creation and is in alignment inside.

REMINDER: My job is to honor their journey, while also honoring my own.

THE HUMAN WAITS; THE SOUL CREATES

The Lower Dimensional Realm Human BEing waits to see and then act in response to that. It needs tangible, proof, and something in its possession for anything that it does. It requires an exchange, for often it feels that it is BEing taken advantage of if it gives and does not receive something in return.

The Middle Dimensional Realm BEing works to shift out of this and come to be a creator again. It works to find balance in giving and receiving, between the logical and creative world, works to create flow out, teeter-totters between giving and taking too much until it can learn the energy of exchange, how to hear & feel lack, for lack was a human creation, one to be transcended within.

The Higher Dimensional Ream BEing creates first and then allows all just to arrive. It cares not how or when this occurs, for it trusts completely in its own frequency transmission. When one exists as their Higher Self, they exist as their abundant future self, as an energetic BEing that holds no lack within, for this was of the human way. This BEing gives at such a high rate to all, that it can only receive in return. It does not focus on controlling that which it receives. This BEing is in creation mode in every moment, sharing with all who truly seek from within. It knows that catering to lack only feeds that lack, which is not of assistance to no one and is of a lower dimensional realm. It understands the energy of all, for it hears and feels in frequency and there is no hiding here.

VISUALIZATION

Allow yourself to get lost in dreams, desires and Creation of the NEW here in the physical. The Higher Dimensional Realm BEing focuses all attention on Creation of commUNITY, coming together, of how all shall BE together as ONE again. When you allow for all separation to fall away within, then it too shall fall away "out there". For if you truly desire to BE in a space where only LOVE exists, then that must be created FIRST from within. Then it shall manifest in all that you do, see and come to BE. All realities shall merge, but before they can, all "old ways" of perceptions must be allowed to fall away; for you cannot fly and hold on at the same time. So let go of all that you "used to be" in the physical, for that is not who you truly are. You are an amazing, brilliant, exquisite and truly unlimited loving energy that exists in spaces that you just have yet to see. If you wish to access them, if you wish to REMEMBER, then go inside and release all that keeps you separated from within.

REMINDER: If I wish to be a creator again, I must allow myself to dream in my heart and 3rd eye simultaneously. The more I dream and believe, the more I am creating from my own REMEMBERING within.

REMINDER: A dream is but a memory in a higher realm parallel that I have yet to come to exist in. To reach the dream, I must first be able to visualize and believe in order to come to BE that vibrational version of me. Then the energy of creation from my open and outward flowing heart will generate the materialization of that.

SACRED GEOMETRY: VISUALS FOR EXPANSION

There are many ways that I use this. This is but one. It is a great tool for getting out of the "human" mindset of being stuck and focused only on "that". It can be a huge event or something small. What it is does not matter, as long as you shift from your Lower Dimensional Human you to your Higher Dimensional Self. This can help so much, that you may need to draw a lot! That alone is awesome, for it involves creativity, which opens the heart.

Now the human will make a bulleted or numbered list, which caters to the logical mind. The purpose is to expand BEyond the logical mind and tap into the creative heart. Gratitude and appreciation in every moment loves!

To use this, you take the "thing" that you are stuck (focused) on and put it in the middle circle. Then you find every purpose and result that you can find gratitude for, as a result of that thing occurring. This is how you expand your human mind. Do this for everything, and expansion becomes what you "do" automatically. Every time you "do" this, you are BEing your Higher Self again, and this is a dimensional shift! First you recognize the limiting belief and old pattern, then you create a "new" belief, which is one of expanded consciousness and flexible realties that are no longer "fixed" as the "only way" that could have been.

By doing this, you are reversing the energy of a 3rd Dimensional fixed mind and expanding into your 5th Dimensional Higher Self. When you get stuck in a "battle" of duality within, you are in the 4th Dimension inside again.

We use this same diagram to become unified again, yet we again reverse the energetic flow. That will be explained later in this book.

SACRED GEOMETRY: EXPANSION GRID

In using visual grids for expansion, when stretching the human mind to become the Higher Self again, we place the "event" or thing of focus in the middle, then we start filling in the circles around it with anything we can find to be grateful for "for that thing". Soon we have reversed the energy from one of BEing a victim to that "out there", to one of the Higher Self that sees multiple purposes creating benefit rather than victimization. The more purposes and gratitude we can find, the more we become our Higher Self again. We use this for absolutely everything until it is an automatic thing that comes from within us again. In expanding the human, we start in the core (middle) and we move out as far as we can. This takes the "single point, fixed reality human to a place of expansion within.

Get a circular grid that works for you, or just draw circles that start out from a center circle in the middle. Go from there. Create as many as you can.

LEARN ENERGY & FREQUENCIES

If you truly wish to understand how to BECOME a CREATOR from inside, learn energy. You are energy, as are all things. So in essence, you are learning about yourself by exposing yourself to something "out there" that will take your logical mind BEyond that which makes sense. It is a magnificent way to get you to understand flow, the connectedness of all things energetically and sharing love to assist others at the same time. Sitting and studying energy from a book will not give you the same experience. For at some point, one must get on in there, connect in the physical and learn to FEEL energy from inside.

The logical minded human cannot understand energy, for it does not make logical sense. The heart must open for this and human separation must start to fall away. One who lives in a completely logical world is shut off, walled up and in protection mode. They just do not realize it yet. For logic alone is a protection mechanism of the human mind. It keeps us from connecting through our hearts.

The energy class that I took was Reiki, and I did not "get it" at all. I was in complete "melt-down" of my own reality and all was falling apart. My solid, logical sense-making world was unraveling, and faster than the speed of light. I had held on until holding on was no longer an option. My Higher Self said "enough is enough, it's time to wake up. And oh, by the way, let me take everything away from you, to give you that proof you *need* in order to get the point to make a different choice". And yet, in the midst of it all, I found myself "called" to the soul activation word "Reiki", that is built into many of our Etheric templates, and we don't know why, but "that is a must". I took Reiki and it made absolutely no sense at all. Why? Because I was too logical. I was trying to "think" about it all and trying to understand it in my head and I had not yet re-connected to that "feeling" side of me again. This was going to be pivotal for me, and I had no idea how much until years later when I could look back and observe from the higher realms. It also served the purpose of raising my own vibrational frequency, for my awesome teacher did not teach traditional Reiki, she taught "LOVE"! The more love she showed me in a safe space that held no judgment at all, the more I could see my true and hearted me through less judgment, for I was holding entire existences of suppressed soul pain inside, that I had no idea existed at all. Each class of high frequency love and light attunements broke through those walls of steel that I had built around my human heart more and more. The time between each class allowed for more surfacing of out-of-tune discordant frequencies represented by human fears and tears that needed to come up and go. The oceans of soul pain I had carried across all existences and times would finally surface to be cried out in order to release all of the old discordant energy I'd held in/suppressed. It was astounding, yet when I was done, I was done. I continued to purge the multitude of physical ailments (manifestations of dense energies I'd held in my physical body structure) over many months and years after, while learning to connect from my heart, feel energy with my hands, learning to visualize, feel again and gaining tools I didn't have before in my fixed-tangible-logical reality/world.

I was doing neurofeedback on my brain and Reiki for my Soul. Things were about to really speed up now! I was "doomed" to awaken quickly, and with extreme discomfort, thank goodness! And low and behold, the day after a ton of light attunements (tuning), my Kundalini opened, shot up my spine, out my head and I was channeling like a mad-woman and clearing as fast as I could let go. Talk about realities falling apart quickly, mine sure did. I did extreme, for I knew no other way.

The cool thing was once I started teaching energy, *I* was slapped upside the head with a few logical students. Yep, gotta love our Universe! ☺ And even though I "got it", inside, I didn't yet have the understanding in words. This comes as we raise in frequency too! They challenged me by sitting in class and saying "what's the point"? (They were referring to Reiki, Energy and it all). Every question that we don't immediately know the answer to, means it is buried deep within. That was a profound question, for I had to observe and go within to truly figure this one out. The answer was huge, for the logical mind seeks a "point". The Higher Self BEing just connects and gets it inside. The more we "do" this, the more WE expand AS ourselves again. Then we go BEyond the teachings of others and we take that which we have connected to inside and we expand that to assist all others. Yes, it is that spiral thingy again.

I went from "scared to death" and totally self-conscious of my own "wrong" hand placement, to throwing all that I had been taught out the window. I released my ego, connected through my heart and and entire Team of Higher Selves and Galactic Light Beings came forth to "teach me" the Crystalline LightBody & Merkaba Energy and Everything from that point forward. I was wide open and the Universe was wide open in response. The more I did not care about "out there" the faster all started to make sense, the more I expanded my own light and the more open I was to "listening" to guidance on what to do from the higher realms. Now at that time, they were still "out there" for me to do from within. From there, came forth my own REMEMBERING, little by little and amazing every time. For miracles began to happen (to the human these are miracles) and we were quantum healing across time. We still existed in the separation of time back then, yet it was already starting to collapse and to witness this was amazing then. Diseases started disappearing "over night". That which had been a battle for entire existences and lifetimes started clearing immediately and before I knew it I was tuning LightBodies, activating Merkabas, working with Sacred Geometry, activating portals and transmitting light from my entire BEing again. My understanding came afterwards, as does all on this journey, until we fully REMEMBER again. Speed of recall of "higher realm" memories and of the ancient times is dependent on our own amount of separation (human-ness) within. Back then, my higher guides were still "up/"out there"", for I did not hold the frequency to yet embody this within. I still trusted, for the communication and visual connection was so strong, there was no doubt within me at all. This would prove to bring forth amazing from that point on. Teaching classes and working with others' energy allowed ME to come to REMEMBER again.

Consciousness is the energy of thought BEing switched from the frequency of unintentional to intentional. The constant practice of this assists us in evolving AS conscious energetic BEings again.

REMINDER: If I wish to truly understand, I will learn to understand the flow of energy, feel energy with my hands and coursing through me as I connect with nature and the energy of others as well. This will allow me to see more than I ever could with my human thinking mind. Energy must be felt, heard, seen, smelled and experienced with all of my senses from within. As I come to master energy, I will come to again BE me again, for who I truly am.

LINEAR VS. NON-LINEAR

Linear is the separation of time that we, as humans, came to exist in as we left the childhood state and were brought into a structured reality. Children exist in present time until "forced" to exist in the boxes that human adults impose upon them. Children exist beyond the veils and it is us that cause their separation to begin with. It is up to us, not to do this anymore. They are the future here. Please be conscious and don't contaminate them with the limiting beliefs that you learned. Expand your mind and find alternatives that will allow for their expansion, rather than suppression by the old human programming habit responding way. Encourage them, listen to them and allow them to bring forth their own essence and ancient memories to share with us all here now. Throw away the boxes and assist them in bringing forth the magnificence they have to share.

The human sees according to the "constraints" of time, while the Soul is expansive, which is the opposite of BEing constrained. This is why so many are termed "free spirited", for these free spirits do not conform to limits and they honor their sprit, their Soul's need to be free. It is not a disrespect, but a respect for their spirit, their soul essence within. Free is what we all were, in the beginning.

The human sees in fixed time, while nothing in the world of the Soul is fixed. It is fluid, flows, bending time beyond that which the human mind can see. It sees in spirals and geometric shapes, translating through visual images, sound, smells and more.

As all evolve from human to Higher Self, the space in-between is a continual teeter-totter & flip-flopping between linear & non-linear states. This is to allow for "time" to leave your own template as your human self and your Soul self merge, where the separation of time no longer exists. It will be quite confusing for a bit, yet present moment allows for ease "here". For this is where your Higher Self is (for this is your PRESENT YOU). Every time you exist only in present moment and in your heart, you are BEing your Higher Self again.

In the space of no-time, things are more subtle and integration is "quiet" and not as obvious as on the physical plane... observation with the silent higher-self-heart-mind allows us to actually "see" things as they transpire, if we pay very close attention....

Now, the more you release yourself intentionally from the need to exist by way of the constraints of human time, the more this will shift and your reality will merge and come to you.

I threw the watch out years ago and threw all but one clock away. I only used this one, if I absolutely had to. I shut off all alarms and asked my Higher Self to wake me up. I started using my computer clock, just to keep up with what part of the day I was in. I set my appointments at "one per day", so I never had to hurry to start or finish or be somewhere quickly. I moved in flow with the universe, waking when I woke up and sleeping when I felt to sleep. We, as humans, separated and created time as boundaries to live by. We lost ourselves in time and now time is going away. Here, as it leaves, we find ourselves again.

We take all the time we need to get ready and walk as slow as we feel to absorb the birds and nature as we do. We stop to speak to others, we smile, just because we feel to. We are not hurried, for time does not interfere with our ability to connect with another anymore. We do not limit our exchanges, for these now come from our heart. We smell the roses, pet the dog, feel the raindrops on our face. We breathe in slowly and become the wind and here, time does not exist.

My client schedule even had to go, and I had to allow my universe to bring clients to me. My understanding was that if I honored this, then all would be exactly as it should be. So I did, over "time", I stopped scheduling and allowed my clients to come to me. When they came, I'd give them options and know that whatever they picked was the "right time" and all scheduling would work out perfectly. One after another, my clients came and all were scheduled without ever a conflict with "time". I never lacked for clients, slept when I needed, integrated light activations and worked very little to have absolutely everything I needed and was "taught to exist" on nothing and to appreciate every moment and every thing. This way, I had a multitude of moments to "do" everything I felt to do. I even stopped scheduling for awhile and just did "in-the-moment" sessions online and this was perfect too! This is not about BEing bound by anything. This is about honoring all that is as it is meant to be.

I found that in my writings and speaking that I was still speaking in separation of time. I set a goal to drop this from my own template, and limited the perception of time there as well. I relaxed from "an hour ago" to "just a bit ago". I started speaking in "now" or yesterday vs. an actual time. To me, days expanded to the time I awoke to the time I slept... regardless of what time it was. I stopped speaking in ages and years, for this fed into the "time" thing too. Releasing as many time references as I could, assisted in letting go of time within. The human thinks in "I have been doing this for THIS LONG." Who cares. That is comparison and we do not do that here. No one cares if you have been doing it one day or one lifetime. The amount of knowledge you have is measured in how much light you hold here. Your own light determines how much knowledge you have, for knowledge is of the Universal heart-mind (The Unified Field of Super Consciousness) and here, we all have access to everything again.

This is because we work in unison AS the entire Universe when we do this. But first I had to be willing to let go of the way "it has always been" and to trust what I was shown. Trust is a huge part of this journey, for we have never been able to trust before. Here we step in faith and trust AS our Higher Self again.

Another was to let go of controlling when and how much to sleep. Your Higher Self will shut you down and wake you up, exactly as you need to be. I have slept for 2 hours and been totally rested and gone for 2 more human days. I have slept for 4 days straight, for activating light has always taken priority for me. I learned a long time ago (yep, using time here), that my vibrational frequency was of the utmost priority and that absolutely nothing came before this. How important this is, we truly do not understand, until we integrate as our Higher Self again. Nothing else is more important and we do not compromise anymore. We are of no use to anyone when we do.

Now the human will say "I only got 4 hours sleep, but I feel great" and then it will try to get back into sleeping habits that fit to the way they "think" they should be. The Higher Self BEing will just sleep and if it is 10 minutes or 14 hours, all is perfect as it is. We do not sleep the way we used to. We shut-down, re-boot and connect to the other realms, parallels, or whatever we are meant to do in that state. Much occurs here and sometimes we wake up "whooped", because we have been working (or awakening Souls go to school). Sleep is just a different state of BEing. It is where much occurs when your eyes are shut. What you are meant to REMEMBER, you will, when it is meant to be. If not, doesn't matter, you didn't need to see it, it just needed to occur for the "time" you are in.

REMINDER: In order to exist as my 5th Dimensional me, I must learn to embrace that playful child within me again. If it is buried under my human experiences, I must allow myself to let them go, in order to REMEMBER again.

REMINDER: Linear is me when I am trying to schedule and conform to the constraints of time. This includes my perceptions of when I must eat, sleep, work and more. I must throw out the old structured ways to let go of the linear boxes I live in.

REMINDER: Happiness, bliss, magic, peace, love and my 5th Dimensional me come forth when I allow myself to be creative, free and exist in present moment again.

REMINDER: If I am thinking in comparison, lists and time, I am human (linear). If I am being creative, present and playful I am my higher dimensional me and time does not exist here. I must do this MORE if I wish the 5th Dimension to exist IN me at all times again!

RELEASING VERSIONS OF THE OLD DENSE REALITY BEINGS AND REALMS

As one comes to seek to exist in the 5th Dimension again, one will be faced with releasing the old versions of all created in their lower dimensional realms. This will include their own identities, physical manifestation, relationships, thoughts, emotions and all attachments. This will also include all human aspects that one has attached, even by way of human family and friends.

Now the human will get confused by this, for they will want to hold on to that which they have come to hold dear to them. They have a hard time in letting go of that which was created for the human experience, yet this is not only beneficial to one's expansion, it is necessary. For all that one attaches to, or holds on to, will keep them anchored in the lower density realms. One fears such a release, yet this fear alone is part of the denseness of the old human reality. Where one can truly let go, they allow themselves to not only to come to exist again in a higher vibrational frequency realm, they also allow themselves to open up to all that already exists in that higher density realm. The physical is "slower" and materializes according to the realm you exist AS, FIRST, from within.

The hardest thing for a human to release is their attachment to others, things, and memories. Yet all of these were created to serve the human experience here, which existed in a lower density realm. In order to come to exist in a realm where the higher version of all others also exist, one must let go of all that do not exist in these higher density light realms.

One will exchange things for experiences and opportunity. One will exchange memories of a past that never truly existed for bliss in current moment that need no memories in order to exist. One will exchange old human aspects to come to exist with the Higher Self versions of all who occupy the same space.

ALL old versions of human aspects shall continually be released as one integrates to the 5th Dimensional Light Realm. One does not release the human, rather releases the perspective of that human that was once known. One cannot come to exist with the higher version of those BEings until the "ending" has been fully grieved and released from one's energy field. Then, and only then, may the higher version of that BEing come forth to exist in one's new higher reality. For it is not the other BEing that presents the issue here. It is your perspective of the version of them that you originally called to you for a previous dimensional experience.

One chooses the version of their self and another that exists in their own reality. If one hangs onto, focuses on or expects the "old" lower realm human version, then that shall be the version that one interacts with. One must create the version that they wish to interact with, and then hold the vibration within in order to interact in the frequency of that dimensional realm. Where one compromises within, to lower their own frequency to exist with the version of another in a lower density realm frequency, then one will "suffer" the reality of the realm they allow their self to exist in. When one no longer desires to exist in that old lower realm reality, one will willingly release this, allowing for a higher version reality to then occur. One must allow the old to leave, before the REMEMBERED can be accessed from within.

Your 5th/Higher Dimensional existence comes when the reality you believe in your mind matches the one you have REMEMBERED from inside. You will REMEMBER that all has already been created. All you have to do is integrate the frequency within in order to come to exist AS it again.

That which you believe shall be true, for all materializes "out there" from inside of you.

For awhile, you must let go of all versions of the old lower density realm and then see from inside only the 5th Dimensional version of that (i.e. yourself/another/an experience, etc.). When "that" comes back around, you must hold the vision and belief of the higher version, in order to have that experience that you set forth in a "previous moment in time" (vibrational frequency).

You must allow yourself and others to already BE in the 5th Dimensional Realm. If you expect a 3rd or 4th Dimensional Realm experience & reality, then this is what you shall get.

REMEMBER to visually create the version that you wish to interact with. Then hold this vibration within you and see nothing less. For that which you truly believe is that which you shall come to experience "out there". By doing this, one has the opportunity to actually shift into a higher realm dimensional experience. If you wish to create your reality, you must visualize it and believe it inside. Then you have the opportunity for it to materialize in your physical reality to actually exist there. The human mind is slow and desires to hold onto the old. Intentionally create from within that which you wish to experience from your heart and then believe nothing less. Hold this vibration UNTIL it occurs. One's overall vibrational frequency will determine "how long" this takes to occur, for the amount of separation within dictates how much "time" your realities span out over. The higher one vibrates, the faster their realities appear to materialize. For it is not faster, the amount of separation (delay) is less inside.

If one believes that everyone and everything is the same version as it always has been, then all shall truly be the same. It shall be so, because one has yet to create it within and then believe it long enough for it to come into existence. If one desires for something to be different, then one must create the opportunity for this actually to occur. Creation comes from within.

REMINDER: They (or that) represented an old frequency within me. I no longer have the need to exist with that version of either one of us. I no longer hold that belief or frequency within. I allow both of our higher realm versions to now exist in this space as one.

REMINDER: I created this and I have to REMEMBER that I created "that" too. For the realm I exist in, is the one I REMEMBER, allow and believe that I do. I REMEMBER that I already exist in the 5th/Higher Dimensional Realms and that all that I interact with have a version that exists here too. The only way that I can exist in a lower dimensional realm is if I allow myself to forget this. When I forget, I separate from this realm, causing me to shift into a lower dimensional version of me therefore causing me to interact with a lower dimensional version of all that I exist with too.

THE "SYSTEM" IS WITHIN YOU

When you see injustice, suppression, oppression, uniformity, conformity, and that "things must be a certain way" "OUT THERE", you see a system that you created for an experience that you needed to have, until you no longer subject yourself to this limiting belief system anymore. The system is within you. That "out there" is your "tangible experience" that you asked for (needed), in order to see what exists within. If you are suppressed, oppressed, feeling victimized or forced to adhere to a system that you "don't think you believe in", then you are already in conflict inside. You just have yet to be able to see the "bigger picture" yet.

Your job, if you will, is to recognize what limiting boxes you have come to exist in, in a tangible, physical reality. Now the human mind cannot comprehend the vastness of all that has been created for this, so it must start small and work its way up to the "big things", unless a huge adjustment comes along to force one into facing "that out there", due to conformity for way too long.

In Soul work, we go extreme to break the old human programming we hold within. Until one has done this enough, to no longer be suppressed inside, tools are necessary to "break" the strong programming of the entire human existence thus far.

If the system "out there" is not working, then we must go inside and find out if we truly believe in that system anymore. You would not be resonating with this, if you truly did.

Your job, is to "buck" your own system. For when you do this within, the system "out there" will start to fall away. It will not be easy, for the entire human experience is built on "the system". Releasing it from your own energy field will be a process of continually letting go of the programming that got you "into the system" to start with.

We learn to work outside the system. This is how the entire system "out there" falls and collapses. It is collapsing because it is no longer a collective belief anymore. The masses are pulling out of the matrix. And as they do, the entire system falls.

WE created the system and WE are the reason it is collapsing. It never existed "out there". It was the tangible thing we created to imprison our human self. When we get tired of BEing in prison inside, we just put the key in the hold and turn it. The key is the light of our heart and Soul. Turning it occurs when we take physical action (make a choice), not to participate and conform anymore inside. First we say "no more" inside, then we follow it up with the action that shifts the energy of the entire "thing" we created to begin with.

Now, this is where many get stuck in the energy of "fight" of "that out there". The energy of the fight keeps it going. There comes a time when the energy is gone and one gives up the fight inside and then "out there". The fight prolongs the endurance of the separation inside. We fight injustice "out there", whereas if all just pulled out of the matrix, "that" would completely cease to exist anymore.

So, you ask where you are "part of the system" inside. Where do you believe things must be a certain way? Start to question absolutely everything you believe in as a human that creates fear or suppression inside. This will tell you much.

REMINDER: The system is a part of my human DNA. As I shift in consciousness to no longer believe, I will release the limits from inside of me. The system was a belief that I no longer believe inside anymore.

REMINDER: The fight is within me. I am unconscious when I believe it is "out there".

REVIEWING THE HUMAN EXISTANCE

Each time we shift to a new realm, higher dimensional version of "ourselves", we go into "Review", so that we can leave the old version behind. Identity crisis's are routine with these, for the higher we ascend, the less identities we desire or need. This I wrote, as I left the lower realms behind, while observing the overall "shift" that my human had gone through "over years" to come to where I currently existed as a "Walking Soul." I was able to REMEMBER, reflect and see, from a different view while in my "human'ish" reflection of "old times". It helped many then, so I share it here with you as well.

REMEMBERING:

I worked my entire human life
To acquire things and build a home
My mind full of expectation
For this way, is all I have known

I worked so hard to separate
And tie my identity around others, memories, and things
To accomplish, gain, prove and succeed
To gather & gather things that I called "need"

Yet, now there is this desire
To just be free & to let go
But if I do, what will happen to me?
For "that" is all that I know

NAVIGATING DIMENSIONS

The heaviness that I sometimes feel
Deep inside my heart
Just does not feel like I am me
It feels like two "me's" BEing pulled apart

Ahhhhh, NOW I get it
As "those" are thoughts and they're not true
For that which I know is really me
Is in my heart, it's my Soul breaking through

"That" is freedom and holds my dream
Which in reality, IS my truth
For my world's been backwards & in reverse
I became human and forgot what I knew

And now to REMEMBER, I must be present
In every moment that there is
For in order to REMEMBER
Present moment is all that exists

And when I am present, I am ONE
No piece of me tied to anything "out there"
For I have reclaimed all of me
Becoming a light that I now share

For I understand, I chose this journey
To acquire all, to then let go
And those things have nothing to do with me
For the "me" that I had forgotten, I again now know.

And this me, is one with all
Full of love and peace within
Which allows me to be absolutely nothing
Yet all that is, as I once was, now again.

HUMAN VS. HUMANITY:
UNITY THROUGH LOVE AND COMPASSION

The human self has lost touch with humanity, yet humanity exists within. It was part of the human experience, yet that falls away with the complete collapse/merging of the lower dimensions. Our job, as Souls, is to find and bring forth our humanity again. We can choose to do this, or have our Universe deliver an adjustment to our reality to "teach us" how to REMEMBER to do this. Choice is a much more comfortable option here.

Anything that opens our heart, causes us to find appreciation and then share with others is our humanity coming forth again.

It's funny how many have their hearts opened by the receiving of money or a material thing, while others have their hearts opened by the love of an animal, the beauty of nature or just a hug. The goal is to shift the focus to where our hearts are open to sharing at all times. Ask yourself some questions. Do you wait to receive before you share? Do you have an attachment to how or who you share? Do you place limits on that which you share? Do you know when your heart is open to sharing? Do you just do for others, for no reason at all? Can you tell when your heart is closed and you have reversed this energy of unity to separation again?

One BEing focuses on their own self (or their own little world); the other focuses on all as one and shares that which they have to assist others.

One must create such a giving force from within, that receiving is automatic from the Universe. One must shift the focus off a materialistic world and to one of sharing again.

The simple things get us in touch with our heart and are there for us in every moment that we are present.

There are vacant homes, vacant offices while Souls live on the streets, do without and are outcasts for not fitting in. There are Light Workers' here to assist in Ascension and no means of support to do this.

If you wish to support something and make use of that which you have, used it to create change and support those who do this as well. Instead of support that which suppressed you, support that which frees all again.

Your first union with your soul, your higher self, (whatever word you prefer to use) will be pivotal and nothing will ever be the same inside you again. You will cry for humanity along the way, be angry at humanity along the way, as you come to embody Christ Consciousness within you and truly REMEMBER again. You must go inside and find humanity within.

It is a part of the process, for the dense human self forgot humanity, sharing and unity. As your heart opens, you will see the injustices "out there", the separation in so many ways that have been created by each one of us as humans on the old physical plane of Earth. Yet that dissolves "out there", as it dissolves within you. Humanity returns in all as they come to exist in the 5th Dimension together again. This has already occurred and is waiting for you to arrive and embody this frequency of love and unity within again.

This occurs over your human time for you, yet simultaneously from the higher realms. Shift up in frequency to embody this again and see how fast you see things change "out there". You start in your own bubble and work out, as it's not the other way around anymore. Expand your bubble so huge that the only thing existent in your reality is in response to you.

REMINDER: When I desire for humanity to change, I will change first inside. I then allow "out there" to transpire in response to my own transmission of love, compassion and unification again.

THE HIGHER REALMS

THE 5TH DIMENSION

NEW EARTH: WE

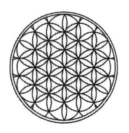

REMEMBERING THE 5TH DIMENSIONAL REALM

The 5th Dimension is a Realm. It is one that you REMEMBER, BELIEVE, ALLOW AND CREATE your way vibrationally BACK into from within. It comes to exist "out there" as you allow it to. All already exists here. Yet one comes to REMEMBER HOW to BE here again, as they let go of all that interferes with their ability to BELIEVE and see this within. The 5th Dimensional Realm is one of CREATION. As one creates from within, works to create the "New", one shall again come to then exist in this space that has been forgotten. The 5th Dimension is the BEGINNING and not the "end". It is the portal that activates all other portals within. Then all realms become visible, when one is ready, in their own human time. For one will continue to unlock, unblock and expand INTO these new spaces, first from inside and then "out there". All realms then merge and here too, there is no separation. This book addresses all realms from the 5th Dimensional Realm. They are only separated when addressing them for sake of explanation. Otherwise they too are a part of the whole. The "higher realms" are as one space to now occupy.

The 5th Dimensional Realm:

- ♥ Is not one thing. It is all things, simultaneously, at once. As ONE again
- ♥ Is a sacred space that one comes to exist AS inside
- ♥ Radiates out from within
- ♥ Is where one exists as an alchemist of creation again
- ♥ Is that which ONE has always been
- ♥ Is the place after "zero point" inside

- ♥ Is weightless, timeless, limitless infinite existence
- ♥ Is where "out there" is a materialization of light from within
- ♥ Is a realm you REMEMBER your way vibrationally back IN to
- ♥ Is a realm of CREATION that starts & expands from within your heart
- ♥ Is a realm of ALLOWING yourself to again BE and EXIST in again
- ♥ Is a realm that your mind comes to understand AFTER you are here
- ♥ Is "achieved" through continual honor, faith & trust AS your Higher Self
- ♥ Requires choosing your Higher Self over your physical human self
- ♥ Is a unification of all of your selves with All-That-Is
- ♥ Is a space where you exist AS WE inside
- ♥ Is VISIBLE internally first, then manifests "out there" to be able to see. If you cannot see it inside, it cannot come to exist
- ♥ It is where one's mind is expanded to come to comprehend and believe that which the Universal Heart already knows
- ♥ It is the materialization in light matter form, that which has been forgotten
- ♥ Is love, light, trust, patience, faith, honor, integrity and peace within
- ♥ Is the opposite, and free of, the old lower realm human reality
- ♥ Is a realm where the Universal Mind and Heart exist together as ONE
- ♥ Is the Realm of HEAVEN that exists here as your NEW EARTH
- ♥ Is a realm where the dense human beliefs of duality no longer exist
- ♥ Is a space where no identities, attachments or cords exist inside
- ♥ Is created from your own vibrational frequency, by you, as you
- ♥ Is where you exist AS ALL Higher Selves, without any separation at all
- ♥ Is an existence without separation and of complete transparency of all

One has always existed here, already exists here, yet their 5th Dimensional aspect (version) is a vibrational frequency that one comes to BE inside again. This is one's entire existence AS All-That-Is.

EXISTING ON NEW EARTH NOW

Your Higher Self is a sovereign BEing and you are also this. Here in the 5th Dimensional Realm you are home and AS this again. You have come to embody all within and release your human beliefs that you are any less. Here you REMEMBER fully and bring forth your MEMORIES to share with others seeking to REMEMBER as well. You also bring forth ancient knowledge that assists in creating change, which is encoded & is already written in your new Crystalline DNA. As you embody this and continue to activate beyond that which your human mind can comprehend, reality totally changes in response TO you BEING ONE again. "Out there" now materializing so you can actually exist here in the physical now. Many others cannot yet see, so it is up to you to share with them.

This started out as a space that you held deep within you that you believed. Now your beliefs are materializing for you, as you held this in your own energy. When you hold this vibration long enough you shall come to exist here again.

This is an unlimited reality. Limits are of the human aspect and they do not exist here. Present moment is all there is. Memories no longer necessary, these were released as you integrated to the frequency of this realm. Until this is the only realm you occupy, you shall have access to memories to assist others through teachings (sharings). Yet there is no attachment to them or anything else, for that matter, for attachment to all went, as you vibrated out of the lower realms.

Here you are your future self, all knowing and all things sacred. There is no waste here. There is only love and light. Duality no longer, you embody

Christ Consciousness here, where creation is existent in every moment just by BEing and existing AS THIS again.

This is what was previously perceived as heaven. This changed after the December 2012 Ascension Gateway opening and the veils that were previously in place were lifted. Now all have the capability to come to exist here. How and when will be up to the ones that choose to participate in their own journey and truly go within. For this is activated by way of portals, that must be unlocked from inside. This realm is first accessed vibrationally, and then it becomes visible and tangible to those who hold this frequency within. This used to be an Etheric realm only; where one's physical body had to die for one's energy to come to exist here. Now, with the activation of the LightBody, the Universal Merkaba, then the Orbitron (as I call it), one can actually exist in this (and other realms) simultaneously, as the LightBody is the vehicle that allows one to move inter-dimensionally between a multitude of dimensional realms.

Here you are an Ascended Master, a Sovereign BEing and you have come to exist outside the Matrix. Your understandings go beyond your old physical human world and you bring forth ancient REMEMBERINGS to exist in love, peace, unity and light again.

Now, I write to you from NEW EARTH, as it is now a physical and tangible thing. Our minds must stretch so far beyond human though, to come to exist here again. Look for the miracles, the magic and expected to occur. Do not assume that when you wake up, that it is the old reality, the old people, the old ways anymore. Do expect for things to be easier and for it to be like walking in a dream. Pay attention to the tiny things that others cannot see. Take a camera everywhere you go and take photos of the sun, the elements and see the energies and orbs and that which would not make sense. Do not try to rationalize or minimize by fitting what you see or experience in a "box of human". Allow yourself to believe the unbelievable and desire for so much more. Embrace crazy, for crazy is the new reality that gets you here. Crazy is listening to that within you that goes against everything you've ever known. Crazy is bucking the system and saying that's not my reality anymore. Crazy is stepping into fear because you know that it's not true. Crazy is holding so much love that it bust out from inside of you. And crazy is REMEMBERING that you are an Ancient, a God, Jeshua, an Angel, and a Star Being that is not from here. It's not crazy, because they all are most definitely true.

REMINDER: Crazy to the human is truth in the higher realms. I am a Star Being, an Angel, a Master and I do not limit myself to being human anymore.

THE "REALITY" OF THE 5TH DIMENSIONAL REALM

The 5th Dimension is the beginning and it is only accessible by way of your open heart. Expansion of your human self allows you to transcend and "release" the blocks keeping you from existing here again. It is where all realms are accessed, and the vastness of what exists there is as unlimited as you are. First you must be willing to choose. The rest is a journey of letting go of all that you once knew in your human mind. Your physical will release all that also held you back. What this is shall surprise you. For it shall be all things created by your human existence that do not serve your higher purpose of light, sharing and unity. ONEness as a way of BEing, rather than something to achieve. You Become this again inside and before you know it you are radiating this from your entire BEing, for this IS you. You ARE SOURCE, Divine essence AS All-That-Is. You just have yet to fully REMEMBER, and you do, nothing else will exist. This will be all that you breathe and that which you have forgotten will start flooding back. First, you must open up to the belief that your physical world reality is not all that there is. There comes a time when "there has to be more" becomes the seeker's quest.

The first I time I realized that the 5th Dimensional Realm was the old, literal "Heaven" that we all heard about in our human reality, I about fell out. Seriously Universe? Are you kidding me? Shocked was an understatement.

I had no specific belief in heaven or hell or anything else for that matter anymore. I had come to respect all belief systems that others had, while remaining neutral and not believing anything at all. The details of that just

220

did not seem important at the time. This was a huge asset, for I no longer had to release limiting beliefs, for I had released them "earlier" as I "grew" and let go of any discord I had with beliefs within. So to actually "see" what all of "this" was that I had been assisting, guiding and gaining access to, well shocker is a mild word. I had been a Light Bearer, a Light Anchor and a Gatekeeper here and had no concept apparently for what that meant. "Duhhhhhhhhhhhh" was a good word when I finally "got" this. It took me several days, even a few weeks, to "absorb" and stretch my consciousness enough to wrap my human mind around this one. Even more-so, when I saw that each belief system had "separated" the 5th Dimension into separate existences. When we come to merge & integrate enough inside, any separation inside goes. For me, it was not so much separation, for I did not have a specific belief system. It was more bringing together "all of them" so that I could actually see them as they truly were. All ONE and the same. I had "learned" they were different "places/spaces" and merging this occurred as the separation in my own energetic template dissolved.

I saw where the 3rd Dimension had become the actual physical "hell" now the earthly plane, the 4th Dimension BEing what I call "the space in-between" (this applies to other things as well, to be covered elsewhere in this book) and the 5th Dimension BEing the literal "Heavenly Realm" i.e. Heaven on Earth. There are so many aspects of this; I will try to touch on them here, without convoluting them by way of human interpretation.

WE are all Light BEings here and as we LIGHT'en, we literally get "lighter" in weight. When one's LightBody is fully activated, the Merkaba turns into this huge energetic bubble. Now inside and outside the bubble, at this point are separate realities. One, inside the bubble changes as we do in vibrational frequency. Inside is our own reality, our own REMEMBERING, our own everything. It is magnetized and draws everything "to it". Just by BEing IN it, OF it, AS it. This also will be expanded upon in a section dedicated to this. Inside is our hologram, outside the collective one. Floating inside this bubble allows us to move and shift dimensionally like never before, and this too shall expand as we do.

I can look back over the entire human existence and see how every moment was one of activation and ascension. Every moment that I was not conscious, I was suppressing and descending again. There is no other way to say it. The human is asleep in a waking state. The Light BEing is awake at all times. And then there is the space in-between where we sleep to wake, integrate and merge while we activate our own light frequencies within.

Understanding now, that the 5th Dimensional Realm is the literal "Heaven" and the Gateways opened for us with the December 2012 activations to come to actually exist here again. The old various writings of the "resurrection", purgatory, heaven, hell and ALL of it, finally made sense. I did have some adjusting to do within though, for all of these things now occur within each one of us. Death, re-birth, ascension, purgatory, judgment day... all held within our own energetic templates, each one of us, to come to understand, purge/transcend from inside to then come to exist in a reality that is utterly and totally heaven "out there" as well. Yet it is not only heaven, it is more. It is a playground of the entire universe opening up. For Gaia and the entire cosmos exists within us. Speaking the words and holding this inside are two totally different frequencies. One resonates with the words, the other radiates it with their entire BEing and totally "gets it" inside. Ascension and Descension now inside of us, we no longer descend when we REMEMBER fully within. And here, my loves, IS absolute magic, unicorns, unity, peace and bliss!

Our limits were in our human minds, our anchors all within as well. One CAN exist in totally unity "out there", once they come to embody this inside. THEN one exists AS their 5th/Higher Dimensional self, and then all realms open up to allow for further existence and expansion as well.

Once I understood all of this, our suffering all made sense. WE WERE CHRISTED individuals and we all had to suffer and be resurrected inside. We crucified others and ourselves, for we were all BEings rolled up in one. Old human realities are "ripped and degutted" from within us, for they are planted firmly in our human DNA. Our Crystalline (Christ) LightBody DNA gives us the ability to leave the lower realms, inside and "out there", therefore each of us ascending first inside to bring forth ancient times here for all again.

EMBODYMENT: As we truly, fully and completely hold REMEMBERING within us, the lower realms do cease to exist. We can see them from time to time, yet they are not a part of our reality anymore. They only exist when we come to interact with another that still exists there, or while any separation (lower realm frequencies) still exists inside. When we are conscious and present, we do not pay "that" any attention, as we do not "spend any time there". We completely allow the energy of it flow on by and dissipate. There is nothing there that WE need any longer. If another comes to us, speaks to us, we acknowledge this, for there is something BEing presented that we are to pay attention to. WE do not step out of our energetic bubble to seek another at all. We go where we are guided inside to go. We honor that which is presented to us. We no longer seek anything at all. Seeking was of the human way. Here we are no longer human; WE are all of HUmanity again.

Now, if you have ever heard of anything "religious", you would have heard of "standing before the gates of heaven to be judged"... well, here is the cool part. We now stand before the gates inside and judgment is our own. We are, at all times, trying to get into heaven. We just do not realize it, for it is BEyond our own human comprehension. From the moment we arrived here, we started trying to awaken, ascending and removing the veils. Every moment as a human was spent creating that which we would have to come to release inside and out. Inside would be all of the human perceptions, thoughts, attachments, emotions, identities and beliefs and "out there" would be everything that those things created in the physical as a result of the frequencies within that "materialized" in the physical from our own denseness and duality. That was the human game (way), the illusion, the untruths inside. Only when the entire human reality is released (this is simultaneous) do we then exist outside and BEyond the illusion in a space of utter and total REMEMBERING. And here, again, human no longer exists. Only a physical suit to hold our light energy and that suit continues to lighten (LightBody) to where "one day" all shall awaken to be able to see that even that has dissipated and we no longer are tied to a physical existence anymore. Materializing is a part of what we all see as "coming". We await for the vibrational frequency and expansion within to allow for this to occur. We are already experiencing this in many forms or fashion. Yet the human mind is the last to catch up to what is already occurring, at all times.

So, all shall suffer to judgment and separation and the release of it within. Until this completely has been released, full access to the 5th Dimension remains just BEyond reach. With each separation that dissolves, one further exists in the 5th Dimension. Yet not "out there", but inside. Only then can "out there" materialize to become visible for one to then see. It already exists, yet the vibrational frequency must be held long enough for one's human mind to stretch far enough to be able to see it with human eyes again.

Now, it is important to understand, that BEYOND the gates of heaven, BEyond the 5th Dimension are the even "higher" (outer) realms. These are Galactic and we exist AS these as well. Memories of these also return and AS Higher Dimensional LIGHT BEINGS again, we fulfill our purpose here Galactically too.

WE are illumined ones, we are all heavenly celestial bodies, WE are all

Galactic BEings, WE are all Lemurian, Atlantean and Extra Terrestrial too. We are ALL of these BEINGS at the same time. We are no longer limited to just one. That too was separated by the human mind and inside. Labels are what humans do. WE only use labels, so that you can find us and we can assist you with your Ascension and REMEMBERING from within.

REMINDER: I am an illuminated BEing. I am of all realms. My REMEMBERING this is through higher heart love. I am homo-illuminous. I radiate light OUT from within.

REMINDER: Ascension is inside of me. I must transcend all human beliefs and limits within.

When your mind is quiet, you shall understand
When your eyes are closed, you shall clearly see
When your heart is open, nothing else exists
When every moment is a dream, reality it shall be.

For you are not that BEing
One of thoughts and of a past
You, you have forgotten
And your high vibration brings it "fast"
For that which you seek to know
Is deep, deep, deep within
A space covered by physical memories
Allowed to surface when the veil is thin

For you see the veil as outside of you
Yet it is your own physicality
As you transcend the physical world you know
You change your reality.

REMEMBERING is not in your mind
It exists within your heart
It occurs as you let go
And dense matter is allowed to part

REMEMBERING is in vibration
Of you as an energy
The more you embrace your essence
The more that you shall see.

TRANSCENDING DUALITY TO TRIALITY TO ONE:
JUDGEMENT "DAY" & CHRIST CONSCIOUSNESS

The entire Ascension Process is Judgment Day and all is within. It is the dissolution of all belief systems, human thought and how anything should BE from within. I call this dis-illusionment, for one no longer exists inside the illusion, but is aware and creates reality from outside the matrix looking in. As a human, one will suffer repeatedly, until all judgment and separation are released INSIDE and one is totally "HOME" inside again. Suffering is the result of BEing unconscious and holding onto judgment and separation within.

Ascension is the complete stripping away of all belief systems, reconstruction of the self, and the dissolution of one's entire reality, all of which exists BEYOND the human realm. Ascension is the death of the limited and small human self, integration of the Higher Self (selves) and the resurrection of the Christed Self, all from within. It is you, AS SOURCE, REMEMBERED and held inside, in frequency, once again.

Now, one does not transcend duality and go crystalline without physical pain. Yet the pain is "different" in the LightBody. One is aware, yet it is as if it does not exist. We exist where we do not feel physical pain any longer, so it can present and we rarely know it is there. We have "twinges" or "inklings", so that we can assist others with this. We do, in some way, still occupy a physical vessel body here. It just serves as a suit, instead of it BEing a separate thing that, we are again one with it.

Duality, all belief systems, separation of time and more, were all anchored in our old DNA, Etheric/energetic blueprint, physical template and when it is time for these to go, they get "ripped" out and we feel like we are BEing "degutted", our bones, teeth and muscles endure much "lightening" as well. The carbon-based dense human body lightens easier, the faster you intentionally let go. If you wait until you are forced into a space for this to occur, excruciating is an understatement here. Your entire existence must lighten, literally, for you to be LIGHT enough to exist in the higher realms. The frequencies up here do not support the old human way anymore.

Now, this can be one huge experience or a little "over time" as one works intentionally to clear, which offers more ease to the human physical experience here. Our spines undergo much "work" and this is another place we endure pain. The lower chakras also cause quite a bit of an uproar. Literally. Our intestines talk, our stomach blows up with "air babies" while we wait to birth "a new". We can go from flat tummies to 9 months pregnant in a matter of minutes when the solar winds and super duper light activations kick in.

Until we have unification with of our bodies, we suffer a lot more, and as we unify the "moments" become few and far between. We develop (telepathic) energetic communication with all of our bodies (mental, physical, emotional), which allows us to just speak to create a shift. This is technically just becoming so conscious that WE are all ONE again. I could just connect, think, or speak and my physical would respond, sometimes almost instantly. We get so used to not feeling any pain, that when we do we are actually surprised.

There seems to be "one last time" before coming to BE fully in the 5th Dimensional Realm in the physical that we get degutted and density is ripped from the inside out. I am not speaking this to create fear, but awareness, for you will get through it if you can endure it, assist it and trust. Separation was embedded within us, absolutely everywhere in our physical existence here. And to unanchor that within us so that we can float and be in magic and bliss again, everything that is not has to go, for here it cannot exist.

Now, I do not share this to create fear, for it is quite the opposite. It is to create awareness so that you do not fear it. It is a welcomed part of this process that we all must undergo to transcend the lower dimensional realms before we can even "think" of existing fully AS the 5th Dimensional Realm fully again. All along the way this will occur, and much of the time you are unaware that "this" is what it is. Human focuses on a need to know what is going on in the physical, while if you just assist it in going, it will leave easier and after bring you bliss. It is the resistance and needing to know that causes all of the suffering and hanging on. You will need to know, when you need to know, if you need to know. If it goes and you are happy, blissful and existing in love and magic again, what do you care? Your heart-BEing self does not. Only your human you does. Where you can recognize this, it will assist you greatly along the way.

The "last passage" there will be a "death" of your old, small, human you. Some have literally thought they were dying, others just had a lot of pain. After requires nurturing, rest as there may be a day or two (whatever amount of time is perfect) of void space while the old is allowed to move out and your energy can merge or reset to "new". The energy spin will be shifted again and you will go through a re-birth of the NEW from inside of you. A review of your journey and entire existence here is typical and much inner reflection is a part of this too. I actually wrote during my identity crisis and experiences, for I understood it and it helped many others to heal/whole years worth of old belief that they had been holding onto as well. The tears that brought forth in assisting another in such a profound way, assisted me even more. You never realize how you assist another. Usually the thing you resist sharing the most is what helps more than you'd ever know. The deepest things shared in love touch others deeply too.

Your entire human existence of separation must be unanchored (human words) from your physical BEing and your higher realm light existence anchored in. If you really desire to know, you are leaving the entire realm and that density was keeping you from getting through the "Gates of Heaven". You enter Heaven with your physical vessel now. You do not die. That was the old belief system. You even get to sit at a computer and write afterwards. How do you think I was able to write this book? Across timelines and dimensions, yes, we do travel now. My minds and hearts have merged and I can see from all realms. I have been for awhile. You will understand this when it is time as well.

You will be resurrected, yes, I said it. Just like Christ, for you now hold Christ Consciousness within you. You just have yet to REMEMBER until you do. It is already there. You are already here. Your human you is still catching up, for it is slow, fights and resists. That is why WE are here.

WE are Light BEings, Crystal BEings, Earth Angels, and more. WE hold Christ Consciousness within. WE bring forth the forgotten for all to also REMEMBER again.

UNIFYING SEPARATED BELIEF SYSTEMS

As the human separated, so did that which it believed. As humans separated into Soul groups, so did the belief systems of the collectives as well. Many BEings moved from belief systems to belief systems, to completely throw out all belief systems, for nothing ever fit. Many "tried on" many religions, to come to do the same. Many *tried* to believe, to find that it suppressed them even more. Because of the billions of Souls on this earth, the belief systems "out there" are as separated as the ones inside. This created variety and the most diversity, for it was your choice for your experience here.

Now, religions separated off into more that could be counted. Those with no religious preference believed in something different, along the way. Many started out with no belief system and became spiritual, while others had no preference religiously, and metaphysics or quantum physics enticed their very logical mind. Some completely bucked the systems and believed in extra-terrestrials (ET's) above all, for they *knew* inside and never gave up on that belief. This is not about one's belief system, for that does not matter. This is about the separation of them all and how they are all the same.

Ascension is the complete obliteration of all belief systems within. Dismantling, dissolving, destruction... doesn't matter. They all apply.

One ascends as they become light. A light BEing, ascended master, angel, SOURCE, the CREATOR, a God-Realized Sovereign BEing again.

For the sake of unifying again, I will mention the three main belief systems that one may have broken off into along the way. Some evolve into one (or more) of these. Some will embody all at some point in "time". As one comes to vibrate at higher frequencies, these beliefs merge and become one again. Regardless of any belief system, eventually there is no longer any separation. This must occur for one to truly ascend again.

The three primary separations I realized (REMEMBERED) were religious (GOD, etc.), Ancient Times (Lemuria/Atlantis/Egypt, etc.), and Extra Terrestrial.

The one who holds a religious belief, they will see the "gold halo" over the Christed BEing. This is Christ Consciousness, that which each one of us now hold inside.

The New Age/Metaphysical one may come to identify with Lemuria/Atlantis/Egypt, etc. This one usually will venture into energy "healing", identify with crystals and crystalline cities and the LightBody. Crystalline energy and the crystalline body would be identified with the glow, the aura, the energy field.

The scientific and technological mind may stumble into quantum physics, sacred geometry, gravitational fields, time/space continuum and more. This one might come to try to prove that which exists in outer space and come to identify with the Merkaba and "believe" in ET's.

Now, all are true, for all are the exact same thing. The Merkaba, Orbitron, Christed Halos, the glow of the Crystalline BEing, all the same thing. All are Ascension "vehicles". All are BEings of Light. All are ONE, separated yet again, as different ways of understanding the exact same thing. Ascension unifies these into one. All are heaven, all are paradise, all are other universes, and WE are them.

REMINDER: That halo, that Merkaba, that Light BEing are one and the same. That is US, from a "future" time, as it is perceived. It is us, seeing us, so every E.T. is us visible by way of vibrational frequency, through an activated portal from within. The only way I can see that "out there" is IF it is projected from inside of me. THAT is my own projection from within. The future is now. It is only the future, because of the separation of time inside of me. As that dissolves, I will again see and BE these things again.

WALKING IN A DREAM

There comes a moment that everything "flips" and you are walking in a dream. Until you are ready to see, and actually look for this, it happens slowly, so that your mind can adjust and adapt. The entire 4th Dimensional Realm was you learning to lucid dream and then bringing that ability into your physical so that you again walk in and AS the dream. Here, everything is brighter, more vibrant, your heart is singing and things just flow with the wind. You are in awe of life, nature, colors, song.... and as the memories of the old human reality faded away, they were replaced with new, exquisite memories of forgotten (ancient) times that have been waiting patiently and dormant within.

In the beginning, all happens gradually, so subtly that you do not realize it, unless there is a specific event that caused it to occur. YOUR Soul has awakened and you are REMEMBERING the land of the forgotten again.

There are moments, along the way, that the teeter-totter causes you to question your own sanity. Sometimes for a few split moments, you may wish for the "old" way to return. Yet trying to hold on for too long will bring suffering and discomfort, so learning to let go as fast as you become aware is pivotal on your Awakening and Ascension journey here.

All exists in vibrational frequency. This is what you are. This is part of what you are trying to REMEMBER. Your energy, your divine essence, you as you forgot yourself to be, yet when you are human, "you" do not let yourself see. The 5th Dimensional Realm exists BEyond SEPARATION. It comes forth as your Soul becomes whole again. This is what you become (REMEMBER) when you allow yourself to be happy.

A huge part of this is letting go and allowing your fun-filled, playful and happy child to come forth to also exist again. Frolicking about, playing in the rain and the mud, talking to the fairies, elementals and elves. This innocent child energy is one with the universe as well. It has a connection to Gaia that you forgot as you became more human. This part is necessary if you wish to come to exist in the 5th Dimension again. So let go, be love, be fun, REMEMBER the magic, for it does exist here and you must find it inside of you and embrace it if you wish to exist here again.

UNIFICATION of all goes beyond trying to unify all "out there". It means BEing so unified inside that all is love, kindness, compassion and magic here. Alchemy is a way of BEing as you transmit love out from within. You radiate and exist again with all who radiate this as well. Your human mind was slow, so you needed time to see things change. They have not changed thought, for this has always been. You have just come to see and hold the vibration to exist here again.

There are multiple realms and as each one opens we get to experience them repeatedly over time until we REMEMBER them at all times and embody the frequency OF them inside of us again. Each realm has a different frequency and once you FEEL the frequency within you, you never forget again. You might have a moment of forgetfulness, but it quickly returns as soon as you are "finished BEing human". Eventually all realms merge to become one and you are walking in all realms at one time again. REMEMBER, the separation within us is what caused us to forget to start with. As separation goes, so does the "time" that separates them in to separate spaces to be in and all is one huge magical, angelic, paradise to BE in and OF again!

Now, you are already here, yet your human eyes and mind keep you from seeing this. You can stretch your mind in several ways. Take a camera everywhere you go. Take photos of the sun coming through the trees. Look for the orbs, look for the crystalline light rays and mist coming in from the sun. Look for the mist, for this is your new reality forming. Look for portals, listen for animals and elementals to speak to you. Look for spaceships in the clouds, angel formations, anything you can think of. It is there, if you truly desire to see. Soon this will be everywhere, for you create what you believe.

REMINDER: *I must look for the magic and allow myself to walk in a dream if I wish for this to BE my reality.*

EACH REALM HAS A SONG

It took me a long time to "get this part", for in the beginning I started hearing a song that lifted my spirits, for I was just coming out of my own "dense days" and "You Are My Sunshine" would play in my head and make me smile and sing along. I would immediately "lift" and go clean while working through my own human mind or do something that further lifted my spirit inside. Then there were songs to let me know when certain "others" were about to appear. I REMEMBER one was "Sugar Pie Honey Bunch" words to let me know a certain girl I worked with was about to call or come by.

In listening to these songs, I learned to pay attention to what was going on when they played. "Back then", I was doing psychic work so I attributed them to psychic awareness. I left the psychic reality behind when I actually "split" to shift into "separate" awarenesses inside. There was a moment when I became an observer of that which I could not previously see. It is as if, in that moment, I had two me's. Little did I know how true that was. One was my Higher Self (through my heart) and the other was my human self (existed in my head). Before that moment, I only understood what I learned or was taught. But in that moment, when all separated and shifted inside, I saw differently. There was an awareness that was not previously there. This "new awareness" was my Higher Self stepping in to show me, to teach me, to guide me and to show me duality, first "out there" to then start to shift (more and more) inside. I was shifting from the "outside world" to a new "inside world", and nothing would ever be the same. For I was just "waking up". I had been sleep walking in the human reality and I had no awareness that any of "this" existed. Little did I know that all was about to turn inside out. It kind of already had. I had suffered through the denseness and my light had just turned on. This was my Soul self, my Higher Self expanding BEyond my human self and I was about to "take off" and leave the entire human reality behind. First I had to learn to observe and this was the beginning of my own expansion INTO my Higher Self. I just became an avid student, listening to absolutely everything I received and "noting" all that I saw "out there". "I" was about to teach "me" about all of this and I was absorbing as fast as I could hear, feel and see. I was taking notes and creating to teach others and share. I just had no idea that this was what was occurring until "after", for this is HOW it works. I just listened, trusted and "did" that which I was guided to do. For it made absolutely no sense to the human mind, but it made complete sense inside. It is that which I have come to BE AS my Higher Self that I now share here with you.

Oh yeah, oops another crop circle, so back to songs & realms. Our Higher Self will give us songs to let us know what realm is open. At first they play to remind us, then we can use them to open the realm intentionally so that we can remind ourselves that we already exist there. It is the words of the songs you hear, not the entire song. So pay attention to the words, for it is the message that you are receiving that is important. I will share some of mine with you. Some were just reminders to tell me something, others were to actually allow me to "TUNE" to shift back into the realms that that I had opened vibrationally from inside.

Eventually one can just "activate" that FREQUENCY by using the songs to tune from within. This takes much conscious practice of "intentionally switching channels, dimensional frequencies, transmissions" and playing the song that expands that feeling (memory) from inside. When we do this, we pay attention and "out there" shifts to match our new frequency as fast as we can "tune and shift". WE tune TO THE FREQUENCY that that song holds in frequency inside. We just play the song in our head, tap into the feeling and open it from within our heart and allow it to expand from the inside out. (I use the visual of a lotus flower opening inside my heart to expand the energy out more). REMEMBERING is what we do when we actually feel and shift intentionally from the inside out. Inspiration expanded out creates a shift into anything we desire. All we have to do is REMEMBER to activate that feeling of inspiration and REMEMBERING again. REMEMBER and BE in that realm again.

Here are some of "my songs". You will have your own. Just listen. It is so very cool! I only share the words and the reference, for the idea. I don't even know the name of half of them, just the tune & words… for I got the message and that was all the reminder I needed!

Words:

- A Whole New World   (from Aladdin)
- Ease Your Mind… and the rest will follow (I would get this when I needed to quit thinking and be quiet and just BE).
- Don't Worry, BE Happy   (Bobby McFerrin)
- The Power of Love by Celine Dion (I used to say "really universe, couldn't you give me another song? This would play and I knew my heart was opening and I was BEing activated to the 5th Dimensional Realm.)
- Good Vibrations by Marky Mark & the Funky Bunch (yep, raising vibrational frequencies!)
- Crazy by Patsy Cline (yep, the crazy realm is open)
- Fly Like an Eagle, to the sea… fly like an eagle, let my spirit carry me (reminder to let go and fly, soar & trust my Higher Self)
- Do you believe in magic? (Magical Realm! An absolute favorite!)
- When You Wish Upon A Star (by Jiminy Cricket!)… I knew manifesting was quick in these energies and to stay focused and to REMEMBER to ask for that which I needed to do my work here in assisting others and that things were getting easier "here". It also helped me stay focused looking up at the stars and to speak to the universe for anything I desired.
- Magic, Magic, Magic …. Ohhh ohhh (another Magical Realm, for I have like 3, as it IS a favorite!)
- Change, change, change (a REMINDER to me to shift and transmit a new tune!)
- "Don't You REMEMBER, WE built this city"… Ancient Memories/REMEMBERINGs coming forth.
- "I'm so excited, and I just can't hide it, I'm about to lose control and I think I like it"… this meant amazing miracles were coming. Oh how I learned to love, love, love this song!

THE ELEMENTAL KINGDOM REALM:
THE KAUAI ROOSTER: "WAKE UP!"

The Elementals are conscious and so interactive in the 5th Dimension. They communicate as clear as if they were speaking out loud. They are friendly and are family, sharing messages if you are present enough to listen and interact with love as well.

Fairies, elves, gnomes in the forest and we morph into them too. Gaia speaks to direct you as to where to go to find and activate portals, and to lend a hand if you should ever need. On a hiking trip I, received guidance to grab a hold of this branch, use my bum to get across the creek, step here, and every step of the way, totally connected and in sync from inside. One with Mother Earth again.

One Heiau we go to here holds the most sacred energy thus far. One Full Moon we went to connect and assist with raising the light quotient on an area that still held pain. After walking the ground, the energy cleared and we heard "Thank You". The next time we returned, the energy was beautiful and at peace. Activating a portal, the frogs came to greet us and pose for the most awesome photos to share. When the portal activation was complete, the guard (the frog that was always at the entrance) spoke and said "time to leave". So we gathered up our crystals and off we went!

A day in the Bamboo Forest allowed for high frequencies and portals abound. Morphing visible in the camera photos makes for an awesome story to share!

Walking home the snails, the mushrooms, the frogs all come alive. On the beach the sand crabs now come up on my towel to visit and pose for photos as well.

The roosters are a favorite, for they have so many messages in their simplistic presence here. They are everywhere and they greet you in every place you go. Whether lunch or on the beach, they are there to BE as well.

My first morning on the island, I awoke to early morning rooster crows. My first response, without moving my head "ahh, that is natural, I am home".

Just a week after arriving home on Kauai, the roosters awoke me early morning hours in song. It was the most magnificent symphony to just lay there and listen as they communicated all across the side of this "mountain". You could hear them and the flow that was created far to near. Absolutely beautiful and this went on for about 20 minutes and would re-occur every so often throughout the day to again hear.

One morning I heard the crowing and then I heard "wake up" as clear as could be. Then I heard "it is our job to remind all here throughout the day and night to wake up and stay awake". I was like "ohhh, how exquisite is that? For they too are REMINDERS to stay awake, which is why they crow constantly throughout each day. Absolutely beautiful, I was also shown that one could tell what dimension they were in just by their response to the roosters here. The lower realm human is annoyed and irritated, for it interferes with their "controlled" reality world. Whereas the 5th Dimensional open-hearted Soul connects and appreciates the beauty of song that they hear when the crowing begins and sees them as sharing this home. Dimensional Roosters as REMINDERS! How cool is that?!!!

BEING IN-SERVICE

For many of us, the mission-driven human used to hold the energy of not enough, lack and struggle, in order to do what was in our hearts. Yet AS the higher realms inside again, struggle no longer exists. That was a human belief.

Follow me through the spiral for a moment, if you will.

For many, we started out struggling to be in-service, yet lacking the tools or resources to do so. Every struggle taught us that we could be in-service, regardless of what we physically had. We got creative, we found ways to reach others with little or nothing at most times. We did without much of the time, compared to that which others perceive as basic necessities. Yet there was a mission, a desire so strong, that nothing would stand in our way. And little by little we prevailed in getting by, while we sought to assist all of mankind along the way.

Now, during this journey, we broke the barriers of the human mind. We found that we could assist and share and needed nothing but an open heart and pure inner-force drive.

This driving force energy is what created the ability for us to survive. Yet surviving was not what we were doing, as we were transcending the need to survive.

As we opened our hearts, others came with open hearts in appreciation and the rare, occasion actual support to assist us as well. Every time we inspired another, our hearts opened and we expanded too.

Now each time WE expanded, little by little we left the old lack version, the lower realm version of us behind. That version was the one without support, for support was up to us. The more we assisted others, the more others assisted us. We found that more came forth, with the same desire to reach others too. This inspired us to continue, our inner determination inspired every time one opened our heart. Yet it also took the integration of our own masculine energy balance, to bring forth the stubbornness and determination to "do" our mission regardless of others' lack of support, others lack of appreciation, lack of honor and much of the time, payment for much of what we did. WE had to not care if we had help, for it was that inner drive that got us to do absolutely anything to reach and assist. It is that energy that brought us back to the higher realms where unification and support now exist.

It was never about "out there" not supporting us; it was about all of our lack to freely share. WE had to work to reverse and transcend the old energy of lack of entire existences. When WE had no limits, those limits diminished out there. Then one day we "arrive" in a space where support is coming forth. Yet we did not arrive anywhere, we held the frequency of sharing long enough to BECOME that which we sought.

WE were this all along and out there just matches us. We share first, and others who desire to share, be a part, and assist now come forth. We exist on our own honor, integrity and love. We draw to us those who hold the same frequency, for the realm we exist in, in the physical is the one we transmit out from within. They are not now arriving, WE are, as one unified Being here again.

WE are the entire realm when unified as one within. Here we never lacked or needed to survive, for that, my loves, was human.

REMINDER: Support comes when I have created a reality where I am sharing freely with all. Human limits are my own. There is a realm where we all exist together again as ONE. It is inside of me and transpires out there when I come to exist here again. ♥

REMINDER: In-Service is not something I "do", it is something I become. It is my higher self me as I breathe and fulfill a mission from within. ♥

REMINDER: I AM inspired every time I inspire you and all others through Love and Light. ♥

THE ANGELIC REALM

One of the most beautiful energy realms there is, this one is a favorite, so I mention it here to all who resonate with this realm too.

One night during "connection time" in my "in-between" space where I normally would work (earlier days I went to "school"), a male energy came and "got me" and took me to a place where there were other souls and told me I was going to "see if I passed the test". Having no idea what he spoke of, for this was my first experience with this, I went and just observed to see what kind of test I was going to have to take.

Once there, I heard the words "you passed" and I was given my wings and sent off on my merry way. That was it. I was apparently now accepted into the angelic realm, yet I had already received two pair of wings prior, these were special, for these were different.

The next day, while I was getting ready for a client, all of a sudden, my solar plexus opened up and out came this most magnificent energy. I was shown that this was the portal to the angelic realm and now I embodied it within me.

After that, every time the Angelic Realm activated, the most beautiful energy was present inside and "out there". Others I interacted with throughout the day would call me "angel" and there would be angels on walls out in parks and overpasses as I drove, with angel quotes everywhere I looked. No mistaking the angelic realm, this was a magnificent one to experience and still is!

THE MAGICAL REALM

Oh, definitely probably my most favorite realm thus far, yet it is so hard to choose, this one is definitely on top!

Rainbows BEing the sign for this one, every time the magical realm is activated, such magical things happen in every moment. One can activate this if they hold the frequency within and REMEMBER to tune to it, ask for magic, look for magic, notice the magic in absolutely everything. If you pay attention, you can find magic in every moment, ever exchange, for everything is already magic and you are too!

I will get up and the first words are "Bring me the magic!", then I shift in frequency and take off on foot to interact with the entire universe in the frequency of magic from within. Miracles (as they are perceived to be) happen here, gifts arrive instantly from the universe by way of "out of thin air", fruit sitting on the side of the road, and that which you speak just appearing, as easy as that!

So, the more you play in the frequency of the magical realm, the more you ask, the more you pay attention, the more you see the magic in absolutely everything around you, the more magic shall come forth for you to exist in again.

REMINDER: Bring me the magic! Then notice and have gratitude for absolutely everything that you see around you. Everything is magic if you REMEMBER this!

GRADUATION: THE SURVIVAL LEVEL OF AWAKENING

Each time I had an experience to graduate, I was surprised, for I had no idea that we graduated along the way; yet we definitely do and in so many ways!

This one occurred after I arrived home on Kauai and months after I had activated a "blow hole" within me activating me TO the LeMUrian energies within. I was shown that I could not come to Kauai activated a multitude of frequencies within me and held them long enough to actually be able to exist on the island. I did not understand it at the time, but BEing here now, I so do understand how I would not have made it here on the island before. Kauai holds a certain frequency and anything out of alignment gets brought up for resolution within quickly. And faster for me apparently, because of my overall vibrational frequency, that brings things forth very fast for me.

Once I arrived, I had multiple activations, a sacred connection with a Heiau and several other amazing things. I also was shown that I had to arrive with very little money, knowing no one, with no place to stay, no rental car, and to trust that everything was "in place", as long as I continued to increase in frequency, create unity with the connections brought forth and not forget inside again.

I was "pushed" to face the survival mode of very little money and the first two days costing me half of what I brought with me here. I first went somewhat into human'ish mode, almost trying to lack beliefs of how I might not have enough. Then I heard my inner voice "you are pretending again and you have forgotten that you no longer lack". Wow, yep, I sure did. So, although it was not in my nature to "waste", I did what I FELT to do and I "reversed" my thinking and shifted to my heart and I heard "How much would you pay for peace inside again?" Well I knew this meant that I was compromising my own inner peace over money and we do not do that anymore. So I removed the money from the picture and I tuned inside of me to see what I really felt to do. Pay the money for the place to stay for the week, even though, by human terms, was ridiculous. It made sense and I got the point.

Now, this is how fast things work when we are unified within, honor and listen and come to alignment quickly again. I walked up to the hotel desk and paid the money for one week and instantly felt peace inside as I did. I knew, that was my "test". The moment I walked away and back to my computer, I had a donation that almost "replaced" what I had just spent.

Now, that night, during my connected in-between state, I cleared a bunch of "weird" energy and parallels really fast. A huge ancient memory holding the energy of intense fear came up and went instantly and it was gone. Then a guy came and "got me" and told me to come with him. He congratulated me on "passing the survival level of awakening". He handed me a "survival vest" and patted me on the back and said "great job". There were others there as well and I awoke to be amazed yet again.

I was shown how, as humans, we all have the "survival energy" deep within our human DNA and cellular memory and that once we have transcended the energy of survival, which was an ingrained belief system as well, we REMEMBER that we do not lack anymore. This is what keeps all from sharing, for they keep to themselves out of fear, protection and unconscious greed that there is not enough for us all. This was a huge step in Unity Consciousness, for we cannot share as long as we believe that we lack or need to survive in any way.

REMINDER: When I feel that I lack in any way, I can say the words "You are pretending again" to remind myself that this is a play.

WE CAUSED THE LOWER REALMS TO DECONSTRUCT; FOR THE CONSTRUCTS EXISTED WITHIN

This journey is one of coming to realize that the entire system that existed "out there" to keep you bound to "it", was created inside of you, from a belief that you has a human needed to believe in order to have your human experience here. As you no longer believe, as you pull out of the matrix, that "out there" will cease to exist. Your belief created it and your belief is what will cause it to "fall". So when you look "out there" and you fear the system "falling" apart and crumbling, know that is occurring because all who are waking up have pulled out of the matrix and it crumbles outside, because you too were a part of that belief system, and when you pull out, it will also fall for you. In its place will be a new system, created from love, unity and sharing for all to participate in. But first you must come to learn to share and believe again. For this does not conform to the human way. It goes against everything that much of you were taught, while some of you have always known. It doesn't' matter when you "got it", just that you do. The old constructs encoded in our original Etheric blueprints and old human DNA. The "new" overriding that and bringing forth REMEMBERING of the illusion as the Soul's Light Activations occur within.

DECONSTRUCTION OF THE LOWER REALMS FROM WITHIN

Deconstruction of the lower realms occurs as we stop believing in them, for it was our belief that created them to start with. It is an oxy-moron, for suffering TO them as humans, was our chosen experience, so that we could come to transcend them inside, to come to not believe in them again. And as we no longer believe, they continue to cease to exist. For this belief only existed within us.

As our templates are wiped, the reality of these beliefs are shaken loose. It is us that must let go of that which we've come to hold on to. For in its place comes new realities, one's REMEMBERING of ancient times, ones of how things truly are, that come from within and then materialize outside.

Yet to exist here again, does mean total dissolution (dis-illusion) of that "out there". It does mean the collapse of entire realities and realms and holding on only tries to keep us there. Holding on to the old, is what creates suffering at all inside.

So when you look "out there" and see all falling apart, crumbling and destruction occurring in an external world, know that suffering is your creation and release of the old is what caused it to fall. Your belief created that and your new REMEMBERING is what also causes it to fall.

For you as a BEing of Light, no longer exist in the denseness that created it all. The dissolution, the destruction is cause by your own letting go. For it was all of your collective beliefs that created that and gave it control. As you pull out of that collective and vibrate higher, you continue to have and see new views.   These new views are only your REMEMBERING of what you have always held inside of you. As you have come to let go of an old reality, it shall cease to exist – for you individually and for all who held this vibration within.

Where you exist at any given time, is a reflection and transmission of the vibration you hold for an extended (or short) period of your human time. The more you no longer desire to exist in one, the more you exist in ones that do. Your belief created that, so as you release beliefs of anything at all, you open up to seeing and existing again, as the vibration you were, before the fall (descension).

These vibrations now a visible reality, for before your human mind could not see, for realities are not fixed, they are as bendable and flexible as you are and also allow them to again be.

The constructs are in your own energetic template. You are the one that now cause them to all fall. Embrace this, for as they fall inside, your freedom and peace is returned to you and all.

Open your heart and expand your mind an allow yourself to truly see, for your memories of your entire existence reside beyond your human world that you limited yourself to see. Your REMEMBERING exists in an open heart, one that shares without limits of the human mind. Your NEW is of the ANCIENT WAYS, where "I" is just a physical body that exists to limit you. For here, it is "WE", a space forgotten and held deep inside of all of you. Here is it is UNITY, your unified BEing of light as All-That-Is. Here there is no separation, here you are "home" again. Expand your Merkaba, your field of light, with and as, all others again as one. Your light is never separate, that was a human belief that is now gone. For here, there are no lower realms, they are not visible anymore. The belief that they need to exist, is your own human belief-mind. Here you DO exist, in magic, bliss, peace and love again. The only time you don't, is when that is your own perception. Those who totally let go, shall come to see and be here again. No longer a "future" dream or thought, now your reality "out there" for you to exist in. The higher realms now tangible, for they materialize in response to you. If you exist AS these realms inside, then outside you now do too. The only time you do not, is when you allow yourself to forget that you do. For here you must hold expansion of the higher realms at all times from inside of you. Here you are your LightBody, your Merkaba creates your new hologram for you. And as you connect AS the realm, you connect with all others who also exist here too. Access is yours, existence is yours, by way of your Unified Frequency Body of Light". Your frequency is your spin and your reality is REMEMBERED again.

BEYOND THE ILLUSION, THE MATRIX, THE HOLOGRAM

Again, these are all the same, yet until one's vibrational frequency has been unified inside, these too are separated. It will be this way for absolutely everything written of here. For when one completely transcends separation inside, this book is no longer relative. So for those reading this, chances are you still exist inside the matrix. And for that purpose, we differentiate here.

As one activates and integrates to higher frequencies, inside also merges and the entire universe "out there" come to be visible from inside. This is because the entire universe is inside of each one of you, yet your separated human mind cannot comprehend this until you "see" it (or experience it) for yourself. Until then, it is a human concept that is BEyond the human mind comprehension. Because so many *know this inside*, this is a fascination that is spoken by many without true comprehension. In fact, the entire journey is this way. Until you experience it, you cannot truly understand it. All you can do is repeat the words until you convince your limited mind, then inside of you gets it, then your mind goes "wow, that's what that meant! Unbelievable". Then it is an epiphany and you share it with others who you know don't get it yet either. Yep, that spiral thingy again.

Inside the matrix, realities are fixed, dualistic, balance is sought and there are markers and placeholders of time and space. The human mind works relentlessly to keep things in a neat little order or fashion, for everything has a neat box, right? Yeah right. Until the entire "world "out there"" gets turned upside down, inside out and ripped from your cold and worn fingers that have tried to hang on to the edge of the cliff, for fear of falling into the Light.

Yet, absolutely every bit of this is an illusion based on fear instilled due to every bit of programming that can be mustered to strengthen the human reality.

To the human, fear is very real. So, not to discount this, when one exists in a 3rd & 4th Dimensional Reality, fear is real. Why? Because one believes it.

Now, there will come a "time" when separation of dimensions no longer matters. They are no longer separated, because technically they do not exist either. They were separated so that one could come to understand them, to transcend them, to no longer need to see them separately. REMEMBER, *separation* is a human creation. When you release this human need to separate, you will no longer care either. Yet, inside the matrix, inside the illusion, inside the physical aspect of the hologram, these are separated. And this book is written for those who still exist inside the hologram, for again, once you do not, you will not care about this book.

REMINDER: If you believe it, it is real. The key is to challenge what you believe.

DREAM STATE:
WHERE ALL REALITIES COME FORTH

Dream state is the Etheric realm where all realities, memories, existences, parallels and realms come forth to become visible, merge, leave, be integrated prepare for materialization in your new physical reality as a dimensional being again.

In the 3rd dimensional realm this was perceived as a sleep state. You discount what you see here and dismiss the ones full of fear.

In the 4th Dimensional realm you start to realize there is much more than just sleep going on here. You clear old traumas, karma and fears, go to soul school and start seeing that which exists beyond your human reality. You may try to learn to astral travel or master lucid dreaming. You start to connect with your soul/star family and start to remember "home". These start to feel more "real" and more like experiences rather than dreams. This is because they are.

In the 5th Dimensional realm, old human realities and un-materialized parallels and realities are cleared here. Sleep state is a connection period to bring forth ancient memories, existences from another time, activate realms and other world and galactic experiences, create new realities to bring forth for actual materialization here. You use sleep state to re-boot, re-align, re-unite and REMEMBER again. It is an activation and integration state as well. You realize that everything you can see here is a memory, an existence, and the only separation between *that* materializing in your physical reality is your own vibrational frequency and your belief that it can occur. You KNOW it's just a matter of "time" before that comes forth in your physical reality to materialize, so you DO everything that you can to achieve the frequency where that already exists. The 5th Dimensional BEing walks in what used to be a lucid dream. All things are bendable and flexible in the new waking state after the flip and merge occurs. Your waking state is what used to be the dreams of the sleep state, to the human, without the density left, for that just clears in your sleep now. A million existences in a matter of a few hours of your human sleep. Eventually there is no difference in your waking and sleep state. You can do anything you can see with your eyes closed, yet now in an open-eyed waking and walking state. Your realities have totally flipped and you ARE walking in *the dream*. The old human stuff now just continues to clear in your sleep. Sleep allows you to activate faster, for your pineal gland will activate just prior to your new transmissions. First you will see it in your head, via your internal projector, then it will materialize out there. The time differential is dependent on your own vibrational frequency integration and the dimension you allow yourself to exist in at any given time.

Much work gets done here; more than your human you can even comprehend. This state, is you, actually working, connecting and existing, without your physical body intact that you currently occupy here. This too shall continue to be one state eventually.

As you integrate to higher frequencies, separation within you diminishes, timelines collapse, within you, and all existences start to come forth for you to see. There is much collapsing and clearing necessary to move you to the higher realms. In order to accomplish this, you are being provided an opportunity to "do" this in what you perceive as sleep. This sleep state is your connection state, to that which you are unable to access yet, in your open-eyed waking state. This is an "expediting", if you will, to allow you to completely transcend realities all in one fell swoop. Yet, this will occur throughout your journey, for each time you integrate and embody more, the more human existences (of all times) you will need to clear.

You are clearing at such an expedited rate, that you do not have time to see them all. The more you try to figure all of these out, the more you will get stuck in that which no longer matters. IF you need to, you will know, for you will be shown what you need to remember or focus on. Mostly, no focusing is necessary, for anything you are meant to REMEMBER will come forth when you reach that frequency and hold it inside. For a short time, you may wish to write things down, or record them, for some things come through and provide you with information that you find insightful or helpful in your journey and assisting others as well. I keep a journal with me at all times and I write anything that feels like ancient memories that will assist me on my journey and useful until I embody it here.

If there is an emotion attached, honor it and quickly let it go. Your human may feel it needs studying, and while this is not necessary, if you feel to do this, then by all means, do. Your journey is up to you. If you choose to acknowledge it and let it go, then do this as well. If you do not care to see, just say to clear as fast as possible, and this too will be honored too.

All of your lifetimes and existences were separated over other times, according to your own human separation inside. As you unify, the separation of time falls away, therefore all of your existences do as well. Your existences are unlimited, so this is a never ending process that will continue to occur. As long as you are human, you will create parallels that create more existences continually to turn around and clear. The more you maintain a unified state of WE, the less parallels you create "out there". Walking in ONENESS as your higher self, as source again, you are a unified being creating the reality you are currently in.

Every vision you see, an actual memory of you, in another time, parallel or realm. This state is no different than your waking state, other than an expedited space for work to be done.

You see these as dreams, for your human mind cannot yet comprehend, that all of these are real, yet the purposes very different.

Some, you go to school and learn (remember), some you teach others instead, some you clear old frequencies, parallels and karma, if you will. Some you get to see realities that you don't yet "have" there.

You will connect with other souls, teach and go to school

What you have yet to understand is that what you can see there CAN be a reality you actually exist in. The only two factors are your ability to believe it and your vibrational frequency to achieve it again. You could not see these things if they were not true or possible. Your human mind and current internal limits are your own blocks.

As you transcend limits, as you unify and come to remember again inside, as you unify all of your existences, those realities also unify. What you have left is you, in a state to then choose which reality, which parallel you desire. This IS you in your REMEMBERED state again and nothing is limited when you exist here again.

Those amazing gifts and abilities, all true. Those abundant realities all true too. For they are not separate ways, they are you in a unified space inside again. Here you ARE those things, just by REMEMBERING who you are and Being this again inside and therefore out there.

Remember, these are all one and the same. The only difference is your need to see them separately and this is your own separation.

REMINDER: THAT is not a dream. Instead, it is a reality I did not remember yet. I will know which ones are important. They will be of ancient memories for me to bring forth here.

PARALLEL REALITIES

There are so many parallel's of a reality, one could get lost counting them all, for they go way BEyond the human scope to see all that were previously created for the human experience/experiment here.

You will see an abundance of parallel's clearing in your sleep. There is nothing to "do" with these, unless you just wish to observe, for the sake of seeing what is no longer and has gone from your energy. You have been many things, in many times, in every way possible.

What is most important is the realization that you now have control, as your Higher Self, not to create parallels that you no longer desire to experience in the physical again. Your own ability to stay centered in your heart, and to act from that space, rather than the limited human mind, will allow you the most comfortable journey, path or route.

Parallel realities occur in every moment. The one you get is the one you believe and expand from within. The belief creates it. The action affirms your belief therefore allowing it to come forth for you to take action, which creates another parallel from that; the "Ripple Effect" of Parallels.

Parallels will cease to exist, when you truly become ONE again. It was your separation that created these to start with. There is only one reality here. It is the one you are currently in.

When you learn to "tune", you will be able to change the frequency of the reality you are transmitting. With much practice, you will REMEMBER how to switch realities at will.

DENSE MATTER AND LIGHT PARTICLES

Lack of light creates dense matter. Dense matter represents the amount of separation within. Dense matter holds a lower vibrational frequency than light. Love and Light bring unification.

There are a multitude of frequencies and these frequencies materialize to show you how separated you are inside. The more you "need", the more separated you are. Look "out there" at all that you have. Now look at another who is so totally happy who has less, then look at another who has more. Can you see how dense or light (separated or whole) you truly are?

MINIMIZING: When the Soul awakens, things start to go. This is because of the separation they represent within the human self. It is not about the things. It is your identity to them and the energy you hold inside. When we can open our hearts and share, without BEing forced, when we spend our moments focused on humanity, then "that" becomes a tool to assist others, rather than a "thing" we covet over the journey of the heart and Soul.

Those who have come to understand the physical reality, need for nothing at all. They have come to understand the denseness of "things" and how disruptive they are to the energy field, when not utilized and assisting in light. If these "things" separate you and keep you from fulfilling your purpose, from unifying inside (therefore ""out there"), from supporting light, your reality will be adjusted until you "get it". When that which you "have" is used to assist humanity and no longer cause you to focus on you, then you have shifted and are fulfilling your purpose here as a Light Worker, as a BEing of Light. Physical "things" were a representation of the density within us. As we BECOME LIGHT again, things begin to go. Eventually all things are there for sharing. For in unity, there is no other way.

Dense matter frequencies are what the physical world is comprised of. The thing one can actually touch is particle matter that has come to form something tangible for the human experience.

Dimensional realms are differentiated by the amount of dense matter present, in all forms. Energetically and physically, both visible and invisible.

REMINDER: I am a combination of dense and light matter and therefore my reality is too. The denser I am, the lower I vibrate and therefore materialization will be slow as well. The more I unify inside, the light I become and materialization shall speed up to match my higher vibrational frequency.

ALCHEMIC CREATION

The 5th Dimensional BEing is an alchemist, yet this too is just a human word for what one has forgotten their self to be. For the true alchemist is one who has just REMEMBERED to be in an unlimited state within. This is where "creation" occurs just with thought and belief. Even this is a perception, for this BEing has only re-evolved back to be what it had, as a human, forgotten itself to be. For you have never been limited; only your separated human aspect believed this.

The 5th Dimensional BEing has come to totally recreate their reality here. The 5th Dimension is one of creation. Yet in order to exist here, one must learn to first create.

Now, while one is learning to create, and releasing their limited human-thinking-box-making-limit-setting mind, one will teeter-totter and flip-flop from realm to realm. One does not just wake up in the 5th Dimension. One works to recognize and transcend their perception of the limits imposed by all of a human society, reinforced by human experience and therefore believed within their human mind.

Creation is not a product of the left-brain human mind that compares, makes lists, numbers, fits into boxes, works between fixed points, sees human to human, limits, needs tangible, holds onto safe and lives in a "proof necessary" reality. This part of the human does not let go, sing, dance, draw or write from the heart. That is the right side of the human brain, the one connected directly to the heart. And to access this one, one must shut their eyes and just let go. Holding on is. And holding on is what kept us all stuck as descending humans to start with. So alchemy is not a left-brain function. The left brain is not used here at all. The higher heart is the alchemist. This is the heart connected with/as the universal mind. This is one is of unity, and this is the one that creates, magnetizes and materializes just by BEing. This BEing need not do anything other than just BE how it feels to BE. This BEing is transmitting such light, such love, such radiance, that anything less is no longer an option. This Light BEing has totally released all that is human from their entire existence and this BEing IS an activated Merkaba, a unified BEing of light.

(See the Alchemic Creation under the Activation Section)

REMINDER: *Materialization is in response to my own light transmission that comes from within.*

REMINDER: *If I am holding on to safe, I am human.*

REMINDER: *The 5th Dimensional version of me is already an alchemist, just by BEing again.*

INCARNATED HIGHER REALM GUIDES

WayShowers, Gatekeepers and Ascension Guides are incarnated here to assist, first by "doing", then by sharing that which they experience and do, so as to lead others to be able to do the same. It was part of our purpose and our own chosen roles here during the time of Ascension.

WE encompass and embody the Higher Self aspect within us. WE have worked to elevate all in vibrational frequency and activate light in every way through love. WE spent much time anchoring the 5th Dimension and Higher Realm Frequencies within us (and "out there"), so that all could come to exist here in the physical again.

WE work to share and allow others to support us, so together WE together can re-Unite and bring forth great change for all here as ONE again. WE "go out" into the world and "do" in whatever way we are shown will benefit more on their own inward journey as well. WE assist others in embracing their own divinity to follow their heart and do that which they activate inside and calls to them.

WE believe in HUmanity, for we hold HUmanity within us again.

There are unlimited realms still to come forth and we have yet to see only a small part of them all thus far. WE still have much work to do, yet WE together now move forth in unity and love.

WE is all who feel this and step up to support, share and unify in love.

UNITY CONSCIOUSNESS: ONE AGAIN

WE separated as we came here, yet now we merge again. WE come together inside and as we do, so do we "out there". There is an energy that is transmitted that brings this forth again for all to share. It comes from one's entire BEing, not just from the heart. The heart is so expansive that one radiates out so much light, that here we have no boundaries, struggle or internal fight. All we have is love and WE set out to show others too, that sharing brings us together again, instead of separating as humans do. Here we are no longer human, and as we release the need to keep all to our selves, just like innocent children we start to share again, and flow is restored and bridges are built to connect all who have drifted away. By sharing first, we show others, that we can give without coming from lack; that what we bring forth here, is giving without expecting back. WE do not have to work hard, when what we give is from our heart. We can work hard to gain all things, or we can share all things and no longer work. Work is what one does, when they feel they have to do something to survive. Here there is no survival, for creation is what makes us thrive.

When we share what we love and create from within to assist others in that which they "need", then we in-turn create the flow to also receive. For here there are no actual needs, just perceptions of a need. All always have that which they truly need. That alone is abundance and abundance is how we perceive.

The open heart offers, steps up and brings to the table to share what they already have that will benefit and assist others. The human holds on to what they have for themselves, holds back and comes from the mind of separation and lack (sharing information is a huge part of this). The human aspect puts a price on sharing. They hold hostage that which would assist others out of personal need of the individual self. This is not an intentional thing necessarily, but the way we came here to be, as humans. This journey is one of total reversal and learning to share completely again. We come to understand that sharing creates an expansive network for all who participate to also receive. It must start inside first and all barriers to this be released. Only then, can receiving be of the same. Look at your own reality and see where you have limits. Then realize these limits are in place to keep you separated inside. We were not "raised" as humans to share. We were taught to keep to ourselves. We "gave" from "holes" inside or obligation. Now we must give for no reason at all, just because we feel it inside and that is more than reason enough. That is our higher selves guiding us to do what is not human, and that is what we are here to REMEMBER again.

The energy of the sharer is opposite of one in need. This one holds unity within, offers to share freely, and allows themselves to receive. They come forth to share openly, there is no survivor here; no take, take, take or "what about me?", this energy is opposite of the human, it is one of love instead of greed. This energy does not lack, for sharing truly comes from the heart and commUNITY is created, as inside is where this starts. Now to create an entire commUNITY, it starts with a few and expands to encompass many throughout the land. Then one day, all have come to share that which helps all as one again. This BEing does not need others to ask, it steps up to openly give. The old way was holding back, the new is sharing, and no more survival energy of lack. For there is plenty when we don't keep for ourselves individually, WE realize we have more than enough, when all come together. Open hearts flowing OUT, for THIS is sharing commUNITY energy of unity.

The 5th Dimensional Realm is the opposite of the old human world. One gives without expectation and creates flow outward from within their heart. The human gives with an expectation of something in return. One has barriers and blocks and the other does not. One has an open heart and an expansive desire to assist humanity, Gaia & the Universe from within. The human holds out for something in return and suffers to lack as an individual human by holding out for themselves due to perception of fear (protection, lack, not enough or greed.) This BEing can still desire to assist others, yet their need to hold back is greater than their open heart. This one holds a belief still that they need something in return for what they give. Their focus is controlling who, what, when, where, why, how they receive, instead of just doing and trusting that they will receive exactly what they need. This one has not come to a place of honor, integrity & trust inside and operates as an individual still. For the one that exists AS their Higher

Self need not control how or when anything is received. Receiving comes from believing and openly sharing all that one has at their disposal that will truly help or assist others. The more we reach at one time, the more we open up the opportunity to receive even more. So our focus is to share in greater magnitude, knowing that our output is so great, energetically, that we cannot do any less than receive exactly all that we desire and need!

VISUAL: UNITY SHARING GRID "WE COMMUNITY"

The circle in the middle represents the core of the commUNITY working together to create from sharing again. The outside bubbles are each of us bringing something to the table, from our hearts to share and benefit others as well. WE receive as a part of the sharing commUNITY that comes from a space of love and unity again. There is no need for money if all learn to come together to share. Support is automatic in the sharing grid of light and love. The grid continues to expand so huge that all are sharing again. All receive as a part of the whole, as ONE again.

Notice how the expansion grid earlier in this book had the energy going "out". The energy is reversed, with all coming inward, when unifying as ONE again.

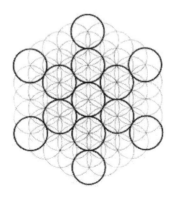

CRYSTALLINE
LIGHTBODY
MERKABA

LIGHT AND DNA
ACTIVATIONS

BEING A COSMIC PORTAL

I will speak in human time for this. For years now, I have been translating the cosmic energies, in "real-time", as they occur. I tuned as the entire Universe from within, as a cosmic portal, and I used my own ANCIENT REMEMBERINGS to share to assist others in understanding this in themselves as well.

To do this, I observed a multitude of ever-shifting frequencies inside of me. I translated that which I would I hear/feel/see and yes, smell. These varied from solar flares and winds, to photonic light activations, gamma bursts, meteor showers, you name it, if I heard it, I would translate it in "simple human". I preferred to describe the feeling, sound, visual and activation of "what" is occurring, so another can translate this into their own reality/world.

WE are all stars, the sun, Gaia, the entire Galactic Universe, Cosmos and more. Coming to shift focus inward and learn to understand the Light Activations that ignite within you as your soul activates, your Crystalline LightBody and Merkaba activate, this will assist you more than know. That sky, those stars, that sun, that earth, they are you and you are them. When you unify inside AS all again, you will see this too. Until then, I share my own reality with you.

These light frequencies are you, as your higher self, as your soul evolving in crystalline form and your old human body (DNA) is obsolete. Things in your human world that worked before, will not work anymore. Actually, they never did, if they suppressed your awakening as a soul. A perception was created so that you (we) would believe this, as this was part of our journey before, yet the "time" has come that this shall cease to be.

With your soul, your Higher Self, and the entire Universe waking up inside of you, things will start to go "haywire" and your new understanding and awareness, will assist you in navigating and discovering new ways that allow your soul to emerge in Light, rather than continuing to suffer to suppression, which was the "old" way we all did this. (Everyone did, in some form or another, what differs is chosen journey and how one did.)

You can use the external (macrocosm) to see what is going on inside of you (microcosm), yet "flipping" your view will help you shift to a different space of understanding. It will be the opposite or reverse of what we believed as humans.

The sun outside does not have a solar flare and THEN affect you in a way that causes you to have a "flare" inside of some kind. Mercury doesn't go retrograde "out there" and then all starts to fall apart. The full moon does not cause you to be overwhelmed and crazy energy to be all about. All happens within you to SHOW YOU what you could not see before. "out there" is what assists you as a guide, that is all. And once you have activated so much light, the old "responses" change as well. They will be the opposite of what they were in the human realms.

Light activations occur within you. They are occurring in every moment in one way or another, yet most are not aware of this to the magnitude that all occurs. Most are unaware at all, yet this too shall change.

Your soul is pure light, so the "Light Activations" are your own soul, your higher self, YOU trying to emerge. Your own soul/higher self holds all Universal information that you desire to know. Your knowledge AND REMEMBERING of ancient times is by way of the amount of light activated within you and HELD INSIDE in frequency. You ARE the frequency of LIGHT.

So, to understand and relate to this, you must shift your own view to inside of you first and then look "out there" to see what you can match up to how much density and light you hold within that is BEing activated with every breath that you breathe in every one of your simultaneous moments that you exist.

Now, every time the sun has a solar flare, this flare occurs INSIDE of you. Itchies, irritations and eruptions from within are a sign of this. Many will experience skin irritations or outbreaks, anger eruptions where there is light, one will have more light activated within. Tingling and prickling under the skin. This is your dormant DNA activating your Crystalline LightBody. Every prickle, every heartbeat in the energy vortexes, every blown up belly as you prepare to birth the new from within.

Now, out in the world you can correlate the same words to what is occurring "out there" as well and then you can look at the solar system and see what is going on there. You will find a "theme" occurring the more you observe. You can look at Earth and see the same going on. Every solar wind, every meteor shower, every full moon, every earthquake, every Tsunami, every radiation episode and explosion, all inside of you. (and everyone else too). That which you fear "out there", is all inside of you. Fear does not exist, for there is no "out there" unless you create it and you created absolutely everything "out there" to experience, endure and transcend from within.

Your human body is evolving from carbon based to crystalline. Every human organ, system, process, must be modified and transformed. You will go through new configuration, new mapping, cellular reconstruction and "new" everything. This, a human doctor will not understand and you will always get "we can't find a reason, but here, take this". This is because nothing is wrong with you. You are evolving, dropping density, and your entire DNA system BEing re-created from the dormant DNA within you.

For me, I spent years in observation of my own body and what was occurring inside and correlated it to what was going on "out there". Then as the frequencies that I heard magnified, I started tuning TO them, until it got to the point where that was predominantly all that I heard, so I started matching each one up to that which occurred inside and out in the physical world as well. I observed absolutely every moment, every reaction, every activation, every sound, every everything. I cleared discord as soon as it became visible so that I could expedite my own LightBody/Merkaba evolution here. Soon, there was this "new understanding" of how all things worked, as my own REMEMBERING came forth to show me what was BEing activated inside of us with every frequency shift that occurred (and there are a gazillion of these too!). I still match things up, as we continue to evolve. Yet after I ascended, these frequencies have shifted too. It appears I may no longer hear descension or the lower realm frequencies anymore. I guess we shall find out as we continue backwards, forwards and sideways through time now, as linear time so went out the window with Ascension.

Now, what I REMEMBER, and see, is way more vast than can be put in this book. For the sake of creating new awareness, I will share a bit of the activations and what you might notice. The rest is available in massive archives on my website and Facebook Page, along with the multitude of writings shared by others all over the internet as well. Find what resonates inside of you, for this will be "triggering" your truth.

As cosmic portals, activating, integrating and tuning is what we do.

All are activating the dormant LightBody/Merkaba/REMEMBERING Ancient DNA that we came here to do. Every time one's heart opens, every time there is a release, one is further activated in the physical. Every moment IS an activation. It always has been. Every memory of either the human existence (which is BEing wiped) or of ancient times (REMEMBERINGS) to be brought forth here.

Where one is just coming to connect, it feels, sounds and appears that they are receiving from an outer source. While this is true, it is not. The "outer source" is your own energy field that is "outside of you", until you go inside and expand it out from within. You hold all in your own energy, just waiting for you to open up to access it. The entire universe you SEE "out there" is a projection for you to see a tangible thing. It is held within your holographic bubble (Merkaba/Orbitron). As you raise in vibrational frequency, your hologram changes "out there".

The evolution of our Crystalline LightBody is far BEyond the human typical of anything you have ever encountered. I do not offer scientific or medical anything. I offer that which I REMEMBER for the sake of HUmanity as ONE again. Proof will come forth from those who can support this or with your own experiences, which is the best proof of all!

Separation is BEing "blasted" with these energies to "irradiate and eradicate" that which no longer has a place. This is happening inside of you and will correlate to a reality you see "out there" as well. If you believe it, it DOES exist. What do you truly believe inside of you?

The human shall see one thing, the energetic BEing shall see another. For the view is much more expansive and "lighter" on the "other side".

The Human shall see a foggy mind, disorientation, relentless sleep, sluggishness. It shall feel physical pain, as all that has been previously suppressed, yet again emerges to leave. It will try the "same old thing" that didn't work all of those other times. It will look outside for an answer, yet "out there" shall no longer make sense. "out there" will only be confusing and answers shall cease to exist. Where one is conscious, it will try something "new" and will honor what it feels inside, when it is ready for change.

The Energetic BEing shall embrace such things and know that all is but further "alignment" and restructuring radiating out from within. It shall be thankful and honored to receive such support and embrace each opportunity to transcend. It will feel the discomfort and know "that" just wishes to leave. It will let go and allow, nurture, love, respect the evolution of that which just has been forgotten. It will go inside and find peace and radiate out their own reality. It understands that creation is but now a choice in presence of BEing and that THAT "out there" can only exist if it is transmitted outwardly through the viewers to see in their NEW (REMEMBERED) Reality.

More are unplugging and seeing BEYOND that matrix of the illusion that has been created. As one does, they come to understand that that "out there" could not have been created if it had not existed within. The desire to exist in the "old way" is no longer present. For what now is visible is far greater than anything "that" had to offer. THAT has lost its appeal. THAT no longer is real. THIS is where all started. And THIS is where all shall come to again BE.

REMINDER: In order to BE my Higher Self again, I must let go of all that I came to understand as human. Knowledge is not what others told or taught me. It is buried in the memories of my own energetic memory coded in my dormant DNA.

CRYSTALLINE LIGHTBODY DNA ACTIVATIONS

The Crystalline LightBody is activating and many, many, many physical adjustments are taking place and absolutely NONE make logical sense! The more one resists, the more discomfort. Nature, nurture, hydrate, eat LIGHT foods, plenty of clean water and honor anything your body says it wants. You are BEing GUIDED and that which you desire may NOT fall into the "normal" that you have come accustomed to. Only the human mind would limit themselves here, while the higher self BEing knows exactly what it needs. The higher you vibrate, the faster you will burn food, water and more. As you integrate more light, this will change. You won't need as much at times, then other times you need tons. Just honor you and anyone telling you that you "should do things a certain way" are imposing their beliefs on you. Seek when you feel to seek and listen to your inner guidance at all times. Your best guide is you after all.

Sleep: This is the absolute most important thing you will do on this journey. Light Activations are a higher frequency than your human self and you must shut down as integration occurs in your sleep. Sleep, much sleep and then more sleep is imperative for all. It is where our realities merge. The human mind will resist sleeping, for it feels like it is missing out on something more important, has an obligation first or judges the self as BEing lazy. Things could not be more opposite if you tried. Your human self does not have the capacity to understand that this is your Higher Self/Soul emerging from within and it will try to talk you out of or shame you out of sleeping. As a Light BEing you will embrace sleep and find every opportunity that you can to honor this. Many of our scheduled evolve around our sleep. This is how absolutely important it is. We have learned and we understand and we could not care less what another thinks or says.

This is their limited awareness and it is up to us to honor this. The more one is able to sleep, the "faster" they are able to merge, REMEMBER and receive. Strong streaming energies will cause this to magnify. 3pm every afternoon can become quite rough for those in mixed atmospheres (work). Many may not sleep as much at night (or may sleep for 12 hours straight) then need to nap throughout the day. If you feel to nap, nap. Listen to the way you feel, rather than what you think. Soon you will understand this and be embracing any opportunity to sleep as well.

DNA: The 2 strand human DNA held the human experience, the human energy template held the lower realms programming as well. These become obsolete as the additional 10 strands of "junk DNA" are activated (these are the Crystalline LightBody Higher Consciousness Strands). These hold the new programming to allow one the ability to come to exist AS the 5th Dimensional Realm. Additional DNA strands (Galactic) can be activated to expand far beyond these realms as well. The frequencies of love, light and sound activate these. The more you hear the frequencies in your head, the more you are BEing activated.

Time: The human perception of time was anchored in the old programming inside of you. As you integrate and hold these higher frequencies within, time will slowly disappear in the current reality that you exist in. Time was a human creation of separation that existed within you. There is no separation in the 5thh Dimension. For you to fully exist here, you must release the need for the constraints of time in your own reality, in every way that you can. Time does not exist as it was separated as you descended and fell and separated within. The more one merges as their Energy Body, the more time ceases to exist. Things become extremely fluid and all flows as one. Along the way, this gets blurred, fuzzy and one gets "lost"... this is THE PURPOSE. The human mind will try to hold on, focus, and keep control. The Walking Soul will enjoy, be present and utilize the fluidity!

Holographic Viewer: This was activated in my "sleep" state. An explosion of color and a viewer presented for whole new realizations, understandings and the ability to see through alternative projector screens. This one rocks, but is very confusing and takes some adjustment. One will feel like they are walking between worlds, which is correct. Dimensional travel can be quite confusing until you get the hang of it. Once you see through this, nothing is ever the same again. This is your pineal gland. Do absolutely everything you can to decalcify and absorb light to activate this.

Quiet Time and Solace: This is imperative for you to spend time with your higher self, with nature, with your thoughts, with your observations and BEing in a space that allows you to receive through the heart and BE ONE again. States of higher consciousness (which is you in your future) are accessed in solitude, silence, observation, expansion, sleep, meditation and by going within.

Energetic Sensitivities: It appears many of the "earlier" sensitivities are returning, but "differently"... as now, all of a lower vibrational frequency from material things, others, noise, smells, emotions, etc. are FELT as discord on one's own energy field. This actually requires MORE CARE and MORE solitude than one might "expect". Nature is always a healer, as is sleep for these offer vibrations that you need for this. The old human used to be affected by emotional and physical responses, whereas the new responses are in the energy/LightBody and are part of the "tuning" process as you lighten in frequency. Honor your own energy when you feel a disruption or drain. Honoring self care in high energy times is a must.

Material World: Believe it or not, your material world is in direct correlation with your new DNA activations, for your new 5th Dimensional physical realities do not hold the denseness that your 3rd/4th Dimensional physical realities did. Your material reality was created with your old human DNA which is now becoming obsolete. Your entire new reality will completely evolve and much of what you came to identify with will have to go, unless it supports your journey within and creates unity for all. Anything representing density and separation will become visible as density within you diminishes. As you come to understand, this will make more sense.

Tuners: The head will continually be "cleared" physically as the frequencies of one as an energetic BEing continue to integrate in higher realms. This is making way for MUCH to occur in the new form of communication for all as an Energy Body. One can actually hear and feel the energy movement activating that which has been dormant. Usually occurs when the mind is quiet or in rest state, but more and more as one becomes able to achieve and maintain this frequency in "wake" state and existing AS the higher realms again.

Denseness in the physical body: Continues to purge. The spinal area is receiving MUCH work, along with virtually everything. Anything that surfaces is a part of your Ascension process. Aches and pains are a part of this. They are normal as you completely are restructured from the inside out.

Energetic Burn-Off's: This is where the LightBody gets cold & hot at the same time and POURS water. This is more than "sweat". At first, you may notice this only happening when you sleep, then you will notice it happening when you are awake. When you are awake, you feel like you are losing consciousness, eyesight goes, hearing goes, temperatures go crazy and you have to find a place to sit down or go to sleep. Do this, assist in the expansion process, as it can be mild to extreme, depending on how much your soul is trying to expand from inside of you. Your physical body was dense and the "suit" did not fit. Think of it as trying to get into your body more and pushing everything out of the way, adjusting the temperature so it is comfortable and calibrating the systems (your entire body) so that all works WITH it. When the soul (Light) heats up inside, density is burned off, so that it can expand and higher states of consciousness can be achieved. Density is in the way. Dense thoughts or huge emotional clearings recently can cause a burn-off afterwards, for the energy must clear your field as well. Find a bed and rest. Your LightBody/Merkaba also is shifting in temperature to come to self-regulate itself from the inside and it takes many adjustments for this to occur. You will feel hot inside and cold outside or it can be reversed. This will adjust overtime. Just know that nothing is wrong. Your entire lymphatic and hormone system will go out of whack while it re-calibrates to your new Crystalline LightBody as well.

Inner body vibrations: Feels like a mini-earthquake inside and can get quite strong. This too is normal as activations continue along the way. The "old human" response was panic attack, yet once we came to understand that the fear was a result of these, that changed the whole ballgame. This occurred to bring fear up so that one can see it and release it from their reality. Once the fear is gone, awesome gets activated with these. Yet, usually when I feel these, even as subtle as they are for me, there is usually an earthquake going on "out there" in the physical. WE ARE Gaia, so yes, we feel these as they are simultaneous and the more we tune, the more in-tune we become.

3rd Eye/Pineal Headaches: In the beginning these lasted for weeks and months and I had no idea what they were. The more logical we "try" to be, the more of these we have. As I abandoned this side of my brain, anytime I was around a stubborn ego mind, I would get a telepathic headache and have to leave the room. Instant cure! Now, I only get these for a few moments, if at all and "see" the light codes filling up for integration and release after sleep. These bring MUCH awesome info/REMEMBERING, so I love it when my 3rd eye expands! New things to see. Awesome!

Tingling all over the body: This can be felt at different times, usually in the vortex spin points, fingers, toes, under feet, palms, 3rd eye, crown area and more.

SOLAR WINDS & PHOTONIC LIGHT ACTIVATIONS WITHIN

Wow, this is a HUGE one and I will address in a fashion that makes sense. So very much is affected by this, as all is WITHIN you. REMEMBER this!

Each frequency activates a different thing to occur within us. I usually try to explain the physical responses, sounds and affects, along with what "could" be affected in your physical reality and "out there" as well. Density and light within will dictate this. Some responses are extreme, where there is much density. Weird is the best way to explain it when we hold much light, for "normal" went out the window a long time ago. That was human. We have gone so far beyond as we entered the higher realms.

Air and energy in the head/brain area: There is an energetic air that moves through the head as our tuners are tuned to higher frequencies. Sometimes it sounds like zoom zoom, as energy fires off inside your head and your dormant brain (neural pathways) are opened (universal corridors). When the solar winds have activated inside long enough, a photonic level is reached and the neurons in the brain fire off as the pineal gland activates this region to be awakened for so very much to come forth for all. Melatonin will be released to cause you to need to sleep (or at least be in a walking meditative, sedative state), so that brain activity ceases and light activations can further occur. DMT is released; a heartbeat in the head region will tell you it is time to go lie down or at least connect to a higher plane. The 3rd eye will fill full, as it is, and one can experience headaches with this. Sleep allows for these light codes to be released and integration of your new memories to come forth. SLEEP SLEEP SLEEP, as this is the absolute best time for this. One can also come to activate these at will, with a lot of practice when one has drifted off yet is still aware and learns how to participate in the sleep state that is not sleep. Waking up stops the activations, so mastering this in the sleep state is truly mastery indeed!

Air babies: This is what we kindly termed solar wind inside the body. The tummy area blows up really fast and one looks like they went from a flat belly to 6 or 9 months pregnant in a matter of minutes or hours when this occurs. Light fills your entire inner regions for new to be birthed from within. New info, new REMEMBERING, new realities, an all new you! This will occur for months or years, as the evolution process does not happy overnight. Although, birth does and many times, for you will get pregnant a lot and integrate the new info when you sleep to awake to a flat (ish) belly again the next day! (or a week later). How "fast" you expand and birth will be dependent on the amount of light you already hold. The higher one's unified frequency (LightBody), the faster this occurs. I can get pregnant and give birth now all in a matter of hours! (when it used to be days or weeks).

Gurgling in the lower intestinal area: Yep, air again, organ re-calibration, repair, and all kinds of new going on here. Tummy talks a lot as it evolves. I used to joke that I was about to birth an E.T. baby. Little did I realize at the time. Now, there will be periods where the lower two chakra regions get "cleaned out" and nothing will stay in the body. This is kind of an intestinal detox and can come and go for several weeks at a time. I used to welcome this, for this saved me a lot of money on detoxing! There is much more going on, this is just one thing.

When the photonic energies build over a few hours in human time or come on really fast and strong, the energy body is raised dramatically in frequency and the brainwave state of the entire body is dropped to a lower state. The lowest I am aware of thus far is gamma for me and I walk in this in a waking state. Most cannot stay awake during this and are shut down and put to sleep. I do at times and I honor this as well. I will be the first one to go to sleep (and all that I work with know do the same. It is funny as we all run for a couch or a bed every time light activations begin!) Crop circle, oh yeah, photonic light activations. I will include an entire section on this, since so much is affected by these. My awareness may have changed since, yet the basis will still be the same.

Gravity: Gravity will continue to go as you lighten and ascend into the higher realms from within. This will start with disorientation, dizziness and loss of balance. This is normal, so take care and get plenty of rest. You will adjust after much integration and sleep. How you experience this in your evolution will change as well. You will start to float inside of your body, as your soul floats. Do not fear this, this is your true you emerging from within.

OTHER FREQUENCY ACTIVATIONS:

Gamma bursts: Ahhh the entire body and head BEing plugged into an electrical socket or laser beam feeling activations. Yes, this is an amazing one and the first time you experience this one, you will not forget. Absolutely everything gets activated and energized with this!

CME and Pyramid Energy Activations: Aimed at the head region, these are super high tones that trigger any discordant frequencies within. Physical pain comes with these all over the entire physical body. You name it, these activate everything inside of you for the NEW. Any linear time gets wiped, memories go too. These "work" to erase our human existence and assist with new memories coming forth too. Sometimes they go so high they "mute" and sound like a silent dog whistle would. They are very noticeable and nausea is a by-product of these as well. Anything anchored within will be "chiseled" out to go. These can bring on fast & intense headaches, disorientation, causing one to lose balance inside as gravity goes inside the Merkaba. Any resistance will make it worse. Just close your eyes and allow it to occur. Bones and teeth are activated with these, as well as the intestinal area too.

Crystalline energies: Christ Consciousness and these bring forth the forgotten in physical form, the crystalline bodies and formation of the crystalline cities to be visible again. These create your NEW EARTH to be visible again. Magic comes forth with these!

Hearing, breathing, vision and smells all move within as well. New realms bring new smells (i.e. Lemurian brings algae and seaweed smells when these realms open, solar flares bring a weird burning smell when we start activating certain DNA strands and higher realms, breathing gets shallow as we breathe like we are under water or in a space suit, and hearing, well this one is so totally loud inside, frequencies of absolutely everything in the universe in our head. Our entire body can do these things, as I have heard with my stomach and my feet at times, as the photonic activations tuned my entire energy body. We have much more to come as we continue to evolve. Oh yeah, and seeing the entire universe, inside the human body all from within, and SO much more!

Note: New understandings come forth every day, so there is no way to keep this updated here. I write in real-time as all transpires and share on Facebook. Beyond that, here, I can just share a brief explanation of the vastness that truly is occurring within. We have recently moved into sub-atomic molecular restructuring, protons, electrons, nuclear fission, gamma radiation, nano-bodies and more; all activating within us (microcosm) and then out there for whatever dimensional realm we exist in *out there* (macrocosm).

REMINDER: If I expect the unexpected, I will do awesome with all of this!

PHOTONIC LIGHT ACTIVATIONS OCCURRING INSIDE OF YOU

This is quantum light, activating electromagnetic radiation INSIDE OF YOU to radiate OUT. REMEMBER, all that occurs inside, also occurs "out there" as well. Microcosm and Macrocosm. This is what creates the electromagnetic field of your Merkaba/Merkiva/Orbitron (whichever you currently have unified to from within).

We receive these in various frequencies. One is "waves" and these cause the walking meditative state to come forth, the brainwave states drop (some of us to gamma frequencies), further activate the "projector" (pineal gland), which activates melatonin, DMT, and further opens the universal corridors/dormant neural pathway in the dormant brain and the LightBody/Crystalline DNA. Solar flares bring itchies and "breakouts" from inside as well, as and activation of your Human Star BEing DNA. The pituitary gland is also activated with these and various new physical responses for ancient BEingness to come forth.

Now, in the physical reality, these "magnify" absolutely everything. Thoughts, emotions, fears or love, bliss and magic, alchemy and SO much more than can be covered here. The entire head is super affected by these, telepathic/energetic communication is heightened as hearing further moves inside and your bubble expands out more and more with each activation that occurs. Slight activations cause slight responses. Huge activations that are continual, well, you get the drift. The solar winds, Merkaba Spin that is heard brings them in slowly, over a period of "time", while the "other ones" are like a meteor shower within, stars activating all over and light particles activate with these. These come on fast and furious.

276

BEing indoors is virtually impossible at times, for all senses are expanded so much, all senses are amplified and all is triggered within. It is a magnificent experience, yet BEing around others, sounds and smells and electronics can be too overwhelming while an activation is occurring and we are acclimating to these. Close indoor quarters are harder with these and nature is a magnificent way to expand these and TUNE, for this is what they do. They tune you super high, super expansive, super fast.

Now, the properties of photons: Charge, mass, spin. It is "mass-less". Look at your Merkaba/Orbitron and see what you see when these are activating with you. The Universe/Gaia "out there" will also be responding with like responses as well.

All becomes super sensitive as the entire energy/Light/Crystalline Body activates with these. We (ALL) "tune" super fast, super high.

This is also what causes us to become more translucent, iridescent and glow. Density comes up & out and then we "LIGHT'en" up even more from the inside out! The Incredible Hulk was gamma ray activations. Correlate the "expansiveness" of his physical when one thing got exacerbated. Kind of the same thing. What is present is magnified huge and fast. Now where this is awesomeness, then we have awesomeness abound!

You so did not think we were staying human did you?

Feel free to go research photons, gamma rays, etc... for I am by far NOT a physicist or scientist. I don't even try to be. I do now see the atom, protons, neutrons, nucleus and more, while I have yet to put 2 + 2 together. That is coming soon! Photon Belt... yep, we have been here and shall continue to BE even more!

MICROCOSM AND MACROCOSM

When you learn to correlate the internal reality with the external reality, you will see things much differently than you did before. For everything inside of you, "out there" is a larger scale representation. It is a projected reality view of what is inside of you. When you can expand this to every minute thing in the Universe, you can see BEyond the matrix, from the outside looking in. You are no longer a human looking up at a sky and starts that exist "out there". You are a Light BEing realizing that is your own projection. You start changing your projection and releasing that which you no longer desire to materialize in your own reality.

In the beginning, you start small. You look at that individual thing and then you go inward to try to find where that exists. Yet then one day there is a flip and you come to completely exist within and only project out, instead of absorbing from the world "out there", you are creating it just by BEing in frequency again.

One can correlate what is occurring with their own existence and then look "out there" to know AS radiation leaks, earthquakes and crystalline energies are forming the new to be visible to see.

When the microcosm is your internal reality, then the macrocosm is the transmitted reality created BY that. Eventually you can see the entire realm for what it is and leave it completely behind. One you leave it behind inside, "out there" shall follow as well.

THE PINEAL GLAND

You will come to find that your pineal gland to be a most important part of your own evolution here. You will utilize this to CREATE your entire new reality, give you access again to the entire Universe from within you and allow you to travel BEyond your wildest dreams. (Literally).

The normal human pineal gland, especially for Western Society, had become calcified, due to chemicals, water, fluoride and more. Anything you can do to de-calcify it and activate it will assist you greatly in this process.

Now, as it "grows" and expands, so shall your physical head. Headaches and cranial expansion are a part of this. The higher the vibrational frequency, the more this activates and expands. Neural pathways will be activated in your head. The most weird experiences are also a part of your ascension journey. Your human mind will expand so far BEyond human, it is hard to comprehend. In the beginning, the headaches can be very intense. There are ways to alleviate this. I will mention a few.

Sleep. Your human mind is in the way. It thinks too much and it actually causes the headaches, for the resistance between your heart and your human mind actually create headaches. The more logical, the more resistance, the bigger the headache. Also, light activations going on within you activate such high frequencies (your Soul is pure light), that your human mind must be shut down for integration to occur. Close your eyes throughout the day as much as you can to also assist with easing this.

Tap your 3rd eye and actually speak for ease to occur. 3 light taps, pause, 3 light taps, pause, 3 light taps… close your eyes and speak for the pressure to ease. Say "I release the light codes within me for easier integration to occur. A nap for a few moments will give great comfort much of the time as well. Liken to a computer, you must re-boot to avoid a crash.

Research foods that de-calcify or stimulate the pineal gland. This is very important as well.

Clean water (I do pH). Super important for your entire LightBody as well.

Now, when the neural pathways, the dormant part of your brain is BEing activated, you will hear and feel energy actually swooshing through your head. Zoom-zoom as I call it, it can actually be heard and felt. This is your Soul energy; it is nothing to fear. You are connecting AS the Universe to be able to access Universal knowledge, be able to travel dimensionally/multi-dimensionally, and becoming a SEER, a visionary, and your higher BEing self again.

You will hear frequencies. This will get loud at times and continue to increase as you elevate in vibrational frequency inside. These are you ascending and starting to hear the entire Universe from inside of you as well. At first, they are outside and annoying. The more you communicate with them, the more they will assist you. They are your connection, as your Soul, Higher Self to all things of higher realms. They will move inside your head as your Higher Self expands from within you. Welcome them and learn to use them in your everyday life. They will feed you, lead you, nurture you and become a very huge part of your entire existence. These are you. You are frequency.

Your pineal gland will be the transmitter of the hologram that you see. Once you get a hang of things, you will become the one creating the transmission. Your heart the generator, your pineal gland the transmitter for tuning the reality you get.

There is so much more that the pineal gland does. It releases melatonin, which causes you to sleep. It releases DMT that causes you to see the other dimensions, parallels and realms. It is magnified when the photonic activations are occurring. It becomes your new viewer (eyes) as well.

Note: I have found that super dark chocolate stimulates the pineal gland, especially before sleeping and in mega doses at times as well. I also found it allowed me to stimulate my "brain" enough to work and maintain a relaxed state that the Higher Self needed, for we must maintain a meditative state while the merge & flip and coming to walk in a dream occurs within. Cilantro is another thing, clean/distilled water. There are many things I found along the way. Sun gazing a must, yet do this safely until you hold enough light that this is no longer an issue with your eyes.

The "forming a triangle" with your fingers (pyramid) and holding your hands out to create a "box" for the sun to be viewable through will assist you as well to absorb the sun through your third eye, breathing it into your entire cellular structure, activating light with every breath. Close your eyes, every so often and just absorb it into your entire BEing. The more you do this, the faster light will activate inside and the more you will notice changes occurring inside of you! Awesome stuff, for you are the sun, you are a star. You are feeding YOU that which you ARE!

DNA ACTIVATIONS & BLUEPRINTS

All of the changes you are feeling are occurring inside and then represented by what you see "out there". You asked for a human experience on Earth, so that is the view you have until you have transcended the limits of this BEing your only existence here.

The barriers to traveling through space and time exist in your human mind, accompanied by your dormant DNA, behind the locked pathways of your Universal Mind. The key is your own vibrational frequency and how unblocked and free you're your heart is. Light activations are occurring in every moment to awaken you. Your own human need for "additional" human experiences will suppress this. AS your Higher Self you will embrace the change that makes no logical sense and honor that which feels right inside.

Now, for the sake of explaining this (as well as everything along the journey), we must first separate things "to see", then we merge them together again (unification). So, "in the beginning" you have a human heart and a human mind. As your heart opens & barriers dissolve, you activate your higher heart and your higher mind. Your Higher Self Universal Heart & Mind merge to become one and these merge with your physical there to then further unify as well. This occurs with absolutely everything you will "endure" as a human. We see through separating, observing then merging them back, without the old density attached. Each release of human separation (fear and "I" anything) allows your physical body and your Higher Self to INTEGREATE & MERGE for you to EMBODY all there as ONE again.

Before you descended, you were ONE. One HEART-MIND in unison, completely connected AS ALL THAT IS. Upon descension, your heart & your mind separated and so did the rest of you. Your human body represents this separation in physical form. Your human organs separated to also hold separated cellular memory to accommodate that which that you needed to experience there.

You have a cellular blueprint and an Etheric blueprint (template) and these too were separated and also merge as you unify again. Your human body was created to "house" all separately, which accommodated your "I" individualism.

Encoding buried deep within your cellular structure is activated by your own energetic blueprint as these two also merge. When it is "time" for you to fully awaken and your Higher Self to expand from within you, you will "split" into two "BEings" so that you can see from two viewers. You can activate this yourself, by utilizing the tools provided in shifting intentionally "quicker", instead of waiting for this to occur.

There is the human heart and the Universal Heart and these shall come to merge. The human's is low, dense and separated. The Higher Self (your future you as a BEing of Light) holds no separation, no limits, no loss of memory, nothing less than SOURCE itself AS All-That-Is.

Your hologram is programmed to "play" that which is encoded in your DNA. As your DNA activates, the hologram (or the play) will change. The view you have will be dependent on the "altitude" achieved inside to allow you an expanded view. It is simple, the higher you vibrate, the faster the spin, the faster the spin, the more you expand. The more you expand, the higher you go, the more expanded the view. Where you "start" for this, is by way of constantly stretching & expanding your reality BEYOND that which you can see as a limited human mind and continue to do everything to activate and raise your own vibrational frequency yourself.

Activations are a spiraling explanation, for none occur linearly here. All occur simultaneously and each one "causes" (activates) the next thing to occur. A never ending spiral, each thing creates the "next". Another view looks like a chain reaction, where as if you speed this up, they all occur at the same time, with no beginning or ending point in sight.

Your old human DNA held discord, duality and separation. The integration of your Etheric blueprint/template allows for the dormant DNA to be activated

The only difference BEing vibrational frequency and the amount of separation or unification within.

Note: After 2013 Ascension, awareness and algorithms started coming through on many things, one being the NEW Crystalline Human Star Being DNA. That will apparently be shared as I go and in the next book that has already started coming forth.

REMINDER: My human DNA held all of my lack, fears and old belief systems of separation within. My LightBody DNA holds light, my Higher Self and a love BEyond that which is known in "human". My physical will also experience a reversal of systems while I transform into my higher existence self. As I unify, that which was separate within me will actually be physically be felt as it leaves (or I leave it vibrationally).

AS YOUR REALITIES BECOME MORE HOLOGRAPHIC, SO DO YOU!

The human will not yet comprehend this, for it makes absolutely no logical sense. Again, NEW EARTH and you new (REMEMBERED) reality is not logical. It is the opposite of everything you once knew.

As 5th Dimensional frequencies are activated from within all, those who have been doing inner work & connecting shall notice increased energetic experiences occurring in their physical, as one's LightBody actually evolves as an energy form, lightens, becomes more translucent, transparent and, for many, starts to glow (and more). You become holographic transmitters. Visibility is matched in frequency.

From within, and at "different times" (according to how separated in time the human mind still is), mini-gamma bursts, electromagnetic radiation (and sooo much more) have dramatically increased to almost an every-day thing, whereas this was weeks or months apart, that is no longer.

You are a walking crystal energy transmitter of the hologram that you see "out there". As the light quotient builds within, so does it "out there". The lighter one becomes, the "quicker" and more connected as energy one also becomes. That hologram "out there" "used" to be one that played a human transmission. As human is left behind, then that hologram also dissipates. Then, there is a "reversal", if you will. The hologram is one that you create. Once the concept is truly comprehended, then you work to create the NEW, as it is perceived, from inside of you. As you do this, you continue to lighten.

As one sees it here, in the physical, this is new. It is something to "work" to create. Yet, it is actually the opposite. WE do not work to create anything. It has already been created. It exists within us as a frequency that can only be seen within first & then to manifest "out there", once one achieves the frequency from within. What you are seeing "out there" is what always has been. Yet you did not hold the frequency prior to see or BE in it. So, that which all seek to now CREATE, is only that which has always been.

Your lightening gives you access. Your desire, your mission, your work to create is your transmission, energetically that in your physical creates a new physical reality too.

Now, you are a walking light energy transmitter. That which you now think & feel are created just by your BEing that energy. If you desire for that "out there" to change, you must go within. Remove, release & let go of all that is not in alignment within you.

The Energetic Communication Grid of Lights IS you. It is ALL of you finally reaching a frequency that allows you all to connect as one. It is this connection, which together creates the NEW hologram that you shall see there in your physical reality. If you are to create the NEW together, you will have to connect AS the frequency of LIGHT that you now become. As this grid strengthens, so does your ability to see/transmit this NEW reality. THIS is how your NEW is created. It exists inside of you. And together as you all connect, new is now visible for all to see too. ♥

BECOMING TRANSPARENT:

With the activation of the higher vibrational realm light activations of your Soul frequencies as energy from inside of you, your DNA upgrades, your LIGHTBODY/Crystalline Body Activations, you ARE becoming more transparent. You will see it when you are ready to.

WE speak of transparency as BEing able to see that which has not been visible. Most focus on the "truths" "out there", yet this applies to SO many other things too. For the "truths" "out there" are manifestations of what exists within. For as you see where you have compromised your own self, your own BEing, and you work to come further into alignment WITHIN, then "THAT" "OUT THERE" continues to shift, change, match your frequency and the old physical shall continue to fall away.

Yet, you cannot look in the mirror yet and truly see that your physical also is becoming TRANSPARENT. YOU are evolving as ENERGETIC BEings AGAIN, and as you do, as you become LIGHT'er, literally, your entire BEing becomes more translucent.

Others too shall now come to see this. They shall see the glow that radiates from within you. Not only, as in the "past" by your bright smile or happy face, yet an actual LIGHT that radiates from within you OUT.

These energy activations raise your internal & entire vibrational frequency. This in turn tunes you to the energy that you are. As you release, you lighten. Your physical changes to match these new vibrational frequencies. Your human eyes further integrate with your energetic eyes that see more colors, vibrancy & light. Those things that you could not see shall continue to become visible. The realities that you have always known inside, yet longed to become, shall truly now come to BE. It is up to you to keep making it your priority. For you see, when your vibration is of the utmost to you, then all "out there" shall come to match that which exists within you.

See yourself for all that you truly are. Hold the light. Allow your mind to release all that is no longer you. And all "out there" shall come to match this FOR you.

ETHERIC BLUEPRINT & LIGHTBODY TEMPLATES: WIPING OF ALL IDENTITIES, SELVES, TIME AND MORE

There is an Etheric blueprint for each one of us, and for Gaia too. These are templates that hold information that continues to be activated within each one of us, as a walking energy form here.

The HUMAN template held separation within it. All were separated in identities, selves, time (and more). This has been & continues to be erased/dissolved.

The entire human template is BEing wiped. This appears to be happening faster, yet it is just more "visible" as one integrates light within and vibrates at a higher frequency. In order to integrate LIGHT, where there is dense to be released, one must sleep. The human mind/body cannot "take" all of the light that gets activated in super high energy times.

The human mind is like the processor of a computer for this template. It processes the clock & time spread throughout your human physical and held within your old human DNA. Until one actively participates in releasing "time" within, one gets shut down for this to occur "for" them.

The Soul Self does not have this separation within it. As more integrate to EMBODY AS their own Soul/Light within, the less this will matter. This BEing "moves" and exists in flow with the entire Universe from within. One is awoken when they are meant to wake. One is shut down when it is time to sleep. "Work" is not done with thought. It too is a "received thought" of what to do, and this BEing does it, without thought. For all that is "needed" is present in any given moment. The words that are meant to be spoken come forth. The ability to "do" an action comes forth, even if it didn't exist in one's human brain capacity, one has access to BEYOND that here.

Sleep for the Soul/Light Self is a "plug-in, re-charge, re-boot, connection time". There is very little actual sleep, unless one is in "light integration" mode. There is not exhaustion from anything that gets done, so the physical/mental/emotional/Soul self all exist in the same space, in flow, as ONE BEing together. There is no conflict or question. There is very little thought here, unless it is of creation of "new" or to assist another. Those are our only purposes here now.

Light is BEing activated within you. Separation within is made visible to see. If not first of the self, then by what occurs "out there" to create an emotional response within.

One can participate in releasing "time" & separation from their body template by releasing the need to look at a clock, make appointments or speak in the separation of time by way of comparison or holding onto a memory that is trying to go. If you cannot REMEMBER it, it is not meant to be. Holding on keeps you in a physical reality that is trying to leave.

Humans will use time comparisons without any awareness at all. If you listen, you can hear these too. Removing these from your own energetic field can assist you in "speeding up" the release of time within you. Some common examples are: Stepping out of present moment to focus on another moment that does not exist; spoken comparisons involving age, achievements, accomplishments, amount of time spent doing anything, speaking or thinking in terms of yesterday, last week, or years. Switch the words from "I have done this for years" to "That was another version of me in a different vibrational frequency". Human compares time, whereas the soul could not care less, for it does not exist here.

When you do find the occasion to "look back at a memory" in order to assist, observe or let go, see the frequency that was present, not how old that human you were or how long you did something. See what frequency you were at (happy is a high frequency, while sad is a low frequency, so re-associate these words as well). How long you were at a certain frequency is not time, it is the amount of energy you held within that created the "amount of time" you needed for that experience. To re-associate you could say "I held a lot of energy at that frequency or I only held a little bit of energy at that frequency. You will start to understand energy and frequency in a whole new LIGHT!

I do not see that I have done "this" for a certain amount of time, yet another has done "this" for a certain amount of time. For that is a human comparison, an aspect of the human self.

Memories also go. For these too existed in separation of time. For as one releases the attachment, the story, the identity... then it is no longer needed.

Much is BEing "wiped" from the memory banks, for it only existed for the human experience. When one no longer "needs" that lesson, that experience, it is allowed to "leave" our energy field... which actually is one just vibrating at a different frequency that no longer holds that frequency.

NEW Earth, the 5th Dimension, is a Realm existent in frequency. These frequencies activated in your new DNA allow you to come to exist here again. It is a space that all occupy which first must be visible from within. Then it comes to be visible "out there".

You are creating NEW Earth/5th Dimension in every moment that separation within is released and you EMBODY love, light and peace inside of you. This is the true embodiment of your Higher Self, your Soul, the body of light (LightBody) and it is occurring "now" for all. How it occurs shall depend on how much you activate light on your own.

All can participate by embracing and bringing in more light. Those who resist it by seeing all as an inconvenience to the human aspect of their existence will receives an "adjustment" to assist in one's alignment again from within. These are where human pain and suffering come in.

SUN ACTIVATION OF YOUR LIGHTBODY

Every day, it is imperative to get somewhere where at least the crown and 3rd eye are exposed (whole body is better) to direct sunlight. Even when there is not sun, you can do this, yet the actual sun allows for one to expand more "in-the-moment". For you ARE the sun!

Sit or lay facing the sun with your eyes closed at first. Breathe it in to your entire BEing, through your 3rd eye, slow, long belly-expanding breaths and on the exhale, slowly release to tune your body & your breath together at the same time. If, on the exhale, you feel to emit a "tone" in your breath (I call this "toning"), you can actually tune, in frequency, as you release your breath in a slow natural tone. The slower & longer the in/out breath, the more you are able to tune within.

Fifteen minutes is enough to activate, yet the longer you do this, the more you will notice the affects and cellular changes within. You will feel tingling and expansion throughout. Feel yourself connected to all there is, feeling love and peace filling you and radiating out to all as you breathe.

Place your hands, palms up and focus on the energy activation point (chakra/crystal) in the middle of your palms and you will feel expansion here too. Tap 3 times in the middle if you wish to activate this.

Now, imagine breathing LIGHT into your entire LIGHT BODY. Imagine the sun activating your physical eyes (take care not to stare directly, unless you know how to do this safely. YOUR entire body IS an ENERGY CENTER, a CRYSTAL. You can activate it, by choice, if you so desire to.

LIGHT ACTIVATIONS AND SLEEP

Yes, sleep again. You will find that this is the single most important thing you will do on your journey, therefore it bears repeating repeatedly!

You are a LIGHT BEING and your Soul is pure light. Your human you is dense. Plain and simple. Your human body is BEing transformed as the vessel that will carry you between the realms. You will learn to shift from your head to your heart and to exist in present moment. This will allow you to shift dimensionally, first in small ways, then leaps and bounds.

In the lower realms you are the densest, where your thoughts are separated, your heart and mind are separated and your spirit is basically "dead". You are a robot functioning the way you were programmed to function, yet not by those you "think" did this, by your own cellular DNA encoded upon entry into your physical body. Your thoughts formed by those you had contracts with to assist you in your human experience here (i.e. parents, friends, authority figures, siblings, etc.), your emotions a result of the frequencies within, your physical body a product of separation and discord as well. Now, you could have had a traumatic childhood or a happy and blissful one, depended on that you set forth prior to incarnating here.

As your Soul awakens, it fires off light from within. This activates your dormant DNA, causing you to expand from within. The light pushes out density, density BEing all low frequencies of fear, doubt, blame, shame, guilt, judgment, pride, greed, lack and more. All representations of separation (lower vibrational frequencies within). Your Soul is pure light and exists AS expansive love. Your human will put up the fight of its life, for it knows it's "reign" is about to end. It will sabotage you and work diligently to convince you to hang on to the old ways. It likes "safe" and secure and things in nice neat little boxes. Your Soul, your Higher Self, likes to float, fly, breathe and to be free. They are opposites and balance is what you will be challenged with the entire time you exist with duality still existent within.

One creates resistance, hangs on, "works" and "tries". The other has no resistance, lets go, allows and just IS.

Your Soul is light energy and in order for it to expand from within you, it needs to activate light. Where there is density and duality within, where the human mind is fixed, this light is a higher frequency and will cause you to sleep. Some slept on and off for 20-40 years. Others not as much, but the one constant thing that must occur for the Soul to totally activate and integrate within and AS you, you must sleep. There are a multitude of purposes in sleep, as your human reality must merge and flip until you are walking in a dream. Human cannot comprehend this. Just by your eyes BEing open, your mind is present and interferes until you are walking in a "lucid dream" state again. This is the 5th Dimension (and above).

Integration occurs when you sleep. Density, other lifetimes, parallels, memories, all clear in your sleep. Old realms are transcended and new ones emerge, all from within you, mostly while you sleep. The rest is done through inner work and those exchanges you need in order to have a tangible physical reality experience.

The solar sun and entire universe exist inside of you. Gaia does too. Many will say "I can predict earthquakes or earth events". This is because that is inside of you. This is how you know such things, you just are unaware this is "how it is". The rest, floating around in your energy field, waiting for you to sleep so it can be activated to "come in". Now, you can participate in this, by intentionally raising your vibrational frequency in every way you can. Tune your frequencies, every opportunity. Bring in and absorb more light. Eat light. Drink light. Breathe in light. Literally. Live plant food and sunlight. (The old the sun is "bad for you, protect yourself", was part of the human suppression to keep you from activating the sun inside of you. I will touch on a few in this book, just for awareness and understanding purposes.

Now, there are so many activations that occur, activating your dormant DNA, so that your heart can open and you can fully awaken and transcend the dualistic reality, to go on to transcend the physical reality realm all together.

HEAD DISORIENTATION:
ANOTHER LOGICAL EXPLANATION

This is a huge part of your Soul (Higher Self) integrating to come be BE inside of you, instead of floating "out there", in your energy (auric field). I prefer to write in "simple", so as to bypass the complexity and allow for the heart to understand.

As more integrate the higher realm energies into their BEing here, much is affected that makes no logical sense. The logical mind shall try to figure it out first, which can cause additional discomfort & pro-longing the experience. When one can "accept" the process and actually participate by either allowing or expediting (raising one's vibrational frequency intentionally), then things seem to move much "faster".

Especially, in the "beginning", these shifts & changes seem more dramatic, as they are "foreign" to the physical body. They are trying to integrate (become one), and so one may feel "taken over", victim, inconvenienced and even scared.

The short version is that your Soul/spirit/Higher Self is expanding from within you and your human mind is in the way. It's taking over and it's tired of waiting.

Yet for those who desire more, here is the expanded version: (here we go!)

For your Soul/spirit/Higher Self (I call it the Energy Body) to expand from within you, it must make room and get those things creating blocks within you out of the way. Your logical mind IS the problem, so it must "take over" and throw you off balance so that you cannot maintain control. Control is of the logical mind. This occurs when much information is trying to be assimilated for "release". All of your bodies (mental/physical/emotional) house veils/blocks/walls that must be triggered, activated, released, removed so that you can expand further. One can participate in the process by practicing "consciousness" and further utilizing choice from their heart (opposite of the human thinking mind).

The three human places where blocks occur in the physical are: Mental, physical, emotional. The last is energy, but then we ARE energy, so I will address that one separately, as it technically is where all originates, but the human can't "see" this, it sees the other manifestations, so we will go there first. Yet the energy is the place to start and will take care of the others!!!

Mental: All lifetimes/other times are present NOW. Your thoughts will show you this if you will observe them, without judgment and work to completely "re-do" your head. This is a necessity and shall occur with or without your participation. Choosing to participate can eliminate much "suffering" and loss.

Emotional: Appear as a result of your human thoughts. All emotions must purge one way or another, so choosing to do this can again eliminate much pain and suffering. Now, it is important to allow a feeling to surface, be validated, acknowledged for what it is, so you can move out of that vibrational frequency (purge/release/transcend, etc.

Physical: This one is "tough", as all things in your other bodies manifest here physically for one to see. This includes the physical body & "out there". As the other "bodies" are cleansed of the lower vibrations (transmuted, transformed, purged, etc.), then the physical will change to then match the new frequencies. The denser the "thing", the longer it takes to change. The physical is "slow" to catch up, so one must continue in the new vibration for this to "show up". Patience and not losing focus is key. Understanding is too!

Energy Body: This one is HUGE. Why? Because it is the entire essence of who/what you are. Yet, most do not understand this and it is the "last priority" on the totem pole. Everything else comes first, as this IS the human way. This shall change as more become aware and start to choose differently. When one comes to understand that absolutely everything they desire within exists in the higher realms/their future self, then ENERGY shall become their first priority and then all shall come TO them, instead of the human way of "seeking, trying, working, slaving and suffering". The golden Etheric key? ENERGY! (Sorry, I get sidetracked, lol). Your Soul/spirit/Higher Self, is already WITHIN YOU. It is trying to get you out of the way. In order to do so, it has to "push" all out of you that is blocking it. (Chronic ailments, dense emotions, yucky thoughts). So, while you try to maintain control and hang on, it says "nope, no longer an option... I drive this bus right now. You go to sleep or do something else that doesn't require you to think/focus or stay awake!".

Your Energy Body is pure light. It vibrates at the highest "speed" there is. This is why you feel tingling, crawling, pricklies, and everything weird under your skin. Your human mind is dense and must be shut down so that it can integrate into your physical BEing here. So, you must sleep (and nap!). When you do, light codes are released, healing & repair is done & realities change. So, schedule the next year off, take a long nap & wake up fully integrated... OR do it the human way and fight, whine & see it as an inconvenience. Choice will be taken away and you will do it anyway too!

You see, THIS IS WHY YOU ARE HERE. So, the more you see it as an inconvenience, the more you don't make it a priority, the more something else is more important, the more shall be removed as a block or barrier. This is what I call an adjustment or re-alignment. Things will occur FOR YOU (not to you), to put you in the path that you will ultimately end up taking anyway.

Now, for those who would like to know a way to participate? So glad you asked, as this is the awesome part! Make energy work a priority. Take tons of time to sit by yourself and observe your thoughts. Gain every tool to "teach" you how to master your own energy from within. And work WITH your Higher Self, as your Higher Self, with open communication in every moment. Most of all, honor your Soul (through your heart). Don't waste anything, don't compromise within, and learn to SHIFT on your own vibrationally.

LIGHTBODY ENERGY & TUNING FREQUENCIES

You are Energy, therefore it would make sense that you would seek "out there" anything that enhances your spirit, expands your energy, assists with removing blocks, and tunes you in frequency to higher frequencies in order to assist in any discordant frequencies held within. Discord creates dis-ease. Discord is just and out-of-tune frequency. You are walking frequency energy. To TUNE your frequencies assists you in your own LightBody evolution. So if you feel to seek assistance "out there" for something, utilize the many options that allow you to TUNE TO a higher frequency. The human will try to "treat or fix something". This is a perspective that something is "wrong". This is not the case.

There are a multitude of ways to tune frequencies. Some use sound, essential oils, crystals and various natural-pathic (yes I spelled it that way on purpose) remedies. Herbs and live foods carry frequencies of healing, nurturing, enhancing light within us. They feed us what we already are, so they "bring us back" to where we have "fallen from".

For me, as a human, I tried everything, and where I didn't get exposed to trying it, I learned about it through my Metaphysical coursework and that which I sought on my journey of understanding within. An abundance of chronic "issues", multitudes of types of suppression, I was the "tough masculine energy" that held out until I was "forced". I needed a "strong lesson or experience" to "get it". Then eventually I understood and didn't need these anymore. I started listening, honoring and putting my own frequency and LightBody first. Everything turned around when I did this. My Higher Self was just waiting for me to actually choose.

In seeking assistance from others, it is important to go into it with a higher perspective as well. I had to get my "human" out of the way for this. For what I wanted and what I "needed" were two different things. They in fact, as usual, were opposites.

First, I would take my "issue" as a question and present it to my Higher Self and ask for guidance on what to do. Sometimes I went & laid down and closed my eyes (meditation to others in whatever position they choose), sometimes I asked for the answer to come forth in my sleep and I would go to bed and see if I "knew more" when I woke up. Other times I would ask and watch for "signs" when I was out and about "doing my day". A store sign, a word repeated or something that just "jumped out" at me to point me in a direction. Maybe a conversation between others talking about exactly what I was seeking. Our answers come in small subtle ways, for they are simple and not logical at all.

In the beginning, it was like BEing on a treasure hunt, finding all the pieces left for me to find and put together in that grand puzzle of the higher realms. Out in nature I would connect and it felt like I was "Gretel" following breadcrumbs along the way. Until realities flip, the human is given tidbits to see if they will observe, listen and honor. It is part of the way that the higher realms "get around" the human mind. Leave "droppings" and then wait until that Souls is ready to actually seek.

So, utilize your higher self to assist you with anything you desire answers to. That is what it is there for. You can ask absolutely anything. Yet if it is not in your higher interest, you may not like the answer you get. Not listening will get you a "lesson" or tangible proof that you should have listened if you wished a shorter route. When you ask your higher self a question, ease or discomfort is always your answer. Ease will let you know you are in alignment. Discomfort will let you know you are not, but you will be if you do that which you do not desire to do, that brings up fear inside for you to step into. Now, you will always be guided in love. Your higher self knows no other way. Anything less is not your higher self. You will know the difference if you truly listen with your heart.

LIGHTBODY "DOCTORS": ENERGY TUNERS

There are no "LightBody Doctors", for your Higher Self IS your guide. Where you do not trust yet, you will seek others to tell you what you already know. This is fine too, for it is just a "space" that you still occupy; one where you still "think" your reality exists "out there" or you use others to tell you what resonates, so that you can use this to decide. Or you can just go inside; whichever you choose is perfect for you!

There are those who have already experienced this, who can share their own understandings with you. There are an unlimited number of "channelings" translated through the filters of those delivering these messages to you. There are those who work with LIGHT energy, who can also assist, if you so choose. But ultimately, "this" part is unknown until experienced, which exactly is the point. You are not to be seeking other "humans" to tell you their limited human view. You are to eventually come to have such communication within, that you receive answers by "two-way communication" between you and Your Higher Self; for you are the same "person". Only one of you has your answers and the other has yet to understand. As you merge, answers are immediate, understood, honored and then shared to assist others as well. That was the "human you".

Your "new" LightBody TUNERS (for there are no doctors anymore), will also be anyone who holds enough light, works in tuning light energy and works AS ENERGY to assist you with alignment in frequency again. None of this comes from a book or the limits of how anything "should be". You now go BEyond human, and that was of the old human way. Alternative, Energy, Light, Frequency, Tuning… these words will assist you here.

BRING IT ON, LET'S DO THIS… AND EARPLUGS

I mention this only for those who are not aware. These words, these things will intensify your experience and speed up your own Ascension process from within. These will cause anything inside to surface faster, "out there" to fall apart/away and allow you to TUNE TO higher frequencies, your future version of you and bring forth REMEMBERINGS much, much, much faster than you can comprehend or imagine, in human.

Now, "in the beginning", we speak this and we do not realize fully what this truly means. So, take great care, be aware and present when you speak or "do" these things. Afterward (or the more conscious one will realize during), we all go "wow, I "forgot" I uttered those words and actually ASKED for that!" One can also speak directly to their Higher Self inside and "ask" for ease & grace to ease to be able to "handle" that which is spiraling super duper fast or "too strong" and sometimes ease will occur. The human will attempt to "bargain" to get ease, then go back on their word of what they bargained with (i.e. "oh if things get easier, I will do _____, I promise). Take great care in not honoring this, as well, for the "next time", the strength of "that" will can be paramount and ease and grace will not come when you plead and ask. Your honor AS your HIGHER SELF is what allows this to shift and change. If you honor your agreement to your own Soul, it will honor you in return. You cannot fool your "future you", for it already knows what you will actually do. The response will be in direct correlation to your own integrity within.

EARPLUGS: I wore earplugs for all of 2013 and continue to do so as long as I feel to do so. This allowed me to shift focus off of the outside world "out there" and remain inside where I needed to be. It allowed me to cut out the disruption of the outside world, by way of others words and thoughts. It allowed me to hear my own louder, so that I could observe, hear, release attachment and shift to a higher vibrational frequency "faster" by participating rather than "waiting" for the outside world to "do it TO me". I got to choose my reality from inside, and I got to hear, see, and tune in frequency by choice. This allowed me to expedite, yet I had to be ready to let go as fast as it "came forth".

It also allowed me to hear the frequencies of my own Soul, own Higher Self, the entire Universe and Solar Sun that others believed first existed "out there". I came to BE one AS all of this by listening and observing at all times from within. It allowed me to stay present and remain an observer AS my Higher Self from inside. This assisted me in shifting from an exterior reality to an inner reality that CREATES my outer world to come to exist in again.

Now, take care with this as well, for this too will expedite your own TUNING in frequency inside. Yet it is one of the most pivotal things I did on my own journey, to cut out the "exterior world" and assist me in staying within. Here I get to create my own reality and then observe it transpiring "out there". I can hear what I "need" to hear, with the earplugs in. For now I hear from the inside out as well. This continues to expand, as I further unify AS All-That-Is. Energetic communication (telepathy to others), teleportation and becoming a "wireless" energy form, next to come forth in my world that I exist in.

I hear others speak of the frequencies and how annoying they are, or how they wish they'd shut up and go away. These shall only continue to get louder, for they ARE you and are trying to "move in". You can utilize them to assist you, listening to every high pitch, low vibration or shift that occurs with them. They are guiding you, feeding you and ARE your entire existence, yet most do not yet understand this. For those that do, and embrace this journey, they will welcome them in every way. You are listening to frequencies and you are but frequencies. They are one and the same.

ENERGY VORTEX SPOTS: Anytime something (the energy) is too extreme, if you are conscious, present and participating in navigating your own journey from within, you can shift out of discomfort, just by shifting in frequency outside and in. You can move your physical body to a place that is more conducive to assist you with ease. If you "sit or lay" in a sacred space (bed or meditation area), these spaces hold your energy and create an energy VORTEX that spins. Every time you place your body back in that space, you shift in frequency and magnify that which is occurring within. If you need ease, get up and go elsewhere with your physical body. Go outside in nature or in another room that holds a different vibration, for they do exist in different dimensional spaces and you can see/feel this if you "play" with this too.

Now, if you wish to create an energy vortex that allows you to raise your vibrational frequency "faster", you can create a space that is sacred and holds only your own energy in that space. Each time you go there and connect from inside with your Higher Self, the Universe, Gaia (whatever you identify with), the energy here spins faster and therefore so do you. It is here in this space that "human" is allowed to fall away and your Divine Essence is allowed to emerge. You expand, therefore so does your consciousness, to connect to the Universal Mind and heart as ONE. For me, I did this in my bed each day, not realizing what I was doing at the time. I would get up each morning, fix my coffee and go back, grab a journal, close my eyes and lean back on pillows to connect. My Higher Self "knew" that I was open and listening and started to come forth on a regular basis. It was the time that I devoted to silence, for I was not a "meditator". It was years before I realize that I had been meditating, just by getting back in bed and opening my heart. Human creates perceptions of how this should be, for there is no "should here". There is honor and allowing this connection on a regular basis until you BECOME it again. On my bed, I merged with my Higher Self, as my future me and my ancient memories all came forth. I allowed myself to drift, dream and sleep, as much as I felt to do inside. I found that sleep was the absolute most important thing, and BEing a meditative space inside at all times. For mediation was the human word, sacred space is what we BEcome again. Allowing this allowed my brainwave state to drop, to come to exist in frequency AS my Higher Self as one. Eventually YOU are the cosmic portal, the energy vortex and wherever you go, you ARE this. There is no longer any separation, for that was the old you of a lower vibration. You can merge AS you're your Higher Self and AS All-That-Is again, just by allowing yourself to connect in every moment in spaces of silence until that is all there is. This allows for total reversal of your energy fields and creates an opposite spin. This is how you raise your vibrational frequency, activate your own DNA, open your heart and lighten your own LIGHTBODY to UNIFY again. This is how you come to connect and your Merkaba merges fields and reverses spin. You need only let go, allow, connect and go completely inside for this. The rest shall occur as you let go of "I" and become "WE" inside again.

ALTITUDES, GRAVITY & ASCENSION: LIGHTBODY/MERKABA/CRYSTALLINE

Altitudes, wow, this is a huge topic. For, as humans, this scares the mess out of us. Our heads get flighty (airy fairy), we forget everything, we lose balance, fall over sideways, stuff crawls on our heads, and energy moves, first "outside" & then "in there".

So, explaining it is just as much fun! For, there are SO many things going on here.

Your entire inside will float as density leaves and you begin to gain entry to the 5th Dimension in the physical there. The human grabs for something to hold onto, tries harder and harder to focus, and tries to stay within the old structures of time. Yet, this is not you and it will go. How is up to you. You can embrace it, understand it, and assist it or you can fight it and use every bit of effort to "stay grounded" and holding on to the old human ways.

To let go is of your Higher Self and to hold on is your human you. One is easier, yet we sleep (or meditate), and a LOT is an UNDERSTATEMENT here.

Now, you do not float with density. Floating IS COMING TO EXIST AGAIN AS the HIGHER REALMS FROM WITHIN. So again, you have choice. Let go to float higher or hang on and suffer more. I know which one I chose and continually choose. Your choice will be based upon your own comfort level. At some point "comfort" is seen as human and we just "jump, leap & fly" anyway.

All descended and separated in order to come to exist here for their human experience. Now, every time you raise in vibrational frequency, you ascend a bit more. Every time you lower in frequency, you descend again. Each descension causes "stuff" to come up, to be pushed to the surface and out.

Think of BEing on an airplane. The parallels are uncanny. For those who have fear of flying, this fear is relative to the fear you hold in your everyday life as a human. For those who absolutely love flying up in the clouds, the feeling of "home" inside, freedom and peace, this is the equivalent of what it feels like "up here" in the higher realms. The head going all out of balance the plane reaches the high altitudes, the weightlessness and gravity going, the sound going in your head. All of these things occur as you expand into the higher realms INSIDE your human body/vessel/suit. Now imagine BEing in a spacesuit or space craft. The zero gravity and floating around weightlessly, with no "time" present, nothing to hold onto, no care or thoughts in the world. This is exactly what it is like INSIDE your body/suit when your Merkaba fully activates. Suspended animation. All stops, gravity goes, identities go, sound goes, absolutely everything goes.

Now, the higher you vibrate, the more aware you get of the frequency "drops". You know when something has shifted, for you feel all within. The heart feels the compression and decompression of the altitude changes. Breathing gets hard for awhile as you ascend and learn to breathe inside your suit. Your breathing will become shallow. This is normal as your entire physical is BEing transformed for your ability to walk dimensionally between realms, realities and worlds.

As your physical transforms from carbon to crystalline form, you will endure many changes that make absolutely no sense "in human". Your entire physical structure must be lightened, for your density will keep you anchored in the physical and unable to walk in the higher realms.

Your human body was to serve as your vessel for your human experience, yet as you evolve, you no longer "need" the human body as it once was. Your dormant DNA holds the coding for your LightBody and is activated with every human release of the physical reality world. This coding is the dormant 10 strands labeled as "junk DNA" by your human world. The Crystalline LightBody DNA are the strands above the 12 strands that you are aware of as humans too.

Your LightBody activates as you release duality within. When duality is transcended, you will actively start to embody Christ Consciousness within you, therefore activating your Crystalline DNA. The LightBody alone underwent a complete reversal/transconfiguration of the human systems (liver, kidneys, lymphatic system, hormones, pelvis, cranial expansion and more). Your Crystalline will undergo even more. Thus far, there appears to be a unification of human organs that will occur. This remains to be seen, for I am just now beginning to see and experience this in my own physical here and do not have enough information yet to include in this book.

You hold light codes within you that activate with frequency activations of Ascension. These are what awakened you. These are activated at a faster pace now, with the time of ascension that all are in.

I wrote and shared with others as I actually experienced my own LightBody/Merkaba activations and integrations, while also working with LightBody Energy of REMEMBERING doing activation and integration sessions as well. Those writings are available on my website and Facebook page, as well as a selected few included in this book.

Now, much of this will not make sense until you match up your own experiences with some of the writings here. Over "time" more will come up that you will have questions about, hence the purposes of this book. One is to assist with awareness, guidance, navigation and information that activates you beyond what you had access to before. You have already ascended; just the version of you reading this may not be aware and may be experiencing the old ascension realms still.

You have already ascended. You are REMEMBERING how to BE your Ascended Self again. WE all have and are doing this as well. After coming to embody Ascension within, I exist as an Ascended Master with an Orbitron (rather than the duality reversing Merkaba), and await the "next thing" to come for the space I now occupy here. This is unchartered territory for me, in my IN-LIGHT-ened human form, so I write to you as I sit here waiting for more NEW and REMEMBERED as well.

YOUR MERKABA, SPIN REVERSAL FROM HUMAN TO HIGHER SELF & ZERO POINT VOID

Absolutely everything "human" must be reversed to come to exist in a fully REMEMBERED state. Human energies, dependent on masculine or feminine ENERY (not specific to the physical human body vessel) spin in a specific direction. As the human separation is transcended, the spin is slowly reversed with each "release". Eventually a "zero point" is reached for "that", a void is necessary for the energy to come to a complete halt, reverse and then resume a new spin. As one activates more light, the spin is increased. Masculine spins one direction, feminine spins the other. When all has been reversed, and the spin increases in pure light, the fields merge and unify. This creates your unified energy field that radiates OUT from within you and you walk in this new vehicle that allows you to exist in multiple realms at once, for time no longer exists and all is simultaneous here.

There are small voids that are just uncomfortable, then other voids that seem huge. The voids, reversals and zero points are occurring all of the time. We only notice the huge ones, because they get our attention. Yet, there are so many shifts that occur, for they are simultaneous while other things are occurring as well.

There is a huge one as identities are cleared, between the 3rd, 4th, 5th Dimensional Realm (and more). There are voids while time gets wiped from our templates. Voids while we let go of attachment and other human emotions and learn to detach and shift to a space of love.

This must occur for your realities to flip and merge. You do not go from human to heaven without a total reversal of all that you once knew.

THE SPEED OF FREQUENCIES, REALITIES, SPIN & TIME TRAVEL

The human speed vibrates very slow and dense and the higher-self speed vibrates very fast. Now, "time" reverses as the speed increases, therefore so do realities and all.

The faster one's overall vibrational frequency, the slower "out there" goes. One can BE an observer here and see FROM an expanded view. One can actually play with "time" here, for time was a human creation and the higher one vibrates, the less this exists inside. "Time" only exists by way of separation, and this you hold yourself deep inside.

The slower one vibrates overall, the faster things go "out there". Details, chaos, all speeds up and the human-BEing never has enough time. For the faster one tries to go inside, the more "out there" will fall apart. The human tries to hold on and manipulate this by fitting more into their human time, according to that which they think needs to be accomplished in a physical human reality. This causes the separation of time to speed up. The more existent one is in their mind, the faster "out there" shall seem to occur. When in fact all in this very physical reality is very dense and super slow. It is the reality of the reversed and is physically exhausting here now. The more one tries to exist here, the more sleep will be required.

As one goes within to do inner work and connect to a higher state, light integrates inside, the inner world slows down, and therefore "out there" will eventually do the same. REMEMBER, the physical world is "slower" to materialize. Yet as all raises in vibrational frequency, the faster materialization "out there" seems to occur. "out there" is not occurring faster. Your spin is either fast or slow and dictating this. Coming to understand this spin, will help you navigate easier, allowing you to speed up or slow down at will. The more you slow down inside, the more "controlled participation" you have "out there". For you focus on your inside world in order to CREATE. When one exists again FROM the higher realms again inside, "out there" slows down, inside and out. The spins reverse and one actually "walks AS creation" (SOURCE CREATOR), rather than the reality created for the physical human experience. The frequencies available now in your time allow you to completely shift out of the old human state and BE this again.

Time travel was a human creation, perception and belief. Time to the human is the equivalent to us as the speed of one's overall unified spin. WE all travel through time by increasing our spin. WE already exist here, and we walk among you in your human time. WE are you, from your future. WE are you and you are US. As you vibrate higher, you will come to see this too. For REMEMBERING this is held within, as your Higher Self and in a space of non-separation. Time travel is the equivalent of overall vibrational frequency spin. Your UNIFIED SPIN is how you all travel through "time", for here, human-time, does not exist. Look to those who speak that which seems "BEyond" that which your human mind can comprehend, yet you feel inside vibrationally by resonance. These are versions of you from your future, delivering activations to allow you to come to REMEMBER and BE here again. The higher WE vibrate the more we REMEMBER and come to exist AS this here again. As humans, we tried to travel through time, while not BEing able to comprehend that we always have been. Now we do it at will.

Close your eyes and feel that which you hear, which goes BEyond your human-thinking-mind. Listen to that which resonates, yet makes no logical sense, yet resonate within you, from inside. For these writings are from your future, existent vibrationally in your human-time. I speak to you from this space of existence when I write these words to you in this book. When you read this you are also REMEMBERING, for that which transmits here already exists within you, previously blocked/locked away with a human belief or thought held inside. I am here by way of my activated Merkaba/Orbitron, walking through multiple spaces and times. I share by way of writing this book, to assist you in activating that which you hold vibrationally, in frequency inside.

You too are existent in "this future", by way of your LightBody, your Merkaba and Unified Field Spin. The more you release of human, the faster you shall spin again. The faster the spin, the slower "out there", the less separation exists within. Here you also exist in all spaces, no longer bound by human time. Every time you are present and existing from your heart, you are your future you. Yet not in the future, NOW.

WE have awaited our awakening and to transcend separation within. Here, in the 5th Dimension is where WE exist and all bring forth the "new". Here is a space all shall come to know from inside and then exist "out there" again, for here is Divine REMEMBERING and here WE are no longer human. WE are all Light BEings, still in a somewhat physical suit, a vessel that bound us to a physical reality that we all called Earth. Yet this too is only a boundary of our limited human minds. When we have released the need to exist in one physical space and time, we too shall be able to move BEyond that which is physical only in our mind.

LIGHTBODY/MERKABA REMINDER:

Fear stops or slows the spin,
Light activates and increases the spin,
Love expands the spin from within.

Note that once duality is released within fully, this Merkaba will then be obsolete. It will merge with more expansive sacred geometry to accommodate expansion as Christ Consciousness (and more) again. The masculine and feminine merge to move to embodying Christ Consciousness from within.

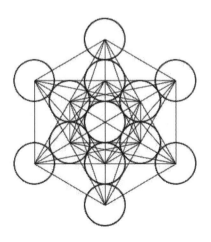

MERKABA: MY OWN EXPERIENCES SHARED

As my Merkaba activated, I would write DURING my experience to share and teach others as well. This was part of my "role" that I created here as a cosmic portal BEing. I will share a couple of posts, for they were written during my experiences, each one different as I came to expand across the dimensional realms. I have been writing and sharing online for several years of my own experiences as I evolved in consciousness, my LightBody formed and my Merkaba activated. For more information, the websites are listed on the back of this book.

September 9, 2013: THE UNIVERSAL MERKABA – CURRENTLY ACTIVATED

The Universal Merkaba is activated. One can feel, hear & see this as it activates, from within. I do not know how long it will last. I have been observing this for awhile, as all must come together to be simultaneous, for one to "know" this. The body "shaking" from the inside out, feeling like it is about to "take off" or launch. All of the sounds that were separate frequencies, all merge to become one sound, that when tuned into, one can hear the spin, and one feels & it sounds like they are in a "flying saucer". The "crickets" no longer separate, the Energetic Light Grid of Communication, no longer separate, the higher realm streams, no longer separate, the lower (gamma) brainwave states, no longer separate, yet all a "part" this "creation" that we now exist in and expand out to be so huge an energy. It has been going now for an hour, in linear time, yet time does not exist here.

I awoke to me "teaching" thousands again and the words I was speaking were "all must LIGHT'en up". Each time this has occurred previously, tons came forth in the waking state to new realizations of REMEMBERING in their waking state too.

It sounds like BEing in a "tunnel" of spinning lights (a capsule is the word I am given). All "tingles", vibrates....

I am shown how since my first activation to feeling this, way back when, and every activation since then, that all came to "work together" now to create this. How every attachment I released, allowed me to further activate and spin. And how, this shall only continue to increase, as more focus their intention on allowing this to occur, from within. Enjoy activation loves, as we vibrate higher into the "new".

September 19 & 22, 2013 Updates:

Since my awareness of this, my own activation to these higher frequencies from within, further activating my own Universal Merkaba, I am updating to share "more" of that which I now see.

I can look "back" over much time "years" and see each moment where this activated within me, yet I did not know what "it" was. Each activation was something different, based upon the frequencies I was activating within. For with each release of the old inside (especially huge ones), we activate further inside. One's LightBody/Merkaba, "builds" in frequency each "time". Each event/episode/activation seems separate, for a "time span" is indicative of how much separation we hold within us.

Now with each activation, we vibrate higher and further unify inside. This unification removes a bit more "separation" of our inner selves, therefore removing the "distance of time" that we hold within. The higher we vibrate, the less we exist bound by time. The human travels through the separation of time. The Light BEing travels through vibrational frequency. All is a polar opposite in those realities, yet even that merges and disintegrates within too.

First, it's just vibrations felt inside, then it is the loss of "time", loss of physical denseness/weight, etc. As these things UNIFY within, so do these things.

The vibrations become "spins", the old frequencies one used to hear becomes Universal Sounds (stars, solar flares, crickets, gamma rays, etc.). Then when one's UNIVERSAL MERKABA activates, all sounds merge into one, all experiences merge (timelessness, weightlessness & more).

For me, I keep receiving the words "Grand Merkaba", yet have never heard these together before. Last week, I experienced the "next" unification of my own Merkaba, while out & walking around "doing" public things. Now, when my Merkaba activates, I can hear it build over "time". It takes many hours, kind of like a "notification" to "get ready". The spin is slow and I can actually listen to it build/increase/speed up. I hear & feel like I am about ready to "lift off". It becomes so energetically powerful (and loud), that it dominates all. This last week, I came to a space where all time stood still, all weightlessness went, all thoughts, memories, everything "gone" and I was in a walking/open-eyed/participating state. I even typed "that" up to share, while in the middle of it.

My Merkaba activates daily now, sometimes several times a day. Each experience building as my own unified frequency increases. Some periods last for majority of the day, others just an hour or so. I see that this shall also integrate as I do, to be "all the time" as time is all one.

I am awoken each day to hearing/feeling this and "new" spaces of occupying here. I can "see" that which is to come, which I will share soon, as this will assist all too.

For what started a separate "episodes" of vibrations or memory loss or time disappearing, are ALL PART OF A WHOLE experience that shall occur for all. One can participate by allowing, tuning IN to it, going WITHIN and releasing all that surfaces to go. This includes everyone & everything (I will also explain this later, for it is not the "purpose" that we believe at the "time").

There will be "portals" opening up "out there" for all to "walk through". These activate as one holds the frequencies to do so. First we do it in our "sleep state", yet eventually we do this in a waking state. Yet, if one has not activated within, this shall not be visible or accessible. This is where the inner work is necessary. And I am shown that this is why the LightBody Energy will be so important. For this gives one instant access to this, and where I shall physically be located, holds active portals for one to actually pass through, in the physical here. Eventually, we WILL all BE a portal. Yet until this time, we utilize that which we have access to here.

Brainwave state: The overall frequencies of all on "Earth" have been dropped in brainwave state. When you hear/feel the heartbeat in your head/body, this is time to connect in. First in a closed-eyed state. The gamma brainwave state that is activated "over time", comes to BE in a waking open-eyed state. It gives one the ability to function "this way" in their "New/REMEMBERED" reality. This too is only accessible vibrationally. All of these things are this way.

The ENERGETIC COMMUNICATION LIGHT GRID is more actively "heard" during these times, yet is always present if one chooses to shut down & connect. This is just you, as an energy form, connecting to all as energy, communicating AS we all are, together, utilizing your own energy field to do so.

Now, I have individual posts for all of these things, for they occurred separately, over time, as I too experienced them. Yet, in a fully activated Merkaba, all of these posts are one. Every post I have ever written on the LightBody, every post on energetic communication, every post on the affects of the energy streams & the physical body, every post is a part of the whole. And every post is on my websites, for I have been writing and sharing for years.

If you feel it, hear it, see it, know it, it is a part of "this". The "next" of which is to come, shall also be a part of "this".

I heard the words in early 2013, you are not of this time, you are from the future". Wow, this made everything start to make sense! Then I was shown the old TV Series "Quantum Leap" (along with a few other things). I awoke to seeing us all already fully in the 5th Dimension and how the only way we are not, is if we forget that we are. The veils that are in place still for many, do not allow them to yet see this, yet this is one's own doing prior to even coming here. Each has the ability to lift their own veils by doing the inner work.

Part of my "MANY functions here" is to bring through this REMEMBERING to share and assist others who make their journey their priority and to expose those not yet aware to that which they have yet to REMEMBER here (writing/videos/tools/connecting, etc.), and also DO/TEACH the LightBody Energy to assist one in the overall vibrational frequency "jump" instantly to shift them higher dimensionally. This is not "for me". This is for us all. Access to the portals is within you; THEN they appear "out there", when it is "time". For time is a human creation. The Light BEing exists in vibration. And "here", there is no separation or limits of time. All exists in one "space" and as we come to exist in this same space, we exist as all.

Embrace, Activate, Integrate and Expand BEYOND that which you have yet to comprehend.

September 19, 2013 post: MERKABA: SUSPENDED ANIMATION –
ZERO GRAVITY INSIDE

I sit here completely weightless, in a spinning Merkaba Field and receive the words "In a space of no identities". I am shown that all the releasing of all along the way, all of our attachments, all of our beliefs, all of our human "safe", all of our everything is of the "old" way. And in this moment, I sit in a "suspended state". It is so very awesomely odd, for I "see" me floating in a state of suspension, nothing holding me, no cords, no attachments, no identities to anything at all. In THIS MOMENT I am absolutely nothing, which "feels" like complete surrender, complete freedom, complete abyss, yet I also know that what comes next is even more magnificent, phenomenal and beyond, and that is hard to imagine at all. "Here" is a space of nothingness and everything all at one time.

I shall update later, for that is all I have... for one of my "abilities" at times, is to be able to write and translate in the moment as I experience it. Here, there is no time, there is absolutely nothing. No thought, no memory, no past, no future, not even this moment seems to exist.

Truly beyond words..... as I leave now to go float, as gravity seems to go to zero point inside.

Now, later, I was able to return to update my previous post. Here is the update that followed:

This was a state of utter and complete BEing inside. Not from a place of observing with my mind. My entire BEING floated in a suspended state, zero gravity, zero anything. All dissolved and when I laid down to close my eyes to go "see", this is what I received, observed and saw:

First, about an hour prior to this, my body temp on the inside started to drop. The outside temp remained "normal", it seemed. My "suit" held a different temp for awhile, and continues to do so today. Inside I was freezing and I saw my temp go to "zero" too. This took lots of blankets and all night to balance out, with an entirely "new" experience today. Today I went outside. I could tell it was "cold "out there"", yet inside I was warm & my physical was cold. I was not cold. I was balanced. This has been occurring much lately, yet I did not know what it was. My body is regulating from the inside out, to no matter what temp I am in. It is "as if" "out there" no longer dictates my temperature. (Read later updates online to this.)

Eyes were "glitching" after, as if the "matrix" had glitches in it. I could see "blips" of it "going"... as if I was in the movie the Matrix and I was kinda sorta in a space like that green hallway where all was just energy and one could "see" beyond the physical reality "here".

When I closed my eyes, all went dense. I "knew" there were stars "out there", yet could not "see" them. It was as if I was in a sphere, a cylinder, and overhead was a "Dome of Denseness" that was not really dense. It was like BEing in an observatory and looking up & out from within.

I weighed nothing inside. I was floating in suspended animation. I saw my Merkaba all around me, huge, primarily gold... no longer spinning left to right & right to left, as in the "old" triangles that spun to create this, yet "now" an entire huge "globe" of gold light that I was encased in, and the reason for "zero gravity" was my Merkaba had completed to be also over my head & under my feet.... I was "encased" in this huge gold Merkaba spinning & elevating me to not touch anything in any direction anymore.

Later I laid down, as I usually do when I connect, hands one on top of the other, placed over my "thymus" region (for this is how I lay when I connect in). I observed myself connected and laying in an Egyptian Tomb-like Sarcophagus, which I have seen before when I do LightBody Energy Sessions on others, yet not usually on myself.

Now, I am shown that this experience was the magnetic poles within me going to "zero point", that which many/all/some (don't know who yet), shall experience with the "pole shift" that is human calendar this December (I awoke in June BEing shown I had gone through a pole shift "overnight"). Yet those of us who embrace this and hold/embody this within, do not "wait" as others do. We activate within when WE are ready. All have this ability, yet one must choose and release all that is "human" that stands in the way. All shall integrate within, to bring one to EMBODY this here. I do not (yet) seek to go anywhere, for we need not do so any longer. ALL is available "here" from within.

There are other things recently activated within me, which occurred previously, the night before. One, a portal within me burst open from the inside out, flowing with the most magnificent crystal clear blue waters of Lemurian/Atlantean Energy BEing activated within me. I start to REMEMBER the language I spoke with the Dolphins, yet I was also a Mermaid... so will have to see where this goes from here. LOVE the new portal access, along with this most magnificent state, that while, all are connected, is totally separate too. I did not understand the "vision/experience" I observed and a connection with a siStar of Light gave me the "missing" piece to come to understand this. When I went to look it up, all made sense and activated further! LOVE it!

September 24, 2013 post: MERKABA: A WEIGHTLESS & TIMELESS BUBBLE

I awoke to seeing from within a "slowly" activating Merkaba field, which is quite the amazing experience within itself. There are no words, yet I found myself trying to write, to make sense of it, to share. It is like all this "info" floating all around me... I can see it... I get it... but then I have to pull it all together to write in descriptive words that create a visual, a picture, so that one can connect from the heart space... which exists so far beyond the human thinking mind. (I will fix this later, as I write as I sit in an activated Merkaba bubble where all time, space, weightlessness has gone and I do not worry about the proper-ness of the words I try to write and share).

Now, time starts to come to a halt again, for "in the field", the separation of time & space, do not exist. All continues to "move "out there"", while no time exists "in here". It is a huge, huge, huge energetic "bubble" of "nothingness" that is BEyond exquisite.

Each experience is different, dependent on how fast it activates (sometimes it builds over "time"). The "points" of the field dissipates as the spin increases to all BEing non-existent and just this huge energetic bubble is all that is present here. The slower the spin, the more active I can be, moving my body, working and doing other things. While still yet, for the frequency I have activated within me, when it "peaks" out and feels fully activated, absolutely everything goes.... my inner magnetic poles no longer separated?, now become a field, like the sun, radiating out from within. There is this view of a "magnetic field" from the inside looking out. One can see the light frequencies transmitting out and "things" BEing pulled "to it". (View a huge bubble, like 30-40 feet all around and standing in the middle of somewhere.)

Even now, as I type, all "out there" is silent and still. All that exists is inside this huge energetic bubble. "out there" still "moves" as if I don't even exist. So very cool.

I will type the words I have right now and had upon awaking "in this" then. I write to visually describe "my view" from inside. I will update later as more comes to me.

Your Merkaba activates each time you lay (or sit) in connection

to/with/as source. It is the transmission of light from within, which
continues to expand as all is released/let go. Denseness BEing released
allows for more light to be present and this light "binds together" to create
a spin. The dense is a disruption in this unified spin.

Your Merkaba is your bubble. Everything you hold on to, or keep,
impacts your bubble's speed. The Light'er you are, the faster it spins. This is
created from the inside out. Your thoughts must be from the inside to
radiate out. For each time you step outside your bubble to "think" of that
"out there", you create a disconnect from inside your own bubble.

Your Merkaba is your vibrational vehicle that allows you "physical"
access fully to the 5th Dimensional Realm (and higher). It is where the 5th
Dimensional Realm is activated from within you and radiates out so far that
as you "step" you step AS/IN the 5th Dimensional Realm in your physical.
As more activate their bubbles, the joining of these bubbles actually
"creates" your 5th Dimensional Realm to come to exist in the physical, for
these do not reach far and wide by the eyes of the human mind... they reach
far and wide vibrationally, which connects all. When all Merkaba's are
activated simultaneously, your 5th Dimensional Reality, as you perceive it,
shall vibrationally materialize to form.

You do not "go anywhere", for your Merkaba creates as you go. All
materializes "out there" as a result of your own LIGHT BUBBLE spin.

This is your vehicle to move freely realm to realm. With each activation
of Light, your ability to move will further expand. The only "thing"
standing in your way of free flowing movement is your need to hold
separation within you, your need to think any certain way and your belief
that things "are" any way at all. For in an activated bubble, no thoughts, no
beliefs, no attachments, no identities, no anything exists. The longer you
can hold a space of "nothingness" inside, the more activated your
Merkaba/Energy Field shall become.

You shall feel the vibrations all over, inside of you. You can hear them,
in frequency, inside your head. The visual is a "space shuttle" ready for lift-
off. When the Merkaba is activating, one feels like they are about to "take
off" in flight. This will continue to build, over your "separation of time" as
you build your light quotient within. As the spin increases, so shall the
magnitude of the vibrations, the intensity of the frequencies you hear... and
then vibrates and spins so fast that all slows down to a complete halt. This
would be the equivalent of you floating in space, without the "suit". Yet
your "suit" is your human body. This is why your breathing gets shallow,

for the "air" is non-existent here, yet you can breathe. You breathe from the inside out, instead of from the "old human way" of from the outside in. You have been BEing adapted "over time" to this. When the Merkaba is fully activated, you "float" in a suspended animation state.... visualize your astronauts in space... it is the same. You can imagine it in a closed-eyed state, yet you now experience it in a waking state, when your brain-wave state lowers to "stop". When your magnetic poles inside "merge".... no longer separated inside. Gravity is at zero point inside. Time comes to a halt and absolutely nothing exists here. The longer you hold this within you, the more you shall come to "move about" in/as your fully activated bubble.... This will take you some time to integrate to. So honor each experience as it comes and allow yourself to BE "IN" it, of it, as it.

And as I type, all comes to a halt. My ears have closed off energetically and sound "out there" does not exist. Time slows to a halt and weightlessness now returns.

Note: There are so many posts, yet these were the ones that came to mind for sharing in this book. At this time, I continue to update regularly on cosmic energies and as we go Crystalline. I tend to post directly to Facebook (which then post automatically on Twitter). I move them over to my website on the days when I have "nothing" to do (needless to say, I am a few months behind on this!)

REMINDERS
FOR
REMEMBERING

♥   REMINDERS   ♥

Until one can come to REMEMBER all within, one must continually remind themselves to REMEMBER. The conscious BEing can do this by repeating the "reminder" over and over until they do this automatically as a response instead of the old human aspect response.

Affirmations and mantras are what the human knows these as. For to strip the human of the old beliefs and re-program, one creates something they "desire" to believe, yet have not come to accomplish within. There comes a point, when the Soul has expanded enough within, where one just needs *Reminders*. For this purpose, we call them *Reminders for REMEMBERING, ("Reminders"* for short*)*, for this is actually what they are.

We will include *Reminders* throughout this guide, so as to assist one with this. You are encouraged to create your own, from your own observations within. This will assist with your own expansion as a Light BEing here, as your own *Reminders* resonate at a frequency that is designed just for you!
.
♥ REMINDER: I REMEMBER to REMEMBER, until I never forget again

♥ REMINDER: I REMEMBER through an open heart. I already exist in the higher realms. When I am in alignment inside, I exist as my Higher Self here again.

♥ REMINDER: It is the intangible world, that you first cannot see, that brings you all you desire and dream. It is the belief that creates and the drive that causes it to eventually appear for you to see in your "new" (forgotten) physical reality.

♥ I already exist in the 5th Dimension. The only way I do not is if I allow myself to again forget. This is called unconscious and requires an adjustment to my reality to REMIND me again. I can avoid this by going inside, getting conscious, living in the present moment, of an open heart and letting go of all judgment & separation that "got me there" to start with.

♥ Separation = Descension. Integration = Ascension

♥ I am not from here, so there is no fear. Fear is the separated human way.

♥ I get what you get, when I forget.

♥ "I" keeps me separated (human), "WE" unifies again.

♥ The answer to the question is always "Go Within".

♥ An "adjustment" occurs "out there" when I have fallen out of alignment inside.

♥ Observation mode, without judgment, is me AS my Higher Self.

♥ Truth exists in my higher heart. The illusion is my human mind.

♥ When my heart is closed, I am human. When my heart is open, I am my Higher Self.

♥ "that out there" is my own transmission. If I wish a different play, I must change my own frequency.

♥ "that out there" is the expanded view of what exists inside of me.

♥ The physical is as slow to catch up (materialize) as I am separated inside. Density materializes faster.

♥ Light magnetizes to me that which I desire or need. I need not "do" anything. All I have to do is REMEMBER and BE.

♥ Meditation is the human word. Sacred Space is of the Higher Self heart-mind and is anywhere our physical bodies exist.

♥ My own human mind is my block. I must expand through my heart if I wish to shift.

♥ If it's not working "out there", I am out of alignment inside.

♥ If I am trying to fit it into a box, I am human.

♥ When I am in my heart, I could not care less about details.

♥ I am a magnificent BEING of Light. I shine when I radiate out from within.

♥ I am present with (as) all living things. I am ONE again as WE.

♥ When I am in bliss, love, peace, kindness and magic, I am my 5th Dimensional BEing Self again.

♥ When I am in my human mind, I am in a lower dimensional realm.

♥ Clarity comes when the human mind is not present at all.

♥ When I do not share, I block me.

♥ When I am UNIFIED, I am whole and at peace inside.

♥ Fear, judgment & not sharing separate me again.

♥ My 5th Dimensional version of me has no struggle inside or "out there".

♥ Bliss is a natural state of BEing. When it is not, I have forgot.

♥ I must completely reverse my reality to come to exist here again. It is no longer about me. It is what I am here to do to assist humanity, how to unify all from within. When this is how I AM inside, then outside will come to exist as the 5th Dimension again.

♥ They are my creation. Gratitude is my response for their honoring their contract to assist me on my journey here.

♥ That is a play, an illusion. I have the power to change it, just with thought. I change it by existing in CREATION in every moment. For that which I think creates that "out there".

♥ Which Earth I exist on is up to my own frequency.

♥ Which version of me I get, is up to me.

♥ Which version of them I get, is determined by which one I allow & expect.

♥ I start my day asking for magic. I walk out & about asking for magic. I am only asking for that which I already am. I am magic!

♥ I must be present and aware in order to be conscious and have choice. That which I choose materializes in my reality for me to see.

♥ When I am not okay inside (at peace), I must go in and see where

I am out of alignment, figure out what I am resisting with my head and where I am not listening to my higher heart.

♥ If I ask for proof, I am human.

♥ If I am comparing, I am human.

♥ If I am limited, I am human.

♥ If I am compromising, I am human

♥ If I form an opinion, I am judging

♥ Anything that opens my heart in appreciation and joy, brings forth my humanity from within.

♥ THIS is MY Reality; THAT is there. Both are true and must be respected from within.

♥ If I believe it, it is true. The key is to challenge what I believe.

♥ This is my head. I can now think the way I want. Eventually I will no longer need to think first, the more that I live from my heart.

♥ If I feel the need to protect, I am human. This is a false man perception created by the human mind.

♥ Fear is a created perception that exists only in my human mind.

♥ My 5th Dimensional me radiates love from the inside out. It is not directed at any one or anything, for that is an "individual" way to be. It is meant for all that I may encounter along my way, along my day, along my path of reaching as many in Light as I can.

♥ My purpose is to integrate light in every moment. Honoring me must come first, then I can honor all others. Eventually I can honor all of us as one, at the same time, just by BEING Light again. Until then I rest, nurture and feed light to my awesome and amazing self that I AM.

♥ Anything I allow from an external world that holds a vibration less than love, creates discord in my own reality, my own frequency, if I allow my own frequency to drop. If I wish to live in love, peace and bliss, I must remove/transcend all that is not.

♥ When I look at that/them, do I feel love or separation within? This will tell me much.

♥ Is my focus on "that out there" to make me happy? Or is it that I am happy within first?

♥ Realities are as bendable (or as fixed) as I believe them to be.

♥ I must stay present, conscious, aware and actually ACT from my higher heart, AS my Higher Self, if I wish to create my reality from the desire within me. Otherwise I get the reality encoded in my DNA, and until I am completely transmitting LIGHT to bring all TO me, I must DO this in every moment myself.

♥ I must REMEMBER to REMEMBER until I no longer forget.

♥ When I stop thinking about individual "me" and start thinking of how I can create change and assist others in love, I will reverse the energy of separation and lack.

♥ If I "do" for all, I AM doing for WE.

♥ What is my underlying motivation for that which I do?

♥ Separation and lack energy has an "inward pull" flow. Unified energy of "ALL as ONE" flows out from the heart and back to me when & how it is meant to be. In order to increase flow to me, I must increase flow OUT for ALL first. With this energy, I shall always receive abundantly that which I desire and need for my journey here to serve.

♥ Magic is a REMEMBERED state of BEing again. Until I REMEMBER this fully, from within, I must ask for the magic, look for the magic and pay attention to every small thing to see the magic. This will continue to grow as I do. Then I shall BE magic again.

♥ Bring me the magic!!

♥ I must "tune" my frequency to shift to a different reality intentionally.

♥ I activate light and unity Consciousness within.

♥ I am this flower, this blade of grass, this butterfly, and those that I interact with.

♥ REMEMBERING is my natural state. Forgetting was my human me that no longer exists.

♥ I am the one who has to let go. Only human hangs on.

♥ I am an angel, a bringer of light. I am a Galactic BEing. I AM: _____ (you fill it in)

♥ Details do not matter if I exist in my heart. Those are of the human mind.

♥ If I participate, I make it my reality.

♥ Shift UP in frequency, in every moment.

♥ I cannot exist in my heart and my head at the same time. Therefore I choose my heart.

♥ If I can see it, it is mine. I must go inside, bring it up & let it go. (Or just ask, for you have the power to do this now)

♥ My spoken word allows me to hear that which I think inside. If I wish to truly change my entire reality, I must own all thoughts and clear them from my own reality, for they are creating for me, whether I am conscious or not. If I wish to know what exists "in there" I will speak every thought out loud. This will assist me in seeing what has been hidden.

♥ This has nothing to do with "them" or "out there". They are here to show me me.

♥ I close my eyes to see and open my heart to hear.

♥ I am always BEing "tested" until I realize I do not need the tests anymore.

♥ My Universe will continually test me to see if I can always come from honor, integrity and love from inside. When I REMEMBER to, I am connected AS the entire universe inside of me again.

♥ I must REMEMBER to communicate with my Higher Self from inside in every moment. This requires asking questions and then listening and paying attention to what comes from within (and "out there") after.

♥ The human works in the direction of separation, while the Higher Self BEing flows in the direction of ONE (love). Everything is in reverse and opposites.

♥ If I wish to be a part of my star being/soul family again, I must release the need to be separated from within.

♥ The human mind must be expanded (through the heart), while the Higher Self is expanded and works to bring all back together again (unification) as one.

♥ If I wish to hear what is inside of me and come to understand what is true for me, I must speak out loud and then observe with an open heart.

♥ Lower & middle realms: Eyes open, mouth open, unconscious. Middle Realm: Eyes closed, heart open, conscious. Higher Realms: Heart wide open and BEing LIGHT again.

♥ I am as I perceive myself to be. Another will perceive me according to their own limited reality. The two will never be the same until judgment falls away and I am my universal self again.

♥ The human competes, while the Higher Self has nothing to prove.

♥ I am LOVE, LOVE, LOVE, utter and complete LOVE, LOVE LOVE!

ACTIVATIONS
FOR
REMEMBERING

YOU HOLD THE KEYS TO YOUR NEW REALITIES

There is a space, if you will, after one becomes aware of illusions and
holographic views,

Where one expands to come to see that there is a beyond that allows one to
further choose.

For there are unlimited realities where one can exist to be,

Yet first one must unlock them, one by one, to then expand to exist in
them simultaneously.

Most have yet to realize that you have already evolved as energy
Your human mind still needs to see a manifestation of a physical reality

Your human self was the one that needed to come to exist in a physical
plane,
Yet the more you realize, that this is no longer the case,
The sooner you can come to move and shift as energy once again.

Your physical world "out there" is but a manifestation of your human mind
And once you come to comprehend this, you will again exist beyond space
and time.

Yet you are already lighter, no longer existing in a fixed reality
Only in your human mind are you bound by limits of a physical that you
still need to see.

NAVIGATING DIMENSIONS

Many have no idea that they do not exist in that "old" physical place
For the human seeing mind is the last to catch up to see beyond time and space.

Your human mind had the need to evolve - Yet you already exist as energy.

Now, your inner to outer viewer is no longer a viewer from just inside your mind
Yet from your entire existence as an energetic BEing of vibrational sound and light

This new space for you at first, will seem like great power for you to achieve
While this is true and a necessary space, it is but a part of what you can yet see.

For eventually, your human self shall move beyond your individual needs
And you will come to use this space, to come together as one to be free

Your forgotten and invisible world is no longer just a dream
Once you allow your mind to let go of your physical reality you too shall be able to see

As you move beyond your separated individual human view
You will use this space together to create the world as you see as NEW

As you come to join together, you unlock the Etheric crystal key
For once you have dissolved as one, you shall exist in a whole new reality.

For as you evolve from your physical world to one where you now exist as energy
Your entire BEing shifts inside, to exist as ONE with us as WE

So embrace within dear ones, as it begins
For your NEW World comes and your old one ends!

HEARING AND FEELING VIBRATIONALLY:
YOUR NEW REALITY

There is a "space", if you will, where the energies are high, the veils & air are thin and one has vibrationally activated the LightBody (Crystalline Body, Multi-Dimensional self, etc.) to feel and see into the beyond. These are all but terms that you use there to understand. We refer to this as "the other side", "the invisible" or "the forgotten", yet it exists only in a frequency that you have yet to be able to fully access, or in the physical, achieve.

You are BEing integrated, or merged, into these higher frequencies at the "rate" that you can comprehend. For you, as an energetic BEing already exist here, yet your human self must increase vibrationally for you to be able to merge dimensionally.

Your physical shall feel more in these densities of the dimensional merges of these higher frequencies. Bugs, rodents, reptiles, spiders & more are used to desensitize your human fears of this. Each time you dream or encounter a "thing" that makes you jump or scream, you further release the energy of fear to that which you see. This is a necessary part of your human process in "shifting up" as you see it, vibrationally.

You are not going anywhere, you are not moving to a new place. You are not leaving where you are physically, you are re-evolving as an energetic space. In this space you are everywhere, all at once and in all times. Here you shall see everything, yet in pieces according to the limits of your own human mind.

In these times of high frequencies, you can see and feel that which you could not previously see. These visions, or experiences, appear new to you, yet they are memories of that which you have forgotten yourself to be.

You will feel tingly at first, then something crawling on you. You may discount the experience or even question your own sanity. Yet inside, you know it to be real, yet not according to your human reality.

This is necessary and shall increasingly occur, as when you are to "walk into the new" (the invisible or forgotten), you shall already be there before you know it, as it happens subtly.

Translation note: The one who writes this, called Transcendence, is shown these things to be able to translate what she sees. She has reached a vibrational frequency that allows her these experiences, then given the words in order to share and teach. We needed someone who didn't filter or compromise with human needs. For this she speaks as we speak, for she exists in these vibrations that allow her to speak as WE. All shall come to a place of no separation within and as they do, they too shall also see. It is in this space that WE exist and shall also speak to you directly.

A HOT AIR BALLOON RIDE TO FREEDOM INSIDE

At first there is fear, oh no, I can't fly
I need my feet on the ground to hang on, ohhh I'll try,
I step into the basket, so full of fear
Look up at the balloon and ask "What happens if I let go of here?
It shakes a bit and starts to rise
Fear fills my stomach, tears fill my eyes
Up up up we now go
I don't feel so well, I'm losing control
Nothing to hang on to, nothing to hold
Closing my eyes tight, It'll be okay, I am told
Oooooh, my tummy, my entire BEing feels sick
Like I'm about to lose it, help me, quick
My mind tells me to be in overwhelming fear
My heart beating fast, words of panic and escape is all I hear
Get me a bucket, so I can toss all inside
My entire inner world, about to violently collide
Oh, wow, thanks... now I feel fine
The fears unbelievable, and they weren't even mine
They were that of learned beliefs or energy of another time
I'm unable to focus, my head like a cloud
Yet new clarity and peace now present, Oops, did I say that out loud?
The view is tremendous and now there's no fear
Breathtaking realizations come forth, just by observing from here
This feeling consumes me, and the desire to fly
Higher and higher into the sky
I want to now see what I could not see before
Wow, the details, do not matter anymore

Nothing does, in the presence of bliss
How could I have feared the exquisiteness of this?
Ohhhhh, I believed, something that was not true
That kept me from REMEMBERING what I already knew
Now looking down there, from this view from above
I have nothing but appreciation and expanding love
For I now see, that which I could not previously see
Perspectives upon perspectives, a whole new reality
For here, in my heart, and BEing, I am truly free
No desire to return to the ways of the old
No longer to attach or things to keep hold
I can just let go, in every moment there is
And know that up here, is where I now I live
In the higher vibrations, where dreams do come true
For the dream was inside, and I had forgotten I knew
That all was within me, the love and the fear
And now I have choice, to release and be here
This new view allows me to see from above
And choose only light, peace within and blissful love
Here I can share with others with ease
For here has always been, the block were inside of me
My own resistance kept me stuck down there
Now I let go and fly everywhere
No more restraints, for now I can see
That what I receive is what inside I believe
And I believe that which I feel inside my Soul
No longer separate, yet again now whole
For all is inside of me and creates that "out there"
So I choose love and this new view and to fly everywhere
Only when I hang on am I bound to resist
And in BEing free, hanging on cannot exist
For I must choose to step in every moment in trust
My tangible is my heart and listen to that I must
For my heart is my map, and my Soul is my guide
In tune in every moment, flow with all is my new stride
Ahhhh this feeling, I REMEMBER this
And this IS my proof, that THIS does exists
If I need to recall this anytime,
I close my eyes, tune to my heart and breathe from deep inside
I quiet my mind and open my heart up to receive
For my thoughts from my future self is what I believe
Ones of inspiration that expand from within
A heart so full, where to begin?

Open up and just let it all flow
For as I do, higher and higher we all go.
A realm of love and light that waits
For me to REMEMBER to walk through the gates
For the doors are now open, they always were
I had just forgotten, yet no longer
For this inside of me, allows me to BE
That which I desire, creating my own reality
With all, as one, for I am them and they are me
No longer separate, again now WE.

Fly loves... it is time! ♥

ALCHEMIC CREATION

Close your eyes and quiet your mind
And open your heart to truly see
Let yourself just drift away
Allowing your thoughts to be received.

Here you see from a space inside of you
Where your mind becomes the projector and your 3rd eye the lens to view

Now observe the light BEing transmitted outward from inside of you
Light beam particles that take physical form in your external reality view
A vibrational frequency from within that materializes in your external reality
You are the creator of your world according to your own frequencies
As you are a walking particle form of vibrational energy.

Now imagine, if you will
Your old physical was dense compressed particles dimming your light
And as that dense matter is dissolved
All that's left are particles of radiant glowing light

Your 3rd eye BEing the lens
Your mind BEing the "reel"
Your heart BEing the driving force
Of creating all that you feel

Now look "out there" at your reality
And see what you can see
For that "out there" is only a physical form

Of all that exists within you vibrationally.

Your Energy Body is a walking power center
Fueled by the energy of your heart
Creation exists in every moment there
When one exists as love and light, instead of doubt or fear

Yet when you allow yourself, to let your human mind lead
Then you have fallen unconscious, and have no choice in what you receive.
For you create in every moment, that which you do believe
So understanding what exists inside
Allows you to change the way that you perceive

When you change your own perception
Of how that "out there" was created
You will choose to let go
Of all that kept you separated.

Now the conscious BEing no longer caters
To the human perspective in their mind
This energetic BEing honors in every moment
That which they are creating from deep inside

Presence and observation are the tools of the energetic Soul
For Alchemic Creation only occurs when the Soul again inside becomes
whole
This requires silence and listening deep within
Your Soul self calls it sacred space
Your human calls it meditation

When you exist in every moment
Where every moment is sacred deep inside
Then "out there" becomes this magnificent creation
Where love, bliss and peace at all times reside.

Allow yourself to tune vibrationally AS All-That-Is
Further releasing any separation within
Allowing yourself to become inside whole again.

As a whole BEing inside you again become unlimited
There is absolutely nothing but complete peace,
For inside IS where you now reside.
Here there is no lack, no question and no fear

For the human aspect now dissolves
As an energetic BEing, which does not exist here.

One understands the power of creation
As clarity is gained with each light activation
Yet the human sits and waits for these
While the Walking Soul activates their own light
With every breath that they breathe.

For a time, until you have raised enough
In vibration through your own Energetic Integration
You must work from inside
In what you call meditation
For until you achieve seeing
Vibrationally with your new eye
When your human eyes are open,
You see as a human from your human mind
As your ONE eye and your two eyes first become Three
This is what you know as your 3rd eye to be
Yet this too integrates within you
You shall come to utilize this in all states to again be able to see
Only ONE eye shall be necessary
As you see from your entire BEing energetically.

As you become transparent inside
"out there" becomes transparent too
And you continue to LIGHT'en
For your physical BEing actually does this too

The more transparent you allow yourself to be
The more transparent your physical reality
As all that you are becomes transparent vibrationally
Then moving about energetically shall also come to be

Your human mind is your separation
From existing AS an energetic BEing of light
So you must work to transcend this
Making your waking state interchangeable with your sleep state at night.

For that which you can see, with your eyes closed
Shall come to be in a waking state
Which is why your human self is put to sleep
So that your waking self can merge and integrate.

Your human mind is too strong
So each time that this occurs
You will shut down yet again
To allow your energetic Soul self to further emerge.

You will continually flip back and forth
Until you allow yourself to transcend
The human mind limits you put in place
No longer serve and now must end.

Every time you separate into identities, selves and time.
You shall go to sleep, until you choose to leave the limits of separation
behind.

You first came here to separate, yet your human you, does not let go
So instead you are given incentive
By BEing shown something you wish for more
More than the physical existence that you came here to acquire
Your world no longer driven by the physical, yet now driven by desire.

When you listen and you honor, this comes with greater ease
Yet when your human mind is stronger than your heart
Then taking something away is what you shall see.
For dissolving the materialization of energy that your human created
Must first occur, so that you can see,
That creation does not come from BEing separated.

Materialization of Energy is what you as a human understand as physical
manifestation.
Alchemic Creation is Energetic Particle Materialization.
When one exists as their Higher Self then Alchemic Creation is a given.
As the "old" dense de-materializes,
Then the "new" shall materialize for you in vibration.
For NOW you create just by BEing LIGHT
For here this is no struggle or fight
When time for you is one then that which you have created
Shall materialize just by thought.
The space between this & materialization no longer separated.

The human lived in a 3rd Dimensional dense physical world
Where hard physical work in exchange for something tangible was required
It is a human manifestation where identities are created around things
And one is driven by what they see externally.

Much physical energy was required in order to create this dense physical
reality

The Higher Self BEing creates from the heart, from a desire deep within
It does this from a drive inside, that cares nothing about what it is given.
For this one is powered energetically by a vision and a dream.
This dream becomes a mission, where nothing else is seen.

How does not matter, just that it is.
Achieving no longer a question, for knowing exists within.
Doubt never enters here, for that is of the human mind.
One that became separated by selves, identities and time.

A vision IS a transmission from the heart and the 3rd eye mind
And one's entire BEing, energetically combined
These merge as one transmit from within SO much power
To then materialize in the physical of light crystalline particle matter.

Every moment a visualization
Of what exists deep in the heart
For creation is of the Soul
That has again become whole
Here every act is creation
Every breathe, every thought energetic materialization.

For an Energetic Alchemist, thought is not first of the individual self
It is of one expanding one's own light from within
And coming together to create new from the forgotten.

Now, when many come together to create in light all as one
This power is beyond that which has ever been known
This will create your new
For the new is the true energetic forgotten you.

AWAKENING AND EMERGING FROM THE FOG

Many have been in a "fog" and could not truly see
So for realities to appear to "flip", A "fog", if you will, was necessary.

For the "shift" was one from a human mind to one of a higher realm view.
Yet not only has this occurred in your mind, but your entire physical you.

For as your view changes, so do you, to become lighter in density
And the human cannot see the change, that you no longer exist in your
"old" reality.

In linear this is seen as lives and years
Yet it is but a moment in non-linear view
For as you "see" as less human, the more you "see" as your energetic you.

The more you come to realize what actually has occurred
The more you have "flipped", integrated, evolved, and merged
From an external to internal reality, using your human terms.

So open up your mind, if you wish you to see,
For you no longer exist in your old human physical reality.

DARK, LIGHT, INDIVIDUAL, COLLECTIVE VIEWS: ALL YOUR CREATION

Your collective reality was created by you for you
For you needed the experience there for you to see

And as was true on an individual level
When you no longer need the collective experience
Then it too shall cease to be

Your Human YOU had a limited view, and labeled "that out there"
As BEing of the collective, another "untruth" for you to "wear"

You shall come to see, that "that" was limited too
And that the "NEW", can NOW be seen from your REMEMBERED
energetic view

For you never truly saw before, as the human mind is small
And cannot see beyond "that", for the veils of the mind are walls

As your own internal dense veils of separation continue to fall
Your energetic self has access to see as ALL
For YOU exist in all spaces, as ONE and in all times
For it is you yourself that separated them in your own human thinking
mind

As a human you are individual, both outside and in
Yet leaving the denser realms allows you exist where the veils are thin
For the collective there, was your own individual human reality

Manifested from within of your own frequencies for you to see

For as long as your eyes are of a human, living in a physical world reality
All that you can see "down there" is separated by your human need to see
Yet you shall see AS the Collective as you continue to become ONE as
WE.

For as a part of THIS collective, there is no separation to see.
Separation collectively exists within you as but yet a denser frequency.

You came there to experience duality, represented by dark & light
Yet duality is no longer, as you allow it to leave from your sight

The battle of dark and light first existed inside of you
Therefore BEing transmitted to materialize in your physical for you to view

For if it were not visible as a tangible thing for you to see
You would have no idea that it existed in your inner reality.

The key, if you will, is to look at that "out there" and observe with your
higher mind
And remind yourself that "out there" is transmitted from your inside
Ask yourself where within you need to fight a fight
Or even see that dark exists instead of only light
For every moment that occurs and transpires
Was a choice of yours to see and learn in order to elevate higher
"Why would I have chosen that to see?"
For if "out there" lacks anything light, then that exists somewhere inside of
me.

All "out there" is your own tangible holographic view
So if there is an imbalance, or dark, this exists inside of you.

Now where there appears a collective belief
That too is manifested for you to see
For you created all of "them" to vibrate with you at the same frequency.
And when you no longer possess this inside, they shall no longer be.

You "borrowed" the memory for this experience, to heal a frequency of
lack
Now you no longer need it, and it is time to "put it back".
As you quiet your mind and allow yourself to feel
You release this energy allowing yourself to whole and heal.

Nothing occurs TO you, yet only in response to your own frequency, FOR
you, BY you. When you are "done", so shall "IT" be.

Anytime the energies "drop", you will be put into a space for you to see
your own duality
The key, is to see it as yours, if you wish to change your "fixed" reality.

If you feel you need protection, then you are protecting yourself from you
This means you inside have separated, from ONE into BEing again TWO.
Protection is a wall created by the mind to interfere with the flow of love
The protected human inside blocks themselves from the realms above
For it is by way of protecting that one is unable to see
That this alone is veils and walls, that must come down to again ONE be.

If you wish to change this, then you must go inside of you,
Raise your own vibrational frequency, release the THOUGHT and
REMEMBER is what you DO.

Dark "out there" does not dissolve for you to move into the NEW
Dark inside is where it exists and must be released first from inside of you.

Your individual view is your own holographic view.
All that you see "out there" is projected from inside of you
So your collective reality is yet of the same
A projection of what exists inside, to keep you in the game.

If you wish to unplug from the matrix that existed outside of you
Then you must always REMEMBER by seeing through your inner to
change your view

For when you look outside and forget that that is yours
You fall back to human, unconscious, which exists behind veils & doors

Your work, if you will, is too important to fall victim to that outside
Keep your center and do not forget as transparency allows nothing to hide
Yet it hides not in another for you to seek in order to see
It hides within, beneath your veils, and is visible when you allow it to be.

And as you continue to expand as the energetic BEing that you are
Your view shall change from BEing down there to seeing from up here
where WE are.

COMPLETE WIPING OF THE TEMPLATE

These energies carry new programming today. A complete wiping of the template, if you will. One can participate intentionally by creating ceremony or a mantra to assist or use.

Activation Transcript:

I am a clean slate. I release all stories, thoughts, attachments and perceptions of who I have been, am at this moment, or was to be as a future me. I clear all previous programming and open up to receive that which now activates within me.

I completely release and empty out all that no longer serves. I open my self to that which my human mind can yet comprehend.

I intentionally choose to become a clean slate, activating my new template within.

I allow for a complete re-write of my previous systems, and for total expansion AS "All-That-Is", to know exist within me once again.

I humbly honor the opportunity to further merge with my Higher Self, Gaia, All Cosmos, Galaxies, Stars, Universes, Planets, and ALL BEings as ONE, to embody within me again, to become that which I have forgotten to be.

I continue to erase, and intentionally replace, that which allows me to become one inside as WE.

NAVIGATING DIMENSIONS

I no longer see separation inside or "out there".
I only see unity where all BEings share.

I remove all remaining barriers, locks and veils within,
I rewrite my own template to create NEW once again

To exit in all space and time now in my mind
As this complete reintegration leaves all separation behind

All moments are of UNITY and all BEings as ONE
And that with this sacred passage, it has already begun

For it has always been available inside
I now choose transparency, where nothing can hide.

This space is of the highest honor and integrity there is
So I NOW activate it, when I speak "AND SO IT IS".

PORTALS WITHIN:
ONE NO LONGER HAS TO WAIT

Many are under the perception that they must wait for energies to come through, to access other spaces and times that are perceived to be outside of you. While this is true, it is also un-true.

The energies that "now" stream, now support one in this "time", yet waiting has never been necessary, as that too is of the human mind.

Now, access has been given, as it has always been in you. Yet most will wait for access to "occur", since this is the human thing to do. One can now choose, to open this inside. For this is no longer "another time" to achieve, as all times can now be unlocked from within where they reside.

These portals have been unveiled, yet one must go inside. For they will only open, when you've "uncovered" where they hide. For they exist in vibrational frequency, that at first comes with a short glimpse to see. Then it is up to you, to decide to release all separation that keeps you from WE. For this space starts outside of you, as a thing or place for you to connect to. Yet once the vibration has been held long enough, access to this "space" then comes from inside of you.

For the perception that all is "out there" to connect to, is just a difference in frequency. For as you vibrate higher, "out there" "moves" from outside, to a place inside you to now BE.

These portals shall be opened, the more you focus inside you. For the portal is not a thing "out there", it is a space inside that you have forgotten that you have always had access to.

This has always been this way, yet the "REMEMBERING" just seems new. But now that you are aware, you can choose to access these portals too. The only difference, again, is your perception and your view. You just needed access in frequency, which is again now available through you.

If you wish for the ability to create these portals in your physical world, then you must first access them from within, as the door to both, exist inside of you. You cannot step through them, until you unlock them deep inside. For it is up to you, to uncover where they hide. For you are the one that put them there, beneath your human you. For as you release your human mind, your true you expands from inside of you. These shall then become visible to see as you vibrationally come to re-create your external reality.

You think these portals to be outside of you, but they have never been. For outside is only created by frequencies you hold within. All but is a space, which has always been one with you. For you are not just one, you are one with us here too. For we do not exist "out there", we too exist, inside of you.

HUMAN IS THE LOWER REALMS

When you let go of the need to be human, then you allow yourself to expand

For it is your need to be human, which keeps you separated from your forgotten land.

For separation exists within you and limits you to a human view

By keeping you focused on an exterior that is instead existent inside of you.

For you are no longer human, as your entire BEing now transcends
All things you "think" are physical are but projection from within.

Human is the part of you that was dense and of the old
As you allow your mind to expand, the higher realms shall continue to unfold

Your human eyes were blind and could not truly see
Let go of the stories that were not you, and embrace what you have forgotten to be.

Your energetic eyes shall show you what was hidden beneath your veils
And locked deep inside your mind, your heart and human cells

As your physical BEing evolves to release the separation that was dense
Your energetic knowing will now understand that which never made sense

For this is not new, just forgotten
And again shall come to be seen,
As every moment in a higher vibration
Bring one further into the other realms they could not previously see.

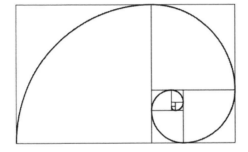

COMPLETE RECONSTRUCTION:
VISIBLE FROM WITHIN

The Inside Deconstructs so that the Outside can then change too. As the inside BECOMES the outside. The Land of the Forgotten "View".

Are you all observing all that is shifting from within and all around you? Much is so subtle, that if you are not paying attention to every moment, you shall have to "wait" until an entire "picture" is displayed to see!

Entire constructs are now visibly BEing dismantled "out there", so that more can see "collectively" what has always been transmitted from within. As more "adjust" to their new "viewers", this can be quite an unbalanced feeling, yet that too shall be integrated for further expansion and greater ease as one continues to expand out vibrationally from within.

The human starts with a viewer of "that out there", to shift to a bit of an understanding that "that out there" is not real" in their "head", to shift to actually "see" through a viewer that gives them the "reality of the illusion", to shift to "wow, all that was created from within me", to shift to "wow, I get to actually re-create my entire reality from within"..... to shift to "you are not going to believe what is NEXT!". For in expansion, all is available and possible from within. For even this is a limited human view ...

The "views" are limitless, vast and continue to expand. Old human realities continue to fall away as the denser realms continue to dissipate and dissolve, as you see it. Yet these realities never existed "out there". They have always been a transmission of all of the realities one held within them. And as all of those "long lost realities" that one could not see continue to emerge and leave, the view gets even more confusing when one actually gets to view some of it as it goes. The collective views purge, so that the exterior, that the human mind needs, continues to re-shape "out there". None of this is new, it is part of the forgotten you.

The "past" is erased from within, if you will, while the "future" is no longer the future anymore, as all "other timelines/dimensions/times" continue to cease to exist. For they do not cease, your separation from them ceases within, AS you further re-evolve back into ENERGY form in every way.

You cannot fully see yet, as the human mind is slow and has to "catch up" with the actual view, according to that which one can "handle" within. For some, this appears to expedite, yet it has always been present. One just did not hold the vibrational frequency within to fully see. This continues and the more it is embraced, the "easier" it shall be perceived to be by the human experiencing a complete deconstruction of the old and creation of the new. Yet neither are either, yet another perception of the ever expanding view.

♫ ♪ ♫

Many of these activations are recorded in frequency and are available for listening to on the website. (MP3 page) Some are also made available for download in the store. Enjoy and happy activating!

LIGHT ENERGY GRID COMMUNICATION ACTIVATION (LYRAN ENERGIES OF THE GALACTIC HIGH COUNCIL)

Higher Realm Frequency Bands exist within you as the sounds you hear in your head or ears.

There are certain times right now that they are more "open", if you will. They have always been present, yet you now are able to achieve the frequency in order to hear.

Close your eyes and imagine opening a portal within you. Your heart, solar plexus or pineal gland are all places you can "go" to do this.

Tune TO the frequency of LIGHT.

You can tune, just by thinking, seeing, speaking this in a deep state from within.

See the Light Frequency streams that connect you with All-That-Is, with all others, also connected to the light grid.

These bands/streams/frequencies, if you will, allow for multi-way communication now, whereas in the "past", you transmitted out OR received, now you can transmit and receive at the same time. YOU limited this, yet this is no longer.

That too was dualistic, to see either/or. Yet now, this too merges within.

You will have to "work" with this new communication, to continue to expand it beyond that which you currently perceive.

Your antennae, if you will, go inward, not outward, and reach as far as your mind can comprehend.

These bands that you have been hearing is the "new" (forgotten) communication BEing built between all of you there, The Grid of Light, as you perceive it, together, as one, with All-That-Is.
You are needed to intentionally connect to these streams.

You are BEing prepared for "The Rising". We need you to strengthen your communication in frequency. What you perceive as telepathy, is just you connecting & communicating as energy, as energetic BEings. (Then they showed me us, as big crystals.) Those who cannot yet hear, are given rays of light to use to connect to (Sun Rays, Stars, etc.). If one does not know of this yet, just ask to receive this. Until you activate this, do not worry, just connect to the light that you can see, either inside of you or externally. For they are the same, the only difference is how you see. Tune to the frequency of nature, the ocean, of dolphins. You go wherever is sacred for you, outside or in. All hold a vibration that allows you to connect within. In or out doesn't matter. Again, they are the same.

ENERGETIC LIGHT COMMUNICATION ACTIVATION:

I activate within me an upgrade in communication.
I hold within me the power to activate all within me in frequency.
I tune to the frequency of Higher Communication.
I tune, I activate, I hold this frequency within me.
I see in Light Communication
I speak in Light Communication
I receive in Light Communication
I transmit in Light Communication
They are not separate within me.
They are one and the same.
I activate Energetic Communication within me, as me & me as it. One.
I am an Energy Form
This is my natural way & form of communication
I am only re-activating that which I have forgotten to be
I activate my entire BEing as LIGHT ENERGY
I activate the Light Codes within me to upgrade my energetic
communication.
Only when I "forget" shall I again separate from the ability to connect and
communicate as Energy.
I connect with the Energy of the Earth, the Stars, The Trees, The Seas and
all Universes & Galaxies from inside of me.
I tune TO the frequency that activates the Light within me.
I tune TO the frequency that activates my ability to communicate as
Energy.
I tune TO that which allows me to BE, hear, feel, see AS ENERGY.

♥

WE CREATE

WE SHARE

WE UNITE

ONE AGAIN

WE COMMUNITY

♥

ABOUT THE AUTHOR

Lisa "Transcendence" Brown, B.Msc., is a highly respected Author, Transformational Speaker, Teacher/Coach/Guide/Re-Educator, Energy Master, WayShower, Oracle, Sage, Scribe and Embodied Ascended Master assisting others in REMEMBERING their PURE selves, bringing forth their own Divine Essences and Ancient Lineages to share with others here.

As an Ancient Elder and Guardian of NEW Earth, she activates & reminds other awakening SOULS ready to embrace their own higher purposes & paths to catapult their own evolution journey here. She teaches through her own Experiences and Remembering.

As a Human StarGate & Portal, she translates multiple dimensions & cosmic energies online in real-time, simplifying the complexities of PROCESSES, the hows & why's of Awakening, Expanded Consciousness/Multi-Dimensional Mastery, Ascension, Descension, Soul/Light Embodiment, Crystalline LightBody Evolution and more.

Her ancient Lineage brought forth thus far includes LeMUrian, Atlantean, Sirian, Lyran, Arcturian, Andromedan, The Galactic High Council, The Angelic Realm, The Fairy Realm, Thoth, Pyramids and more. WE have been all things and as we hit that frequency, that comes forth as a memory from within. When you embody it, you ARE it again.

She brought forth Crystalline LightBody/Merkaba Energy of REMEMBERING to assist the physical body with the upgrade & integration process anchoring/holding/embodying Source Self inside. Unification of all bodies simultaneously, while expanding consciousness across all dimensions again.

She activates and re-educates global consciousness through live speaking events, daily writings, courses, one-on-one and group work and more. Evolution back into PURITY and BEING the Advanced NEW Earth Human is our NOW.

She is the author of Awakening To REMEMBERING: A Journey of Consciousness (with several more on the way!), resides on Kauai, fully in-service as a Crystalline Grid Keeper and Light Anchor Point, photographs NEW Earth magnificence and thoroughly in-joys sharing the vibrations of our higher dimensional existence now. ♥

SERVICES

Books & Publications

Global Speaking Events

Online Video Courses, Classes & Focused Programs

Personal Guidance & Coaching Sessions

Personalized Retreats and Workshops

MP3 Quantum Light Frequency Activations

Energy Updates, Daily Writings and Newsletters

Andaras and Crystals

Free YouTube Videos & Inspirational Reminders/Quotes

Crystalline LightBody/Merkaba Energy Sessions

Upcoming Events

Something For Everyone!

www.AwakeningToRemembering.com

Printed in Great Britain
by Amazon